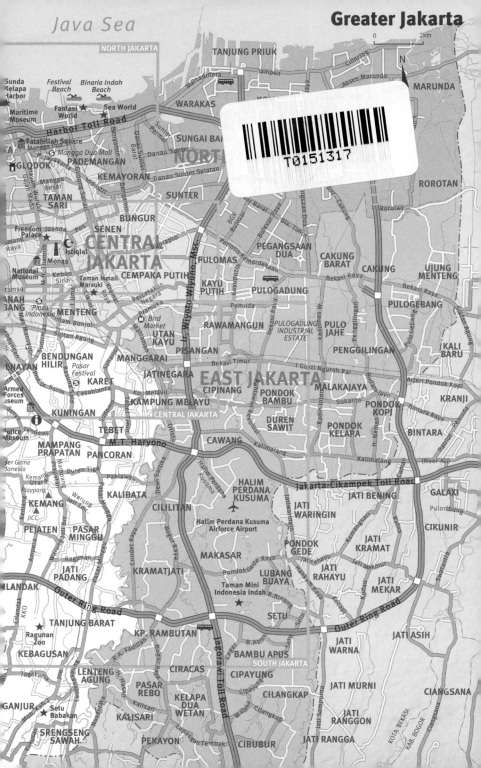

The Tuttle Story: "Books to Span the East and West"

Most people are very surprised to learn that the world's largest publisher of books on Asia had very humble beginnings in the tiny American state of Vermont. The company's founder, Charles E. Tuttle, belonged to a New England family steeped in publishing. And his first love was naturally books—especially old and rare editions.

Immediately after World War II, serving in Tokyo under General Douglas MacArthur, Tuttle was tasked with reviving the Japanese publishing industry, and founded the Charles E. Tuttle Publishing Company, which still thrives today as one of the world's leading independent publishers.

Though a Westerner, Charles was hugely instrumental in bringing knowledge of Japan and Asia to a world hungry for information about the East. By the time of his death in 1993, Tuttle had published over 6,000 titles on Asian culture, history and art—a legacy honored by the Japanese Emperor with the "Order of the Sacred Treasure," the highest tribute Japan can bestow upon a non-Japanese.

With a backlist of 1,500 books, Tuttle Publishing is as active today as at any time in its past—inspired by Charles' core mission to publish fine books to span the East and West and provide a greater understanding of each.

Published by Tuttle Publishing, an imprint of Periplus Editions (HK) Ltd

www.tuttlepublishing.com

Copyright © 2012 Andrew Whitmarsh

Library of Congress Cataloging-in-Publication Data

Whitmarsh, Andrew, 1976-
Jakarta : 25 excursions in and around Indonesia's capital city / Andrew Whitmarsh and Melanie Wood.
  p. cm.
ISBN 978-0-8048-4224-2 (pbk.)
1. Jakarta (Indonesia)–Tours. 2. Jakarta Region (Indonesia)–Tours. 3. Walking–Indonesia--Jakarta–Guidebooks. 4. Walking–Indonesia--Jakarta Region–Guidebooks. I. Wood, Melanie, 1976- II. Title.
  DS646.29.D5W47 2012
  915.98'220442–dc23
  2011031437

ISBN 978-0-8048-4224-2

16 15 14 13 12   6 5 4 3 2 1

Printed in Singapore   1209CP

Distributed by

North America, Latin America & Europe
Tuttle Publishing
364 Innovation Drive
North Clarendon, VT 05759-9436 USA
Tel: 1 (802) 773-8930; Fax: 1 (802) 773-6993
info@tuttlepublishing.com
www.tuttlepublishing.com

Japan
Tuttle Publishing
Yaekari Building, 3rd Floor
5-4-12 Osaki, Shinagawa-ku
Tokyo 141 0032
Tel: (81) 3 5437-0171; Fax: (81) 3 5437-0755
sales@tuttle.co.jp
www.tuttle.co.jp

Asia Pacific
Berkeley Books Pte Ltd
61 Tai Seng Avenue #02-12
Singapore 534167
Tel: (65) 6280-1330; Fax: (65) 6280-6290
inquiries@periplus.com.sg
www.periplus.com

Indonesia
PT Java Books Indonesia
Kawasan Industri Pulogadung
Jl. Rawa Gelam IV No. 9
Jakarta 13930
Tel: (62) 21 4682-1088; Fax: (62) 21 461-0206
crm@periplus.co.id
www.periplus.com

Jakarta

25 Excursions in and around the Indonesian Capital

ANDREW WHITMARSH and MELANIE WOOD

TUTTLE Publishing

Tokyo | Rutland, Vermont | Singapore

CONTENTS

Welcome to Jakarta!

Raised in the Wild Wild West of America with cowboys as my heroes and bank robbers as my enemies, I spent my childhood climbing mountains, building forts and fashioning rafts to float the North Platte River. Channeling this adventurous spirit, I became a leader in the Outdoor Club at university before joining the Peace Corps and spending two years in a small, mountainous village in the Republic of Georgia. Hiking for hours through the scrubby green hillsides, chatting up leathery old shepherds and reveling in solitude, clean air and the tranquility of body and mind were everyday occurrences.

Then I moved to Jakarta.

My first thoughts as I moved into the massive apartment block of Taman Rasuna in Kuningan, which has a population four times my hometown, was that I had died and gone to hell. The buildings were too big, the people too many, the automobiles too dirty and the city too hot. But soon my instincts took over and I began to adapt.

My first action was to buy a map and a bicycle. With these tools I covered massive swaths of the city, venturing into slums, joining street protests, squeezing through markets and following the canals until exhausted. I began to not only tolerate the city, but to fall in love with it. As the years went by and I continued to have incredible adventures, I knew that I was experiencing a Jakarta that most people are not exposed to. I heard a lot of complaints that there was nothing to do in Jakarta except go to the mall, and I knew this wasn't true.

And so it was that, four years ago, I began to scribble down notes on where I was going, what I was doing and who I was meeting so that I could help lift the lid on the steaming pot of mystery that is Jakarta, and in so doing let many others get a taste of the experiences they may have been missing out on.

I hope that as you read this guidebook you feel inspired to get out and explore, to open mysterious doors, to eat curious foods, to talk to intriguing people and to do things you never thought you'd do while living here. Now go and have yourself an adventure.

GENERAL INTRODUCTION

This book contains 25 guided tours, most of them geared towards walking. Twenty of the tours explore areas in north, central and south Jakarta while five others explore attractions an hour's driving distance or more from the city. Each tour contains information on how to reach the start point, the length of the walk, who the walk is suitable for, and facts on the points of interest along the way, as well as cultural notes and recommendations on where to eat and drink.

Different tours have different functions: some delve into the city's history, others focus on family activities; there are walks which link parks together for a green kick, while others amble through village neighborhoods and markets. There's not always an end destination; instead, the walk itself is the purpose.

Many of Jakarta's residents, both local and expatriate, have yet to ride a public bus, rarely get beyond the malls on weekends and have never walked anywhere in the city for pleasure. This is not necessarily for lack of want, but rather due to a dearth of helpful information compounded by plenty of misinformation and a fear of getting lost in the city's maze of chaos. What you now have in your hands, though, is a key to seeing more of the city than shops, and a guide to parts of the labyrinth of streets which make up Jakarta.

The purpose of the walking tours is to introduce you to weird, wild and wonderful places—places in Jakarta you may not have known existed. This will require you to call upon your inner adventurer, cast aside preconceived notions about the city and its people, and ignore the paranoid warnings from your company, your embassy and your friends. So strap on your adventure shoes and pack your adventure bag; it's time to take some incredible photos, experience things that will spice up your emails home and live a life more fulfilling. Very little in Jakarta is what it seems to be. It may take some time to discover this, but like the delicious *es campur* (mixed ice), there is always another layer to be discovered if you dig a little deeper.

First and foremost, though, it's time to shelve the fear of the unknown. Jakarta is no more dangerous than any other capital city in the world. To make matters even better, the local people are helpful, courteous and approachable. Rather than run from them, greet them. Rather than shy from what may be around the corner, take a peek. This is not to sugarcoat the city however. The air quality can be poor, the sidewalks rough or non-existent, the environment hot and humid, the traffic frustrating and the lack of amenities inconvenient. Going on walks in Jakarta requires you to leave home with the resolution not to be critical, to have a stalwart mind and a sense of humor. You will need patience, resilience and water. Your comfort zone will be stretched, your sense of direction twisted and your determination challenged. But along the way you are likely to meet friendly people, discover a unique shop, stumble upon a cute park, step inside a tasty café or come across an artistic mural. You may never get to where you intended, but instead end up exactly where you want to be.

AN OVERVIEW OF THE BOOK

This book is divided into five main sections. The first section gives some tips for successful expeditions into the tangled lanes of the city. Being streetwise, knowing what time of day to travel to certain areas, knowing which mode of transport is the quickest for particular routes and knowing how to give and respond to greetings are the street-savvy elements which will make everyone's experience of their visit much more enjoyable. This first section also covers health and safety basics, cultural do's and don'ts and an introduction to the city's transport options.

The second section delves into seaside north Jakarta, the city's black pearl, so-named because, although to some it is the gem of the city, it is by no means the sort of thing you would give as a wedding present. There are five walking tours exploring quarters of north Jakarta. Three have a historical and cultural flavor, strolling through the city's old town, harbor and Chinatown. The Muara Angke tour takes in the disparity between rich and poor, passing through neighborhoods in which mansions and slums share the same zip code, before arriving at a mangrove forest and fishing village. And the fifth, the Ancol tour, is a blast of seaside fun with roller coasters, a water park and an art market.

The third section moves to central Jakarta, with eight tours exploring both the main streets and the seldom-visited back streets. The Monas tour is steeped in history. The Menteng tour guides walkers through a sequence of parks to enjoy the leafy side of life. A day at the city's central sports grounds is the focus of the Senayan tour. The Markets tour brings together a trio of unique places to shop, while the Cikini tour looks at the arts. Explore the quaint lanes of the Bendungan Hilir neighborhood or make your own *batik* at the Textile Museum during the Tanah Abang tour. The Downtown tour provides a contrast between the upscale malls and the small neighborhoods located just blocks away.

The fourth section journeys to south Jakarta, a huge area of the city which the government defines as encompassing both Kuningan, in the central business district, and the University of Indonesia, which can be over an hour's drive away. Seven tours tread through this part of town.

Some of the city's larger, family-friendly attractions are located in the south: Ragunan Zoo, the cultural and educational park Taman Mini Indonesia Indah, and the fruit orchards of Mekarsari. The Pondok Indah and Kemang tours amble through green residential neighborhoods. The Kuningan tour visits some eye-catching cemeteries, and the Blok M tour satisfies both shoppers and park fiends, while passing an animal market as well.

The fifth section explores some of the attractions within five hours driving distance of the city. The farther you get from the smog and noise, the greener and more relaxing the environment becomes. These drives may mean renting a car and leaving before the call to prayer has finished rattling the bedroom windows, but it's worth the effort to breathe the sea and country air.

Sun worshippers and sailors will enjoy the Thousand Islands tour. The Jatiluhur tour spends a day at a lake. The Bogor tour gets on the train and explores the botanical gardens and a gong factory, while the Puncak tour goes up to the Gede and Pangrango volcanoes. The Pelabuhan Ratu tour gets all the way to the south coast of Java for some white-water rafting and surfing.

Welcome to Jakarta and its surrounding areas, where even the incredible is nothing out of the ordinary.

Safety Tips

On the city-wide scale, Jakarta has endured floods, earthquakes and terrorist attacks. That being said, the city is not a dangerous place to live. There are, however, things to keep in mind while exploring the streets.

CYCLISTS BEWARE The best tip for cyclists is to stay off the main roads. Instead, map out a route to your destination using the quieter back streets. Not only will you be less exposed to pollution and potential accidents, but the ride will be more pleasurable and your map-reading skills will improve. Always wear a helmet and reflective clothing. Fit out your bicycle with lights and a loud horn, and buy a proper anti-pollution mask if you are regularly riding in traffic. Go with the flow of vehicles, don't use your middle finger, ring your bell as needed, stick to the left lane and don't assert yourself too much.

MOTORBIKES Motorbike riders and passengers are vulnerable. When riding a motorbike wear full protective gear or, at a bare minimum, shoes and a properly strapped on helmet. Keep alert. Most road rules are not applied. Poorly maintained roads are one of the greatest threats. Riding at night or in the rain is hazardous: flooded roads can hide giant potholes, uneven road surfaces and broken lane dividers. Watch out for kids and pushcart vendors in the street, motorcycles entering a road without looking and vehicles changing lanes without indicating or looking. If you're riding in the *kampungs*, keep an eye out for marquees and wedding parties in the middle of the road.

PEDESTRIAN CROSSINGS The safety of pedestrian crossing is deceiving: cars won't automatically yield. Do not stride confidently across the street in a display of pedestrian rights. Motorcycles are especially loath to brake for anything and the potential for collision is high. Always look both ways and cross with caution. Be careful about getting into an altercation with a car or motorcycle driver after a traffic incident as a mob is likely to form and you may suddenly find yourself facing 20 people, not just one.

SIDEWALKS Watch where you walk or ride your bicycle, or you may find yourself neck deep in an uncovered sewer. Even in the smartest business and residential areas, it's common to find gaping, yet unmarked, holes in the sidewalks and roads. Sidewalks are often not much safer than roads as motorcycles drive quickly and freely on them. Always look both ways before crossing a road, even a supposedly one-way street, as vehicles, especially motorcycles, often travel in both directions.

THEFT Despite Jakarta's poverty, crimes against foreigners are few. The most likely crime is pickpocketing, with mobile phones and wallets choice targets. Use common sense: always mind your belongings and be aware of your surroundings, especially on public transport, at train and bus terminals, in queues and at busy markets. When leaving the bar at the witching hour, topped up on tequila and chanting the Canadian national anthem, keep your wits about you: take a reliable taxi and note the driver's ID and the license plate number. Don't ask the driver to go by the ATM for you to load up on cash, and don't pass out in the back seat.

WOMEN Women should generally find that they feel quite safe in Jakarta, and that while there may be the occasional stare, they won't feel like their life is in any danger. Ultimately, though, try exploring the city with a friend, always be aware of your surroundings, and if your intuition sounds a warning, listen to it. An ear-piercing scream can often be the best defense. The word for help is *tolong*.

Motorists don't stop at pedestrian crossings.

Health Information

GENERAL HEALTH TIPS Dengue is known as a classless disease as it is mosquito-borne and therefore strikes people at all levels of society. It may be useful to carry a few sachets of anti-mosquito lotion with you, as avoiding being bitten is the only way to prevent infection. Make sure your vaccinations are up to date and you are inoculated against typhoid, hepatitis A and B and tetanus-diphtheria. Take sunscreen with you as a general rule, but especially when you leave Jakarta for the Bogor, Jatiluhur, Puncak and Pelabuhan Ratu tours. Everybody gets the occasional upset tummy. Buy some fresh ginger roots and brew your own ginger tea to help.

FOOD SAFETY Indonesians may have guts of steal, but you don't. Certainly explore the roadside treats served at *warungs* (small informal restaurants), but be cautious as well. Ask for your food *bungkus* (to go), as often the gut-busting microbes are on the dishes washed in dirty water, not in the food itself. Think twice about having ice in your glass: it is usually transported by bicycle or cart and can be well manhandled before landing as chunks in your juice. Pick a *warung* which is popular with locals, drink straight from the bottle or can, and wipe your cutlery first with a napkin.

HYDRATION Keep hydrated in the tropics. You may not realize it, but your body will become as dehydrated as a shrimp cracker. Don't wait until you are thirsty. Start drinking water the moment you hit the streets. Dehydration will lead to headaches, irritability, and lassitude and could end with heatstroke. Cut down on plastic garbage by bringing your own water bottle pre-filled with ice-cubed water. If you feel your mood plummeting during a walking tour, drink and eat something immediately. You'll find that it wasn't your surroundings bringing you down, but neglect of your bodily needs.

Always have bottled water on hand.

Open-air fish markets offer a variety of seafood.

Cyclists rule the roads on car-free Sundays.

Cultural Do's and Don'ts

Due to the polite and accommodating spirit of the local people, a person may commit repeated cultural and etiquette-related crimes and never know it. That being said, there's no reason you should blunder blindly through the city, making grown men blush, insulting elders and giving foreigners a bad name. The following are a few tips on how to be a polite citizen in your host country.

ANSWER THE QUESTION As you walk through Jakarta you will commonly hear *Mau ke mana?* Literally this asks where you are going, but actually it is more a courteous greeting than a question. A lengthy reply is not necessary and the question isn't intended to be nosy. You can either tell them succinctly where you really are going, *Mau ke pasar ikan,* for example, if you are going to the fish market, or with the more general *Jalan jalan* (Just walking around). You *should* respond verbally though, do not just ignore this polite social greeting.

ANNOUNCE YOUR PRESENCE In the narrower neighborhoods, kitchens often spill into the streets. This means you may end up walking through someone's kitchen as you explore the area. Call out *Permisi* (Excuse me) to individuals and groups as often as necessary. With this expression you are politely asking for permission to proceed through the neighborhood. People will be very grateful for this sign of respect and will happily answer with *Silahkan* or *Mari,* meaning you are welcome to proceed. This simple word can unlock both doors and smiles, especially if your presence has surprised someone or you have intruded on a social event.

ACCEPT YOUR TITLE Indonesians politely greet each other with titles. *Bu,* for example, signifies deference for an older woman; *Pak* is the respectful title for an older man. Your title is *Mister.* You'll frequently hear 'Hello mister,' and it is not supposed to be annoying. Say hello back and don't bother trying to correct them if you are a woman.

BE THE BULE You will also often be hailed as *bule.* This is a commentary on your being a foreigner. Though you make get tired of hearing it said so many times, it is not an attack. In the *kampung,* the word will draw the attention of the locals and the delight and interest of the children. A happy smile or nod of acknowledgment is the proper response; a middle finger, scowl or smart-ass retort is not. Often the people calling out *bule* don't realize you understand the word.

GREET GRACIOUSLY Handshaking is acceptable when being introduced to an Indonesian, though don't be surprised if the hand is limp. Indonesians don't go for the crushing handshake and it's not cool for you to give a macho display. Give a light handclasp. Touching your heart immediately after the handshake is very polite. If you mix in affluent circles, get used to cheek kissing. The standard first greeting is *Apa kabar?* (How are you doing?), and the response is *Kabar baik* (I'm fine).

USE YOUR RIGHT HAND Always use your right hand when passing and receiving items from people. In this culture, the left hand spends a lot of time near the bum and is considered unclean.

GESTURE WITH GRACE Try to avoid pointing at someone or something, especially with your left hand or index finger alone extended. If you need to indicate direction or a specific person, gesture with your entire right hand. If you need to summon someone, beckon them with your palm down and wave your fingers. Pointing at or touching items with your feet is rude, and do not point your soles toward someone when sitting down.

Be aware that standing with your arms crossed or your hands on your hips suggests arrogance or anger. Patting anyone on the head, including children, is rude. Men should not touch women, or be overly familiar in social situations, other than for the initial handshake.

SHUCK YOUR SHOES Generally speaking, people should take off their shoes before entering someone's residence. Look for a line of shoes at the door and at least motion towards removing your shoes. Your host may tell you it's unnecessary.

FIND YOUR RELIGION Indonesians are required to have a religion. As a foreigner, you will be required to declare your religion to complete certain paperwork, opening a bank account, for example. It is considered poor form to dispute the existence of any deity. Pick a religion for formalities sake.

STATE YOUR MARITAL STATUS It is common for Indonesians to inquire into your marital status and number of children. They may show surprise or disappointment if you are above your mid-twenties and do not have children. Ask in return how many children they have, and they will be proud to list their children's ages and class levels at school.

COMMUNICATE CLEARLY Remember that a smiling Indonesian is not necessarily a happy Indonesian. A smile can indicate embarrassment or confusion. If a smile is not the response you are looking for, consider that you may be making people uncomfortable or that you may be making a spectacle of yourself. It's not their fault if they can't understand English and it may, in fact, be your accent or mispronunciation when speaking Indonesian.

ASK THE RIGHT QUESTION Indonesians like to be helpful. This may mean they give an answer to a question without really knowing the answer. Rather than admit, for example, that the person does not know where the nearest post office is, your interlocutor may give you their best guess. A tip when asking for directions is to get three people to give you the same answer before considering it accurate. Avoid leading questions like, 'Does it open at 9am?', to which the response is likely to be agreement. Ask open questions instead: 'What time does it open?' Questions about distances may be answered *jauh* (far)

or *dekat* (near). However, often *jauh* isn't actually that far at all!

DRESS FOR SUCCESS A woman showing skin will attract comments. Keep your shoulders, cleavage, midriff and thighs covered anytime you are not in a fancy mall, restaurant or bar. Dress conservatively when walking through a *kampung* to avoid offending less cosmopolitan residents. Unless exercising, men's shorts should reach the knees.

BE A POLITE PHOTOGRAPHER Indonesia and its people are incredibly photogenic. However, do ask permission, *Boleh foto?* (May I take a photo?), before shooting portraits. Most of the time you will not only be allowed but will be highly encouraged. Your subject may mutter that everyone takes their photo and then literally *takes* the photo away and never shares it. Photographers might consider printing some copies of the images and returning another day to share them.

HAVE SMALL CHANGE Always carry small denomination notes when out exploring, and do not assume that people can give change for a bill larger than Rp20,000. You may want a pocket of loose change to give to beggars and buskers.

SHOW PATIENCE Indonesians do many things which other cultures may find impolite or offensive. These include constant sniffing, unabashed belching, hawking and spitting on the street, blowing snot rockets, nose picking, squeezing pimples in public, letting doors slam in the next person's face, gathering in places which block the path of others, walking very slowly, commenting on how old, fat, scrawny or tired one looks, smoking in public places, pushing to enter and exit elevators, queue jumping, shoving at airport luggage carousels, letting their children run amok in restaurants and littering. These things are best ignored. Try not to judge one culture against another. Ultimately, these behavioral annoyances are minor and not intended to offend.

Getting around Jakarta

A car may be the easiest form of transport to arrive at the start of your urban walks, but it may not be the quickest or most adventurous. Add to the excitement of the day and the spirit of adventure by trying one of the numerous means of public transportation in Jakarta. It may be daunting the first time, but from the end of your first successful trip, your confidence will grow.

The following is a survey of some of the various means of transportation available in the city.

Fun, fast, cheap but daredevil Kopaja.

PPD, STEADY SAFE, MAYASARI BHAKTI AND OTHER LARGE BUSES These behemoths carry the largest numbers of passengers. There are both air-conditioned buses (Rp6,500) and non-air-conditioned (Rp3,000). They are useful for long hauls and cross-city trips, and may use the toll roads which can add to the price.

A safe, air-conditioned Transjakarta bus.

TRANSJAKARTA BUSWAY These air-conditioned buses operate along fixed corridors across Jakarta, and are the city's first attempt at a mass rapid transport system. The buses are clean, comfortable and easy to use. Buses run from 5am to 10pm, and the current fare for a single trip is Rp3,500. Although the government officially calls the system Transjakarta, the colloquial name, and the name used in this book, is Busway. Fares are fixed and paid at the start of the trip prior to passing through a ticket-operated turnstile.

KOPAJA AND METRO MINI These buses are fun, fast and cheap, but prepare for a white-knuckle ride. The conductors hang from open doors waving fistfuls of money, while drivers career across lanes pushing through the narrowest gaps in traffic. These buses are best taken during daylight in non-commute hours. Signal you want to alight by standing up and tapping a coin against the roof. The conductor will then holler to the driver. Fares are fixed, currently at Rp2,000 and will be collected during the trip by the conductor.

A familiar powder blue Angkot minivan.

ANGKOT/MIKROLET These are small powder blue minivans with side entrances. They generally hold 10–14 people but many more will squeeze in or hang out the doors during peak times. These minivans are very useful if you can figure out whether they are heading in your direction; routes are marked in the front windscreen. Fares are fixed at Rp3,000 per trip and are paid upon leaving.

TAXI It's easy to hail a taxi from the street or to order one by phone. There is a vast array of taxis in the city, with Silver Bird at the top end of the scale. Bluebird and Gamya are popular and reliable. Cheaper taxis display a *tariff lama* (old fare) sticker in their windscreens. Of the cheaper taxis, Express is safe and dependable. Other

A row of popular and reliable Bluebird taxis.

The more modern blue version of the bajaj.

Negotiate your fare in a three-wheeled bajaj.

personal favorites are Taxiku and the dilapidated Kosti Jaya.

OJEK Taking a motorcycle taxi is the quickest way to get anywhere in the city. There is not a spot in the city which does not have a guy on a motorcycle for hire. *Ojek* drivers will congregate together in packs of 2–20 waiting for passengers. They will provide helmets, but of varying quality. Unlike taxis, *ojek* drivers will always take the most direct route to your destination. Negotiate the fare before mounting the bike. Try haggling for a half or two-thirds of the starting price, but don't give yourself a hernia trying to save a few thousand rupiah. If you speak Indonesian and act confidently, you may be given the real price at the start. Fares could be between Rp3,000 and Rp30,000, but it all depends on distance, weather, traffic conditions and bargaining skills.

BEMO These blue three-wheeled vehicles are confined mainly to the neighborhoods of Bendungan Hilir, Manggarai, Salemba, King ITC Kota and Klender. They are very convenient for short trips. Try taking one from Pasar Benhil in central Jakarta, also the start of the Bendungan Hilir walking tour. Upon reaching your destination, tell the driver to stop by calling out *kiri* (left). Fares are Rp2,500 and are paid at the end

of the trip. Pass the money directly to the driver through the window.

BAJAJ These are wacky, noisy, smoky, bright orange three-wheelers, with the driver in the front and space for two passengers in the back. They are useful and fun for quick trips in the immediate neighborhood. Fare rates are negotiable and are paid at the end. You may want to agree a price at the outset. Prices may range from Rp10,000 to Rp25,000 depending on distance.

NEW BAJAJ The more modern *bajaj* is blue, has four wheels, and is cleaner and quieter than the older model. Fares are a little more expensive.

Pedal-powered becak carry two passengers.

BECAK These are pedal-powered rickshaws with space for two passengers in a bucket seat at the front and the driver mounted on a bicycle seat behind. They are rare now in Jakarta having been banned by the city administration in most areas. *Becaks* can, however, still be found in Bekasi and Glodok, and are common outside of the capital. Fares are negotiable and dependent on distance. Pay on arrival.

Enjoy a ride on a horse-drawn dokar.

DOKAR For a taste of the countryside, take a horse and cart and trot around the block old-school style. *Dokar* aren't very useful for getting from point A to point B as they generally travel from point A to point A, but it's all about enjoying the ride rather than getting somewhere. *Dokar* are becoming more difficult to find, but still operate around the Monas, Senayan, Pondok Indah, Kemang and Kebayoran Lama. Fares are negotiable according to distance and may be between Rp2,500 and Rp5,000 per person.

OJEK SEPEDA Generally found in north Jakarta near the Tanjung Priok port, Sunda Kelapa, Kota and Glodok, these are bicycles fitted with an extra passenger seat. Often toothless and with poor eyesight, the *ojek sepeda* drivers continue a tradition that has lamentably seen better days. They are fun for short, environmentally friendly trips, especially through tight traffic. Fare rates are negotiable and paid at the end of the trip, but don't bargain too hard with these guys: they face enough challenges as it is.

CANAL FERRY Most populated canal banks have simple ferries or rafts to carry people and goods from one side to the other. Powered by pole or by pulling on an overhead wire fixed to both shores, these craft are one of the few non-motorized forms of transport in the city in addition to the *becak, ojek sepeda, dokar* and *lori*. Fares are fixed at around Rp1,000 to Rp2,000 per person.

A canal ferry for carrying people and goods.

Trains are convenient for some destinations.

TRAIN The train from Gambir station in central Jakarta is very convenient for getting to the University of Indonesia, Bogor, Bandung and beyond. Visit www.kereta-api.co.id to get up-to-date schedules. Local station locations and schedules can be more challenging to figure out. Economy class trains can be slow and packed, but bring you up close and personal with a cross-section of Indonesian society. Look out for locals riding on train roofs during peak hours, but don't try this yourself.

LORI No doubt the strangest and least likely way to travel is by *lori*–a homemade push-cart rolling along the rail tracks at Kebon Kosong in central Jakarta. *Lori* can hold four passengers and are also used to transport goods. The standard price is Rp3,000 for 1.5km, but watch out for trains.

When riding on buses and economy trains you will often be approached by beggars and buskers. You might consider taking a pocket of loose coins to give away.

Tipping on public transport is not necessary, but rounding up the fare to the nearest Rp5,000 will be greatly appreciated in taxis.

Using Public Transport

REASONS WHY IT CAN'T BE DONE There are many reasonable objections to using public transportation—each of which is dutifully acknowledged and then dismissed here.

Objection #1: I'll get lost
It is possible that you will board a bus marked Blok M in south Jakarta and somehow alight near the Monas in central Jakarta. You can see this as either a) a disaster and a waste of time, or b) an excellent opportunity to explore the Monas. Getting lost on public transportation is a great way to find adventure in a new part of town. Ask the conductor or any of your fellow passengers if you have a question about where you are or where you are going. If all else fails, get out and take a taxi.

Objection #2: I'll get mugged/pickpocketed/harrassed/groped
Jakarta is a reasonably safe city, with the greatest risks being tummy trouble, broken infrastructure and traffic. If you feel especially vulnerable, get some tattoos and wear an eye patch. Otherwise, use common sense, protect your belongings and be aware of your surroundings. You are unlikely to experience trouble on public transport during daylight hours.

Objection #3: It will take too long
On the contrary, *ojeks* are the speediest form of transport in the city. Other forms of transport may not be quick, but taking public transportation might increase the uniqueness of the day, make for a better after-dinner story and add insight to your overseas experience. Try using public transportation to the destination and taking a taxi home.

Objection #4: It's hot and uncomfortable
It's the tropics, everyone sweats. Wear quick-dry clothing and travel during non-peak hours, with weekend mornings being by far the best. Always carry bottled water with you. Indonesian women often carry fans, so why not tuck one in your bag as well?

Objection #5: I can never figure out which is the right bus
Just ask. Indonesians are incredibly friendly and very approachable. Or pick up one of a number of fairly handy transportation guides from local Indonesian bookstores.

Objection #6: It won't take me directly to where I'm going
Try combining various forms of transportation. For example, take an *ojek* to the nearest Busway stop, ride the bus to the zoo and take a taxi home.

Objection #7: It's dirty, polluted and stinks
So is Venice! But don't let this stop you! Take a bandana to cover your mouth and nose.

Objection #8: I'll be overcharged
If you don't know where you are going, an *ojek* might overcharge you Rp10,000 or Rp20,000. On a bus, the conductor might ask for an extra Rp1,000. Who cares?

Objection #9: My company forbids me
You are not a rare imported species of fish or a vase. Company policies can be overprotective and paranoid; after all, they are looking out for you. Ignore your company once in a while.

Objection #10: I'm a girl
So what? See Objection #2. Travel with a buddy at night.

Now that all the objections have been overcome, everyone is free to choose any form of public transportation and go! The challenge now is to try and use every form of public transportation at least once during your adventure days in Jakarta.

Car Rentals and Taxis
Eazyrent Car Rentals
www.eazyrent.co.id

Trac Astra Rent Car
www.trac.astra.co.id

Bluebird Taxi Group
www.bluebirdgroup.com

Express Taxi Group
www.expressgroup.co.id

Transjakarta Busway Routes

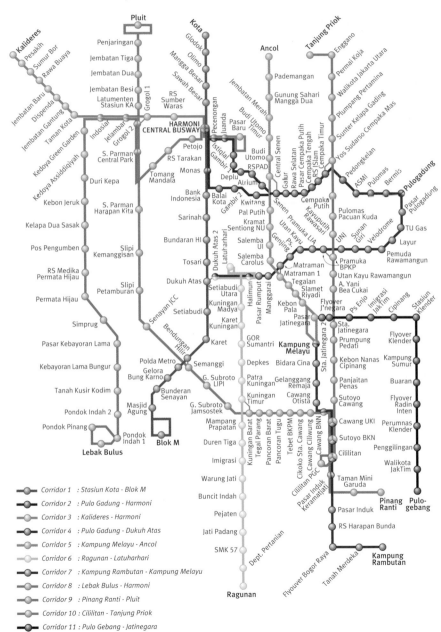

Corridor 1 : Stasiun Kota - Blok M
Corridor 2 : Pulo Gadung - Harmoni
Corridor 3 : Kalideres - Harmoni
Corridor 4 : Pulo Gadung - Dukuh Atas
Corridor 5 : Kampung Melayu - Ancol
Corridor 6 : Ragunan - Latuharhari
Corridor 7 : Kampung Rambutan - Kampung Melayu
Corridor 8 : Lebak Bulus - Harmoni
Corridor 9 : Pinang Ranti - Pluit
Corridor 10 : Cililitan - Tanjung Priok
Corridor 11 : Pulo Gebang - Jatinegara

Planning Your Explorations

Regardless of whether you have been in Jakarta for one day or one year, you may have noticed that just when you think you've got it figured out, there is always a new twist. The intention of this section is to clue you in to some of the inner workings of the city and to give the inside scoop on things you may have yet to come across and may have not even imagined possible. It's very important to read this section thoroughly before setting off on a walking tour, because it could save a lot of time, effort and possibly anguish.

A NOTE ON CITY PARKS Some people will tell you that the only parks Jakarta has are car parks. Unfortunately, that is a lot closer to the truth than we would like to admit. There are quite a few green spaces in the city if you go in search of them. Just consider a few things first.

The term 'park' is used loosely here. Strips, squares, triangles or any other shape of public land that has grass and is dotted with at least a few trees and shrubs is considered a park. Asking that parks have playground equipment, exercise stations and jogging paths is holding Jakarta to a standard it's not ready for.

Don't be surprised if when you arrive at a park you are the only one there. It is rare to find children playing in parks, families strolling around eating ice cream and groups of teens shooting the breeze and sneaking a cigarette or a kiss. Parks, as you might think of them, are so much of an anomaly in Jakarta that the residents don't seem to know exactly what to do with them. Most often, the only other visitors you may find here are snack vendors, a few stray cats and a couple of teenagers hanging out. On the weekends

A modern sculpture in Langsat Park.

and at dusk, though, some parks can get quite busy, especially as young guys often come out to play pick-up soccer games there.

Often there is little to do in these parks except stroll around in circles, sit and read or ponder life, but in a city such as ours, you should count your blessings when you can walk on an unbroken sidewalk without the risk of being run over by a motorcycle or falling into an open hole in the ground. While many parks are formed merely by the junction of a number of streets, and so are not totally free from motorized vehicle noise, there are still quite a few gems that were purposely made and are relatively peaceful and quiet, depending on the time of day.

Also, don't forget that golf courses are basically large green spaces with lots of trees and ponds, so when desperate times call for desperate measures, we count these as parks too. Even if the thought of playing golf abhors you, it's still a great way to get some light exercise, a suntan and escape the rat race.

A NOTE ON TRADITIONAL MARKETS

Nowhere in the country does even the most amateur of photographers have more opportunities to take incredible photos than in a local outdoor market *(pasar)*. With a kaleidoscope of colors, an often tantalizing array of exotic wares on display and a host of toothless, smiling faces, there's never a lack of subject material.

Beyond being great places to capture memories, they are also great places to capture your next meal. With fresh fruits and vegetables going for bargain prices, it's a wonderful way to buy healthy ingredients and save a dime. While food markets abound, many markets sell a wide variety of often unexpected other goods. Looking for a wicker lamp shade? You've got it. Ever wanted a pack of 1,000 incense sticks? It's yours. Can't live without a police costume? Go ahead and buy one! While not every market in Jakarta has been included in this book (there are more than 100), those found here should keep you busy exploring for a while.

When shopping at a *pasar*, it's a given that you should bargain and a given that you will still pay more for something than a local. That's okay. The important thing is whether

Jakarta's Railway Network

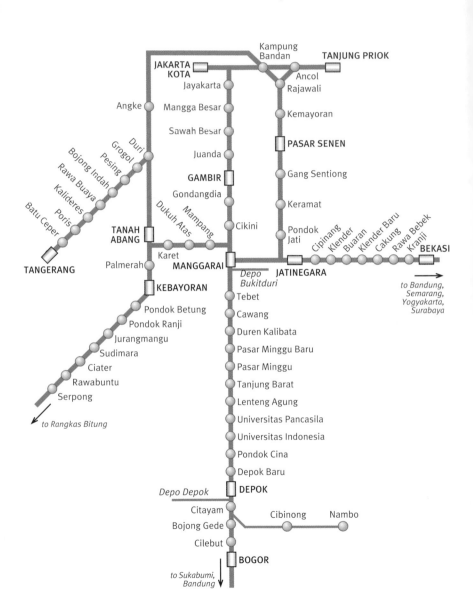

Selling chilis at a traditional market.

you feel you paid a good price and you got your money's worth. Always keep it friendly and wear a smile, as shouting or getting snappy over a few thousand rupiah is never acceptable. One thing to watch for is the pause. If you ask how much something is and the seller pauses for a few seconds before producing a number, you know that it's too high. Make sure to come with small money, because if you have just bargained for 30 minutes to get the price down to Rp10,000 from Rp12,000 and then you ask the seller to break a Rp100,000, you can be sure he will shoot you a soul-destroying stink eye.

BEWARE OF PICKPOCKETS Markets are a favorite hangout for pickpockets, so be aware of your surroundings, don't flash your money around, hold your bags close and keep them zipped, and dress down. Taking pictures is generally acceptable (though you should always ask first), and try to bring a cloth bag for your goodies so you don't end up with 20 disposable plastic bags at the end of the day.

A NOTE ON MUSEUMS Generally speaking, Jakarta's museums are underfunded—and it shows. Be sure to temper your expectations before entering and instead see them as an excellent opportunity to escape the heat and mayhem of the streets while learning a thing or two.

The entrance fees are not listed in this book but they generally range from around Rp500 to Rp5,000. This may not help funding much for the museums, but it does ensure that even the poorest of Jakarta's citizens have a chance to get in.

Most displays are not translated and those that are will say something vague, like 'old plate', which is not very useful. Either bring an Indonesian friend to translate, join an English-language tour, bring your electronic dictionary or just enjoy a stroll about. Learning Indonesian so you can read the signs yourself may be the best option of all.

For the most complete guide to the city's museums, check out the Indonesian Heritage Society's guidebook, *Museum Encounters: Jakarta.* Unfortunately, most museums don't have a website and those that do are in

The National Museum is great for learning about the country's numerous cultures and crafts.

Graves at Ereveld Menteng Pulo War Cemetery.

Indonesian, so make good use of the 'translate' button in Google.

Most museums are closed on Mondays and public holidays. They may also close for afternoon prayers.

A NOTE ON CEMETERIES If you are looking for a quiet place to walk around, away from the street noise and people, it's best to head to where they're dead. Cemeteries are good places to stretch your legs on a bicycle, and they can offer some decent single track. It's also interesting to see how locals bury their loved ones based on their religion.

Throughout the book you'll find various cemeteries noted, a good example being the Kalibata War Cemetery in Kalibata, south Jakarta. It's a large chunk of land complete with wide, clean, solid paths as well as a lake, monument and lots of bushes, flowers and stately trees. To top it off, there are deer in one corner of the cemetery. Most of the graves are noteworthy because of the helmets resting on them.

On maps, the cemeteries are listed as TPU, which stands for *tempat pemakaman umum* (public cemetery). If you are strolling around and trying to find a cemetery, you can ask people for the *kuburan* (grave) or *makam* (tomb).

A NOTE ON INDONESIAN PLACE NAMES
Except in headings, most sights listed in the book are first given in Indonesian, such as *Pulau Onrust*, and then followed up by the English, Onrust Island. The spelling of some words varies throughout the city, e.g. *ojek*, *ojeg*, etc. Generally, the spelling options given here are the most common.

A NOTE ON FINDING YOUR WAY AROUND
When you are looking at street signs, bear in mind that they stand perpendicular to the street they are naming, rather than parallel to the street as you would find in most Western countries. This is crucial knowledge if you are wondering why your map doesn't match the street signs.

The walking tours and corresponding maps in this book reference street names. On the ground, however, it may be challenging to actually spot a street sign. Look for street names given on local buildings or banners. Better yet, ask any of the lingering security guards (*satpam*) or *ojek* drivers nearby. The initials Jl. stand for Jalan (Street).

When seeking directions, ask for the end destination rather than the streets leading there. People may not know the intermediary street names, but they may well be able to point you in the right direction if you tell them the final destination. If there is confusion about where you are going, you might be mispronouncing the name; try showing a written form of the destination. Note, however, that in poorer neighborhoods, or among street workers and *satpam*, people may not be able to read well, or at all. People may also not be able to read maps. The longer someone hesitates before pointing somewhere, the more likely they don't know, so watch out for that look of uncertainty.

Directions to places in the book are, at times, not given with a high degree of detail. This is done on purpose. If you are anywhere near where you are supposed to be, just ask people around you and they'll point the way. It's better than having your nose buried in a map and getting frustrated because the book's description doesn't match what you are seeing. Another reason is that things change very rapidly in this city and a landmark/building/market that was there yesterday may not be there today.

A NOTE ON PEOPLE The walking tours in this book are nice, no doubt. You will enjoy going to new places, discovering novel things, and you'll come home loaded with tales of adventure. But the locations themselves are only half the story. It's the people who make up the rest.

It's imperative that you stop and talk. Take the Senayan walk, for example. Ultimately, it is a walk around a giant sports complex. This doesn't sound so interesting, but if you are there on a Sunday morning, and you stop and take the time to talk to some of the athletes, the families, the drink sellers, the skaters–

whoever it may be–your day will be radically different than if you had not.

If you feel shy, just sit down and hang out and undoubtedly someone will approach you and start chatting. Don't scowl at them, but smile and see what they've got to say. It doesn't matter if your Indonesian is not great, or even non-existent. You can either take this opportunity to practice the few words you know, you can seek out the English speaker in the group, or you can discover the beauty of hand gestures. Remember that Indonesians are not only incredibly kind, they are also incredibly patient. If you say three words in Indonesian, they will exclaim that you are fluent. Try saying three words in French to a Parisian some day and see what *they* have to say!

If you plan on snapping photos of people selling things, a good way to get them to open up and be responsive is to start by buying one of their goods. Imagine if you were a guy who sold drinks out of bamboo tubes and a tourist took a hundred photos with you and then walked off without buying the Rp3,000 drink! It hardly seems fair. Sellers will greatly appreciate the courtesy.

There may be times when you'll need to pay an unofficial fee to gain access to a site, enter a building, go beyond a certain point, take pictures or compensate for taking up quite a bit of someone's time. Usually this is a minimal amount of money, between Rp1,000 and Rp10,000, and the person asking for money will refer to it as *uang rokok* (cigarette money) or *uang kopi* (coffee money). This is likely chump change to you so be nice, pay the fee and don't get red in the face and stomp around. If you are trying to get something done, be proactive by offering to pay this *uang rokok* or *uang kopi* and alerting the person you are ready to go the extra mile to get it done. Often they won't state an amount, suggesting that 'it's up to you'. Pay what you think it's worth and watch for their reaction to see if you have given enough.

A NOTE ON ACTIVITY INFORMATION

Change keeps things dynamic and constantly interesting. For that, we love it. When it comes to phone numbers, e-mail addresses and websites, though, it's not great at all. From the time research began on this book until the time it was sent off to the publisher, more than half of the contact information collected was no longer valid.

CONTACT INFORMATION If an activity or business has a website, all extra information about opening hours, addresses or other relevant facts and figures will not be listed in this book since it should be available on the website. If you try the website and it's no longer valid, it may just require some additional internet sleuthing to find the new website, a valid phone number or e-mail address. This isn't the optimal situation, but it's the reality. Many businesses, in fact, are ditching websites in favor of a Facebook page.

A large number of the websites listed will only be in Indonesian. Make sure you are using Google's latest browser, which comes with a 'translate' button that will automatically translate the website into manageable English.

GETTING AROUND For getting to all the places listed in the book, it's generally assumed that you will come by taxi, take your own car (and driver) or take the Busway. General driving directions are often given, but it is expected that you'll make best use of a map. When it comes to parking, it's nearly impossible to guarantee that the parking situation of today will look anything like that of tomorrow. Most taxis will know general locations, but if there is some confusion, show them the printed name of where you are going as they may not understand what you are saying.

PRICES In most cases, prices have not been listed. Most entrance tickets, parking and admission fees, etc. are Rp50,000 or less, with many only Rp5,000–Rp10,000. If something is quite expensive, it has been noted.

PHONE NUMBERS Phone numbers are generally of two types: mobile phones and landlines. For all landlines in Jakarta, the numbers begin with 021. This is only needed if you are calling from a mobile phone or outside Jakarta. If you are calling from within Jakarta and from a landline, you don't need 021.

OPERATING HOURS Most government-run museums, cultural centers, etc. are open from around 10am to 4pm, Tuesday to Sunday. This may vary slightly from place to place. Note that often things will close during Friday prayers.

WEATHER OR NOT In a perfect world, every person in Jakarta would go around wearing nothing but a pair of shorts, a tank top and flipflops all day, every day, year round. With only two seasons, dry and wet, but a temperature that remains fairly constant, it's not hard to choose what to wear each day. The only question is, umbrella or no umbrella? While the humidity may rise and fall depending on the month, the temperature only varies between 80 and 90 degrees Fahrenheit (27–32 degrees Celsius). Nights don't cool down much, getting down to around 75 degrees Fahrenheit (24 degrees Celsius).

The rainy season is fairly hard to predict these days, but falls roughly between November/December and March/April. It's during these months that Jakarta is hit by its legendary floods, which can ruin the nicest of shoes, so keep those rubber boots at hand. The rain, while it can be inconvenient, is essential for scrubbing the city clean and cooling the air down. When the dry season finally comes, it can feel brutally hot if you are out under the direct sun and the locals, especially the middle to upper class, will avoid being out if it could darken their skin. A general lack of breeze doesn't help much, and tends to drive people indoors to the comforting coolness of air-conditioning.

THE RIGHT TIMING By far the best time of day to be out is in the early morning. If you can manage it, you should get up around the time the mosques start their morning call, the first of five daily prayers, at around 4.30 am. This is not only the coolest time of day, but also the quietest and cleanest. Late evening is nice as well once the traffic has abated and the clubs and restaurants start filling up. Many entertainment venues don't wrap things up until the wee hours of the morning, so you never have to search for a reason to stay up late.

Almost all activities in this book are best done early in the morning—from 5am to 8am. The later in the day you go, the more likely places will fill up with garbage, noise and pollution.

MONEY MATTERS Credit cards are useful at most shops in malls and modern stores, but don't bother using anything electronic on the street as it's a cash-and-carry deal only. Carrying around a wad of Rp100,000 is useful at Plaza Indonesia, but having a pocket full of Rp2,000, Rp,5,000 and Rp10,000 notes is crucial on a walking tour, as many vendors, *warungs*, taxis, *ojeks* and bicycle coffee guys don't carry much change and certainly don't want to break a big bill.

Prepare to bargain as needed for certain things, but always keep it lighthearted and try not to assume you are always being ripped off.

RELIGION RUNDOWN The government officially recognizes six religions: Islam, Catholicism, Protestantism, Buddhism, Hinduism and Confucianism, and woe to the poor fool who declares publicly that he or she is an Atheist. Houses of worship for all religions are found throughout the city and generally there are no issues between different religions worshiping in close contact. Of course, not all is hunky-dory: for example, there are ongoing clashes in Bekasi between a Christian congregation and the Muslims who don't want them worshipping in the area. Islam is the number one religion in Jakarta, with a mosque located on nearly every street corner, though many are no larger than a shed. People looking for an English language church service can check the local papers for listings.

The times you will most notice Islam at work in Jakarta are during Ramadhan, when Muslims fast throughout the day; Lebaran, the holiday after Ramadhan when everyone travels to the villages to be with family; Idul Adha, the Day of Sacrifice, when animals are slaughtered all over the city to celebrate Abraham's willingness to sacrifice his son; and every Friday around noon, when all the faithful head to the mosque for prayers.

HAPPENING HOLIDAYS Red days, as national holidays are called, are numerous in Indonesia and help keep everyone happy. If a holiday falls on a Monday or Friday, the city usually becomes a fairly civil place as people head for Puncak, Bogor, Bandung, Pelabuhan Ratu, Anyer, Carita, the Thousand Islands or Sukabumi to have some family fun. These three-day weekends often mean traffic is light, streets are fairly quiet and, if you want to explore the city, now is the chance to do it in peace. Note: People who stay in town often flock to Ancol, Taman Mini Indonesia Indah, Monas and Ragunan Zoo on these days, so it's best to avoid the destinations locals love.

Here is a list of some of the big holiday days:
- International New Year
- Chinese New Year
- The Prophet Muhammad's Birthday
- Hindu New Year
- Good Friday
- Ascension Day
- Buddha's Birthday
- Ascension of the Prophet
- August 17th Independence Day
- Lebaran/Idul Fitri after Ramadhan
- Idul Adha Sacrifice Day
- Islamic New Year
- Christmas

THE WHO AND HOW MANY Jakarta is made up of every ethnicity within Indonesia, as well as people of nearly every country in the world. The largest groups are the Javanese from Central and East Java and the Sundanese from West Java. While the Chinese do not make up a majority of the population, their influence on both the past and present is incalculable. Two terms you may often come across are *betawi* and *pribumi*. A *betawi* person is one whose ancestors were originally from Jakarta and their mascot is the *ondel-ondel*, large, brightly colored, doll-like statues or costumes with masks and giant spiky hair. A *pribumi* is an original inhabitant of Indonesia.

More than 9.5 million people live in Jakarta, though counting the local population is like trying to count a million meandering minnows in a pond. During the day, the city swells with a mass of commuters who inflate Jakarta to its bursting point, then flood out in the evening, causing legendary traffic jams. Jabodetabek includes more than 26 million people.

The number of expatriates (expats) in Jakarta, however, is a tough number to report, partly because many may not want to be counted due to their less than legal status in the country. The total could be said to be roughly 30,000, give or take 10,000.

YOU ARE WHAT YOU EAT While it seems impossible to get an authentic New York cheesecake in Jakarta, you can get nearly everything else. Of course, you should spend a good amount of time tucking into the local dishes. There are some great, upscale Indonesian eateries that serve some true delights, but often the best food will be dished up from *warungs* or *kaki limas*

(rolling food carts). The standard rule (up to a point) is that the cheaper it is, the tastier.

You may not think that eating food from a roadside stall would be that pleasurable, but many locals will tell you that the true secret ingredient to a good plate of *nasi goreng* is the exhaust off the street. This is why a similar dish found abroad doesn't taste nearly as good. Do note that while eating street food is encouraged, it shouldn't be done with reckless abandon. Try to eat somewhere busy, somewhere relatively fly free and somewhere with its own running water. If something smells or tastes funky, trust your instinct and don't eat it.

Try to glimpse how and where the dishes are bring washed. If the person who is cutting up the meat is also the one handling the money as well as sweeping up, perhaps it's time to push on. Ultimately, try to find a place with a good, long-running reputation and think about either ordering it to go or bringing your own bowl and cutlery.

SAY IT LIKE YOU MEAN IT Although English is becoming more widely used, and a surprising number of Indonesians can use it functionally, visitors to and residents of Jakarta are highly encouraged to learn the local language, *Bahasa Indonesia*. It's by far one of the easiest languages to learn, particularly since most Westerners can read it without having to learn a new alphabet. The grammar is simple, the words are generally short, and it's free of the challenging tonal inflections heard in languages like Chinese and Japanese.

For the true Jakarta explorer, the most important word to learn is *Ayo!* (Let's go!). See the back of the book for a list of helpful starter phrases which should be employed immediately.

One of thousands of roadside stalls in Jakarta.

Jakarta Food Guide

While out and about, look out for and try the following common dishes and snacks.

Eggplant in tomato salsa

Papaya leaves

Padang-style dining

Banana leaf rice wrap

Bitterballen

Satay

Fried tempeh with chili

Corn fritters

Chili sauce

Egg, chili and shallot dish

Fried rice with egg

Stewed buffalo, tourist favorite

Mild and fiery chili salsas

Fried noodles

Instant noodles

Cashew chicken served in pineapple

Sour vegetable soup

Fish balls

Fried snacks

Red chili sauce and salad

Fried bananas

Desiccated coconut and palm sugar rolls

Streetside wraps

Fried streetside snacks

Fermented moldy tempeh

Indonesian meatballs

Vegetable fritter

Steamed fish wrapped in
banana leaf

Croquettes

Rice boiled in palm leaf packets

Steamed peanuts

Guava

Grilled corn

Persimmons

Rose apples

Fresh fruit in vendor cart

Durian ice cream

Jackfruit

Dates

Mussels

Cockles

Octopus

Cubed fruit drinks

Melon juice in recycled cup

Avocado juice with chocolate sauce

Mango juice

Watch out for gasoline sold in soft drink bottles

Kopi luwak

Bottled soft drinks

Palm sugar drink

Iced coffee

Pulled tea with condensed milk

Dessert soup

Banana coffee

Soup

Coffee from bicycle coffee seller

Coconut juice

Jakarta Snapshot

While most people claim to live in Jakarta, in reality they live in Jabodetabek, which sounds more like a mythical beast than a place to live. This is a combination of names for all the municipalities that have slowly been swallowed up by the Jakarta beast. The name comes from Ja (Jakarta), Bo (Bogor), De (Depok), Ta (Tangerang) and Bek (Bekasi). From north to south, the city of Jakarta stretches more than 25km and covers more than 740 sq km. The Jabodetabek area covers 2,720 sq km. Of the 100 largest cities in the world, Jakarta comes in number 24 according to the United Nations and it also has one of the highest growth rates, regardless of government attempts to stem the incoming tide of workers from the countryside. People continue to have fairly large families as well, as every child is considered to be a gift from God according to Islam, adding to the population increase.

Jakarta sits on an alluvial plain, which means it was formed by the build-up of sediment that washed down in rivers from the surrounding highland areas. Regular, natural flooding helped to increase the plain's size, although the flooding nowadays seems more intent on washing Jakarta out to sea. The entire city is quite flat, with the highest areas in southern Jakarta still only about 50m above sea level. There are 13 rivers that wind their way through the city, although not all were naturally formed. The Ciliwung is by far the most famous of the bunch.

Jakarta rests on top of an aquifer known as the Jakarta Groundwater Basin. Unfortunately, the output is higher than the input, which means that the city is not only sinking, with north Jakarta going quicker than the rest, but that the water supply is being tapped out. In addition, there is serious saltwater intrusion into the aquifer from the Java Sea, and local industries continue to pollute all water sources at an unchecked rate. Luckily, there seems to be no shortage of *Teh Botol*, so no one will die of thirst–and as cheap as it is, theoretically one could bathe in it as well.

HISTORICALLY SPEAKING The history of Jakarta before the 16th century is patchy. Traders from India most likely brought Hinduism and then Buddhism to the area, and Chinese merchants headed through the Malacca Strait started visiting islands here on a regular basis in the 15th century. But it wasn't until the Portuguese rocked up in 1513, the first European ships to do so, that historical records become detailed.

At that time, Jakarta was known as Sunda Kelapa and was the port town for the Hindu Kingdom of Pajajaran. As the Hindus wanted to temper the Islamic Sultanates of the region, they signed a deal with the Portuguese that allowed them a presence in the area. Before the Portuguese had a chance to establish a foothold though, Fatahillah of the Banten Sultanate destroyed Sunda Kelapa in 1527 and then founded Jayakarta–meaning 'Victorious City'.

The Dutch came to shore in 1596, unknowingly changing the course of Indonesia's history, in order to establish the VOC (Dutch Trading Company) and capitalize on the spice trade. At that time, there were only around 3,000 houses in the town, a far cry from residential counts of today. The British weren't too far behind, though, as they began settling in around 1615. Until 1619, Jayakarta was ruled by the Sultan of Banten, but it was the Dutch Governor-General Jan Pieterszoon Coen who walloped the Sultan's troops, destroyed the city and built one to his liking, with a castle called Batavia at the center. The name Batavia was chosen in remembrance of the Batavians, a tribe of people regarded as the ancestors of the Dutch people. The name stuck for the next 300 years.

In 1650, Chinese temples went up in Glodok and Ancol, and in 1710 the City Hall at Fatahillah Square went into service. Starting in 1730, the unfortunate inhabitants of Batavia were being ravaged by malaria so badly that there was a mass exodus southward for those looking for somewhere more livable. In 1750, the Dutch murdered 5,000 Chinese residents in a killing spree that followed a period of growing suspicion and unrest. This event, helped by horrendous sanitation issues, led to Batavia's eventual downward spiral. In 1796, the British whooped up on the Dutch, and in 1799 the VOC was considered to be all but washed up.

By 1811, much of Kota had been dismantled or destroyed and new construction was

An early Dutch map of Batavia, the name given to Jakarta by the Dutch in the 17th century.

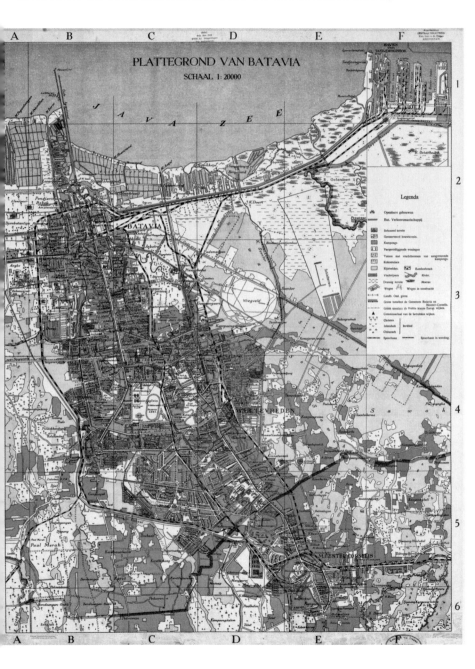

The City Hall of Batavia, 1710–1913.

replacing the damage. At the same time, Sir Stamford Raffles, the Lieutenant-Governor of Java from 1811to 1815, was pushing for an end to slavery across the country. The Dutch came back to power in 1816 and turned the Monas area into the center of business as well as the new hotspot for the rich and famous. Dutch rule lasted until the Japanese arrived in 1942 with swords drawn and a kamikaze spirit, thereby becoming the new overlords and ruling with an iron fist. The city's name at this time, Jayakarta, was shortened to the current Jakarta.

The Dutch, tenacious as always and loathe to give up both the city and country, made a power grab again after the Japanese surrendered the war in 1945. It was then, on August 17th, 1945 that Indonesia declared de-facto independence. Unfortunately, without the American assistance that almost came through, the Indonesian people had to continue to fight for the next four years until the Dutch, outnumbered and outfought, gave in and agreed to grant Indonesia its independence in 1949. The population of Jakarta at the time was less than 1 million and Kebayoran Baru was the newest Dutch-built neighborhood.

Founding President Sukarno had a grand vision of modernity for his newly freed city, and he set about to make it so by backing projects such as the Istiqlal Mosque, Monas and the Gelora Bung Karno Sports Stadium, all connected by Jl. Thamrin running through the middle of the city. With Sukarno's fall from power in 1965, having been ousted in a coup led by Suharto, the job of running the city was left up to Lieutenant-General Ali Sadikin, who worked feverishly to develop and modernize the city, sometimes for the good, sometimes for the bad.

With the economic collapse of 1997, a year permanently etched in the minds of many Jakarta residents, all development came to a screeching halt when funding evaporated. In 1998, all hell broke loose in the city as tanks rolled through the streets to prevent looting and rioting, sparked by inflation, fuel price hikes and utter dissatisfaction with the 32-year rule of dictator Suharto. Armed forces killed four students at Trisakti University in west Jakarta during a political rally, and in the pandemonium that ensued over the following months, more than 6,000 buildings were torched, burgled or destroyed, and approximately 1,200 people died. Mobs targeted Chinese residents in Glodok, and the evidence of these times remains visible to this day.

The latest ills to affect the city were the bombings of the JW Marriot Hotel in 2003, the Australian Embassy in 2004, the Ritz Carlton and again the same JW Marriot Hotel in 2009 and substantial flooding in 2007.

But time heals all wounds and Jakarta, while falling one step back for every two steps forward, continues to forge ahead and to establish itself as a major player on the international market. The Indonesian economy was little affected by the economic crisis in 2008, and growth, development, modernization and waistlines have continued to grow at an exponential and seemingly unabated rate. Skyscrapers and high-rise apartment towers mark Jakarta's skyline like blades of metallic grass, and suburban sprawl devours surrounding farmland and rice fields like an insatiable, wild-eyed beast. The rich line their Lamborghinis and Porsches in front of Pacific Place Mall to ensure they get noticed, and to have any less than two mobile phones is something to be ashamed of.

The incredible forward momentum of the city is simultaneously being tempered though by the city's planners who seem to be on permanent holiday. With the local government continuously demonstrating that it is powerless to create change, the city's future seems, at times, mildly frightening. All this being said, it's the lawlessness that runs rampant in Jakarta that is half the city's charm, and perhaps the chaos and disorder that so well define Jakarta should be something to be accepted as part of its very soul rather than seen as a disorder which must be cured.

Jakarta, for all the airs it may put on from time to time, is and always will be nothing less than a great big village.

Staying Active in Jakarta

SPORTS CENTER

One of the toughest things about living in Jakarta is trying to get some outdoor exercise, mainly because finding out when and where to go can be challenging. The central sports complex is located in Senayan and various sports are mentioned in the Senayan tour (see p. 136). Other sports are covered in this section of the guidebook, and while not exhaustive, it should provide a good start for keeping fit.

AUSSIE RULES RUGBY

Also known as footy, football or AFL, this is a game in which two teams of 18 players each try to score points by kicking a ball between vertical posts at each end of an oval-shaped field. Players move the ball by either kicking it, running with it or hitting

Cyclists wearing Bike2Work T-shirts.

it with a closed fist or open hand. The ball is never thrown. A 'mark' is taken by catching a kicked ball on the full, entitling the mark taker to a free kick. There are no offsides, with possession turned over if an attacker is tackled or held with the ball. This is a contact sport played without padding or helmets, but there are rules to restrict dangerous physical contact.

In Jakarta, the local team is the Bintangs, and although it is mainly an Aussie crowd that plays, the team welcomes people of all nationalities and abilities. The club plays against teams from around Southeast Asia, with adversaries including Singapore, Malaysia and Vietnam. The Bintangs also support a growing junior league for Indonesian teenagers.

CHECK OUT www.bintangs.com

NOTE The location and times of the Bintangs' practices can vary, so it's best to contact them via their website to get updated information. Otherwise, they can often be found at the artificial turf field (see p. 138) next to the outdoor basketball courts in the Senayan Stadium complex on Thursday nights from 6pm to 8pm.

BICYCLING

BIKE2WORK First started in 2004 by a few individuals from one of Jakarta's mountain biking communities, Bike2Work has now grown to roughly 10,000 members. Some want to help create fresher air in the city by avoiding the use of motorized vehicles, others are looking for a fun ride to work while saving a bit of money, while still others are simply sick of sitting in traffic jams.

To become a member of Bike2Work you need only join the mailing list and make the commitment to get to work under your own power from time to time. Some people ride solo, others meet in large groups to commute together. Some ride every day, others just once or twice a week. It's a social thing as well, with Bike2Workers often dining together, getting together on weekends and building friendships. They are very supportive of newcomers and will escort them to and from work until they are comfortable on the roads and on their bikes. They will help find alternative routes, point out bicycle shops, give tips on bicycle maintenance and train you on how to read the traffic.

You don't have to own an expensive bicycle to join, as Bike2Work is collaborating with local bicycle manufacturer Polygon to produce affordable bicycles and helmets. Wimcycle, another local brand, makes cheaper, less durable bicycles, while Indonesia-based United offers models toward the higher end. You can pick up good second-hand bicycles at Pasar Rumput (Grass Market) (see p. 148).

> 'Our dream is that soon every household will own at least one bicycle and that someday riding your bicycle to work in Jakarta will be seen as a normal alternative for transportation.' **Dani Dewanto of the B2W Program and Technical Team**

WHO TO CONTACT www.b2w-indonesia.or.id

GO TO Jl. Ahmad Dahlan #20 south Jakarta

CYCLING IN THE CITY The second and last Sunday of every month is car-free day on **Jl. Sudirman and Thamrin** from the Senayan roundabout to the Monas. The same goes for these two roads every Sunday morning from 5am to 8am (exact times can vary). For those who are looking to cycle among hundreds of other riders to really get a sense of community, and in fact to join the cycling community, there is no better opportunity than this one.

Other sweet spots to go for a ride are the **Monas**, which offers curb hopping and mazes of paths among the trees; the **Senayan Sports Complex** for some short dirt trails, a few laps around the stadium and general exploration; and the **Ragunan Zoo**, great for early morning speed cruises on the sloping, serpentine pathways, plus long stairwells for the brave at heart.

There is also the **University of Indonesia**, which offers a wide, open campus for logging a lot of tree-lined miles with loads of cute girls and guys around to provide distraction; **Taman Mini**, which not only provides a cultural tour of Indonesia, but has enough space for a couple of hours of exploring. **Ancol** also has loads of bicycle friendly paths

and roads, while the neighborhoods just west of there have real bicycle lanes.

For clean, quiet rides among Jakarta's finest, head to the upscale communities of **Menteng, Kebayoran Baru, Kemang** or **Pondok Indah** on Sunday mornings. For those with adventure running through their blood, a ride along the canals and railroads provides a good lesson in socioeconomics; it's slow on speed but heavy on the eyeballs. A fine stretch to start on is the **Kali Malang** (Malang Canal), which runs through the heart of the city. You can hop on it from Menteng where Jl. Cokroaminoto crosses over Jl. Latuharhari.

Be aware that although bicycling is alive and well in Jakarta, the key to safe riding is to ride defensively rather than aggressively. Signal intentions to turn or stop, ride in a group if possible, wear reflective clothing, use lights at night, never ride without a helmet and never assume a vehicle will give the right of way. The rule in Jakarta is to go with the flow, fill the gap in traffic, relax, but always be aware and stay off the main roads as much as possible.

CHECK OUT www.rodalink.com, www.unitedbike.com and www.polygonbikes.com

MOUNTAIN BIKING Tearing around muddy bends, disappearing over steep drop-offs, plummeting down a screaming hillside and occasionally doing a Superman over the handlebars—that's what single-track bike courses are all about.

The **JPG** (Jalur Pipa Gas) cross-country mountain bike course in south Jakarta is not only home to the Bike2Work movement, but also the go-to place to take in some solid single track and get a dose of fresh air. Whether you go for fun or to compete in one of the races (there are categories, for men, women, children, pros and members of the public), the course is easy enough that most competent riders can complete it, while those with skills will still find it challenging.

The 7.2km track combines footpaths, single-track and dual-path dirt roads. It rolls through trees, fields and local neighborhoods, goes over rivers and streams and past a fishing pond. It combines sharp corners, fairly steep but short hills, rickety bridges, muddy sections, fast straight-aways and knobby root stretches. Oh, and don't forget the water buffalo.

The action starts at **Mpok Café** in Kampung Lengkong Timur. It's here that you can pick up all the latest mountain biking news, form friendships, find other cyclists to ride with and fill up on fried bananas and sweet coffee before setting off on a roller coaster ride.

HEADS UP

The course is generally quite safe at slow speeds, and there are sections that some may need to walk. Be careful at higher speeds, though, and try not to ride faster than you are comfortable with, since some sections could send you sailing over your handlebars.

HOW TO GET THERE Finding Mpok Café is nearly impossible without going with those in the know. Head to the McDonalds parking lot in Bintaro Jaya Sektor 9 at the intersection of Jl. Bintaro Utama 9, Jl. Jend. Sudirman and Jl. Maleo. This is just north of the Jakarta-Serpong toll road. Groups meet on Saturday or Sunday morning between 6am and 7am. Some groups will then head toward Sentul and the Puncak area, some toward central Jakarta and others to the JPG or any other number of trails in the area. A new trail recently opened and others are constantly being sought out and developed, so it's good to go back regularly and find out updates.

SENTUL Long known as the go-to place for both mountain bikers and road cyclists who want to ride hard but still stay close to home, Sentul is roughly 45km from central Jakarta. Riders generally head out early on a weekend to avoid traffic and take advantage of the cooler weather.

Bikers meet at the **Star Deli** in Sentul at around 7am on most Saturdays and finish up by lunchtime. Some of the rides will be fairly hard core, running you into the ground. Others are more suitable for newbies. Most rides start in the Sentul Selatan area, just a few minutes from the toll road.

For road bikers, there are some nicely paved stretches of road relatively free of heavy traffic, with some folks starting at the lake next to the park gates near Rainbow Hills. Mountain bikers, meanwhile, can enjoy countless rides in the hills and mountains on single tracks, village paths and plantation and rice paddy trails. There are some long hills out here that expats usually ride up, while many Jakarta locals get shuttled up in a truck before putting on their gear for downhill-only rides.

Top off-road rides include:

HAMBALANG HILL This ride has a couple of good downhill stretches that include riding through a quarry as well as some grinding ascents, including one called The Wall. It starts north of the Star Deli in a *kampung* that links up with a nice road that later turns rocky with lots of climbing. It continues through a semi-rural area that includes some fast dirt downhills. It ends near Sirkuit Sentul.

GUNUNG GEULIS (PRETTY MOUNTAIN) There are many variations on this ride, one of which is to start south of Star Deli and ride in the dirt and mud parallel to the toll road. The route follows the river for a while before climbing, then dropping into the town of Gadog near Jl. Puncak Jaya. From there begins a long series of climbs that end on a ridge looking over the Rainbow Hills golf course. The ride continues until it reaches The Cyclists *warung* at the T-intersection of Jalan Bojong Koneng-Babakan and Jalan Bojong Koneng-Gunung Geulis. You can then take the Waskita path, a fun downhill single track that leads back to Sentul.

HUNTER'S HUT Start at the General's House and take the dirt road, cutting through farmland and forest all the way to Pondok Pemburu (Hunter's Hut), where refreshments are sometimes available. Next, cross a stream, pass a church and follow the ridge-line toward Gunung Pancar, a pyramid-shaped mountain home to the Sebex MTB Bike Park. This park is a wicked single-track, downhill mountain bike course with banked turns, exposed roots, boulders, meter-high jumps, mud puddles, sandbags and daring drop-offs. Although Sebex has an extreme downhill track option, it also has easier side paths for those less daring.

The ride finishes by passing through some fields and a development area before getting back to Sentul. Note: This ride can be done as a circuit from Sentul, but this makes it a long ride with lots of climbing. It's easier to get a lift to the General's House and then get picked up at the bottom of the Sebex downhill track.

Since all these routes are unmarked and can be difficult to find and/or follow if you don't know where you're going, the best way to ride is to join one of the many cycling clubs that come here often. Also, the wet season makes all off-road tracks significantly more difficult. If you're riding after a heavy rain, be prepared for plenty of slippery mud.

WHERE TO GO The Star Deli in Plaza Amsterdam in Sentul is a popular place for cyclists to gather both before and after rides. It has good burgers, beer and flirtatious barmaids, and offers a good place to get cleaned up before heading home.

HOW TO GET THERE Take the Jagorawi toll road to the exit at km 36–Sentul Selatan/Sentul City. Drivers can park outside Star Deli or at any of the shopping centers in the Sentul City area.

THE VELODROME Jakarta is home to a full-sized velodrome, an oval-banked track for cycling, with large angled walls made for ripping laps and training for the next big racing event. It's a bit rundown, but intact enough for you to spend some time spinning your wheels. It has a small section of stadium style seating so friends can come and cheer (or jeer). Open to the public as long as cyclists register in the velodrome office, it's a great place for a rider to feel like a pro. For those with a fixed gear bicycle, the latest trend among cyclists these days, it's an excellent place to get a workout.
Note: There's a good chance local kids will be using the velodrome for bicycling or even for sliding down the steep embankments on their butts. Challenge them to a race, and may the best cyclist win. Also, keep in mind that going high on the banked wall is a thrill but it can be dangerous. Always wear a helmet, and don't attempt anything that you're not capable of.

HOW TO GET THERE Take Busway #4 to the Velodrome stop (note that only folding bicycles are allowed on a Busway bus).

FOR DRIVERS From Central Jakarta, take Jl. Pramuka as it turns into Jl. Pemuda. The Velodrome is on the left-hand side just past the Busway stop. There is plenty of parking inside.

DANCING
BELLY DANCING Get your moves down in a dance studio. Learn to swing your hips with Christine, a voluptuous belly dancing instructor. As a belly-dancing student you will wear jingly belts and learn to sway rhythmically to Middle Eastern music, wiggling and thrusting, shaking and strutting; hands held steady while mid-sections move magically. In addition to belly dancing classes, the dance studio, located in a large converted house, offers hula and Bollywood dancing.

Bollywood movies have popularized moves such as shimmying, arm rolls, hop steps, head swivels and gestures that mimic archers shooting arrows. Just like in the movies, Bollywood dancing requires first and foremost the desire to boogie; after that you'll find yourself exercising without even having realizing it. The music is rocking, the instructor is good looking and everyone around will think you look great in tight, hot pink pants.

WHERE TO GO Jl. Mas Putih, Blok D-48–Permata Hijau

HOW TO GET THERE Take Jl. Teuku Nyak Arif to Jl. Permata Hijau Boulevard Barat, then turn on to Jl. Mas Putih. Parking is limited to the street.

CHECK OUT www.bellydancejakarta.com and www.huladancejakarta.blogspot.com

Scuba diving in the warm waters of the Java Sea.

DIVING
If you really want to enjoy Jakarta life, work all week and dive all weekend. Dive shops in Jakarta offer convenient certification courses for those without a scuba diving license. In

just two days you can finish the bookwork and pool sessions, ready to spend the third and fourth days exploring the warm waters of the Java Sea.

Most dive outfits also offer scuba for kids, refresher courses, advanced open water, rescue and dive master.

Most operators run monthly trips to the Thousand Islands, Krakatau and Ujung Kulon in West Java, and if a person has more time, to Sulawesi, Komodo and Papua. Coral bleaching, dynamite and cyanide fishing and a constant battering of garbage and pollution from Jakarta has taken its toll on the visibility (10-15m) around the Thousand Islands. Still, there are a solid number of good dives out there. Try out the following hotspots.

NAPOLEON AND TABULARASA WRECKS NEAR PRAMUKA ISLAND The ships, the sea life and the coral are what make this dive cool. Its close proximity to Jakarta makes it easy to reach as well.

PUTRI ISLAND This is by far the best-known island for an open-water certification, largely because it has its own dive center. Overnight options are reasonable, and the swimming pool and karaoke bar make it an interesting hide-out for families or party-goers.

ALAM KOTOK ISLAND With its private dive center and basic accommodation, this is one of the best-value options for a quick dive weekend. Although closer to Jakarta than Pulau Putri, the marine and coral life here seems to be in better condition.

PENIKI ISLAND The house reef along the west side of the island is a sloping reef that runs 5-20m deep. Fish life here is good, with batfish, parrotfish, moray eels, barracuda and passing turtles. A wooden cargo vessel wreck on the southwest tip of the reef at 20m attracts schools of fish and some of the larger parrotfish. The focus here is shore dives.

MACAN ISLAND Stylish but basic eco-resort constructed from driftwood and recycled materials. Although the lack of a dive center makes this a pricey option for divers, there are still plenty of snorkeling opportunities.

CORAL LIFE AT SEPA ISLAND The beaches are beautiful and you'll find no shortage of

marine life. Its proximity to Pulau Putri's dive center keeps the prices within reason.

GOSONGLAGA ISLAND The island is actually a sandbank that is entirely surrounded by a reef that extends down 20m. The corals here rival those of Alam Kotok, and a large variety of reef fish have made this their home. Stingrays are frequent visitors, as are sweet lips, trigger fish, lionfish, moray eels, turtles, surgeons and unicorn fish.

HEADS UP
Boats to all these islands leave from the Marina Jaya Ancol. Just check at the office.

TOP DIVE OUTFITS IN JAKARTA Kristal Klear Dive in the Kristal Hotel (Jl. Terogong Raya, Cilandak Barat; www.kristalkleardive. com); Aquasport Indonesia in Kemang (Jl Bangka Raya 39a; 021-749-9045 or enquiry@aquasport.co.id); ODY Dive Center Indonesia in Menteng (Jl. Panarukan 15; www.odydive.com); Bubbles Dive Center in Kuningan (Jl. Guru Mughni 18; www.bubbles-divecenter.com); Lautan Mas Dive Shop in Glodok (Jl. Toko Tiga 24; www. lautanmas.com)

FUTSAL (INDOOR SOCCER)
A curiously miniaturized version of football, futsal is a fast-paced indoor sport that is played all year round. With teams made up of five players and a ball that is smaller than a standard football, the game is lightning quick. It relies more on ball-handling techniques and control than brute kicking force.

WHERE TO GO The following are just a few of the myriad locations to play:
- Pakubuwono Futsal Center (Jl. Kyai Maja Raya 63; 021-724-3088)
- Planet Futsal Serpong at Kompleks Multiguna (Blok B2 #8, Jl. Raya Serpong km 7, Tangerang; 021-539-8234)
- Planet Futsal Kelapa Gading (Kompleks AXC, Building E, Jl Boulevard Raya, #1, Kelapa Gading; 021-4584-2594)
- Pro Arena (Jl. Metro Pondok Indah Blok BB III, Pondok Pinang, Kebayoran Lama; 021-765-8670/021-9407-5700)

FOR A MORE COMPLETE LISTING OF FIELDS, CHECK OUT www.makarafutsal. com/fighting-ground

GOLF

A round or two of golf is more than just a way to get in some exercise or get away from the family, it's an avenue for soaking up a bit of nature and fresh air, something everyone needs a lot more of. Whether you want to practice your putting, have something to prove to your buddies or just want an excuse to dress in funny clothes and drive around in a miniature car, hitting the greens in and around Jakarta is a must.

Of all the courses in the area, the **Jagorawi Golf and Country Club** probably has the most cachet. Although there are 47 holes, it is the 'Old Course,' consisting of 18 splendid holes carved out along the banks of the Cikeas River 30 years ago that captures the imagination.

This is a walking-only course with fairways that are narrow and generally lined with impenetrable secondary growth. Jagorawi's Old Course is sheltered and can get extraordinarily hot, especially for those who tee off in the early morning. Once the dry season has arrived, a post-lunch start offers the prospect of a second nine, in which the temperature drops to a balmy level and all the colors and textures of a late afternoon in the tropics are visible.

Over the years, the course has built up a devoted membership despite the spartan changing rooms and other perceived shortcomings, because it is a golfer's course where it is not necessary to book. The country club also has three pools and offers treks, horseback riding and polo.

WHERE TO GO Take the Jagorawi toll road heading toward Bogor and exit at km 24.

CHECK OUT www.jagorawi.com

From the moment your bags are unloaded at the **Cengkareng Golf Course** to the final check-out with a charge card-cum-locker key, it is clear this is a professionally run business whose aim is to get people back.

The 18-hole course is not easy. In fact, it is tough enough to have been chosen for the 2002 Indonesian Open, although its proximity to the airport must have counted in what were still considered risky times for the country. And even though it occupies a flat, rectangular plot, the designers and gardeners have achieved a remarkable variety of layout and color on what is, pleasingly, also a walking course.

The excellent level of service impresses, from the cold towels at each of the drink stops to the delightful but not over-familiar staff to the low-key clubhouse with its decent dining and proper spike bar. Partly because of its location, the course can get crowded, and there is always the risk of a general and his entourage creating mayhem with the tee-off schedule. You may also need earplugs on two or three of the holes as planes take off nearby.

WHERE TO GO Soewarna Business Park just off Jl. Raya Bandara at the Soekarno-Hatta Airport, just before Terminal 1.

CHECK OUT www.cengkarenggolfclub.com

RANCAMAYA is a development that took off in the booming 1990s, but the sheer scale and location set it apart. As you leave behind the chaos of the Bogor/Sukabumi road and motor down the kilometer-long tree-lined drive, the ambition of the developers becomes apparent. The estate is huge, and much of it faces the still partially wooded slopes of Gunung Salak (Mount Salak).

The golf course is beautifully orientated to take full advantage of the views, especially the first and tenth holes. Different sections of the estate have been set aside for various types of housing, with the top-end plots located adjacent to the course. Some, though not all, of the mini-palaces that have been erected are shocking in their vulgarity. Many prominent Suharto era figures 'acquired' plots here, and a round of golf can feel a little like a lesson in recent political history. Rancamaya is professionally managed, well maintained and has an excellent clubhouse with great views. It rains most days, so an early tee-off is recommended. Buggies are mandatory, and while the caddies are charming, they are certainly not among the best in terms of reading the greens for the lazy golfer.

WHERE TO GO Take the Jagorawi toll road just past km 46 to Ciawi and exit to the right on to Jl. Rancamaya Utama.

CHECK OUT www.rancamayaestate.com

Another excellent choice is the **Bukit Pelangi Golf Course** (Rainbow Hills). This beautiful property sits at an elevation of around 500m above sea level, and this makes for a nice, ambient temperature. To be in the fresh mountain air in the early morning is a privilege. Although the decaying shell of a planned Sheraton Hotel overlooks the course and the clubhouse is below standard, the rewards of playing this tough hilly course more than outweigh the objections.

This is not a walking course, but many golfers are probably grateful for the buggies given the undulations that need to be negotiated. As with most Puncak-based courses, it is probably wise to tee off early. In truth, there are a number of competing properties in the area that can be recommended, including **Gunung Geulis** and **Bukit Sentul**, but playing at Rainbow Hills really offers a sense of being completely away from the maddening crowds of Jakarta.

HOW TO GET THERE Take the Jagorawi toll road to Sentul, exiting at km 36. Go up Jl. Thamrin, take a right on Jl. Bukit Sentul and then a left on to Jl. Cijayanti, following it to the course.

CHECK OUT www.rainbowhillsgolf.com

The **Matoa Golf Course** was built in 1995, reportedly as an act of 'homage' to President Suharto by one of his business cronies. It is located on a compact site among the *kampungs* of south Jakarta near Ciganjur. Getting there entails a tiresome drive along roads teeming with motorbikes and public transport vehicles. But once there, the park-like setting is very attractive and there has been a real effort to plant many different tree varieties, including the eponymous matoa tree.

The course is not the most demanding, especially off the white tees, and unless a drive is particularly wayward, the man-made contours will keep the ball in play. One assumes this is how the former president liked it. The clubhouse is well situated, and ending the day on the terrace watching the final groups putt out with the calls to prayer emanating from the local mosques is sure to make for good Jakarta memories.

HOW TO GET THERE From the outer ring road take Jl. Cilandak KKO. Follow it as it turns into Jl. Muhammad Kafi I and take it to km 7 (note that due to a one-way stretch,

you will need to detour on to Jl. Mabes Polri, then on to Jl. Paso, before getting to Jl. Muhammad Kafi I).

CHECK OUT www.matoanasional.net

FAST FACT

There are roughly 40 golf courses in the greater Jakarta area.

HIKING

Indonesia lies along the ring of fire, which means it's a hotbed of volcanic activity. The majority of islands have bulging backbones made of pointy peaks, many of which reach to heights of more than 3,000m. **Java Lava**, a hiking club that has been around since the early 1980s, is a non-commercial, professionally run group that embarks on 10–12 trips a year to mountaintops across the archipelago.

Generally, people fly out on a Friday morning or afternoon to the city nearest the mountain they're climbing. A chartered car or bus whisks them to a *losmen* (guesthouse or small hotel) and they wake at the whip crack of dawn to begin marching their way up the volcano. Groups spend the night in a tent on the summit, waking at 4am to the sound of porters singing and clanging pots and pans. Then they slip, slide and trundle back down the mountain for a beer, a shower and the return flight home. Trips take roughly 72 hours, so many are close to home. These include hikes up Gede and Pangrango, both of which can be seen from Jakarta, as well as hikes around Bandung and near Pelabuhan Ratu.

Java Lava is designed for the working professional with little time to plan his or her own trips and work out the necessary logistics. Java Lava is not a tourist group or babysitter's club, and is geared toward hikers who have some cash to spare and the desire to witness an incredible side of Indonesia. An experienced hiker leads every trip and most include porters.

CHECK OUT www.javalavaindonesia.multiply.com

Alex Korns, a long-time veteran of Indonesia's hiking scene, has loads of information about trekking in the Puncak area. He can provide maps and guidebooks and can also arrange for a guided hike of the area led by a seasoned professional. His website has a plethora of information to read before getting started.

CHECK OUT www.puncaktrek.com

A newcomer to the trekking scene is **Indonesia Expedition Guides**. This group is the brainchild of local hiking legend Krystyna Krassowska, a British explorer who takes singles and groups all over Indonesia and as far away as Africa. The group also offers Saturday hikes to the Sentul area, trips to Puncak, outdoor skills courses and clinics, adult walks, trail runs, family and kid-friendly hikes and adventure race training.

CHECK OUT www.idguides.org

Horse riding at a Jakarta equestrian club.

HORSE RIDING

As there's nothing better than the feeling of a strong-muscled brute beneath your buttocks, check out one of Jakarta's equestrian clubs. You can either pay for a guided hour-long amble around the grounds, stroll around looking at horses while just enjoying the sense of being out of town and outdoors, or sign up for regular riding lessons.

STABLES OF CHOICE JPEC Sentul is the most low-key and simple of them all. It's located 30 minutes outside Jakarta, just off the toll road and is surrounded by loads of greenery. It's very popular with the expat community and boasts some good quality instructors. The café here is also nice, with some solid grub and a great chilled-out atmosphere.

Sunset on the summit of volcanic Mt Rinjani.

WHERE TO GO Jl. Pasir Maung, Desa Babakan Madang.

HOW TO GET THERE Take the Jagorawi toll road to the exit at km 36. Head up Jl. Thamrin and turn left on to Jl. Pasir Maung.

WHO TO CALL 021-8796-1569

TRIJAYA EQUESTRIAN CLUB, located in Ciganjur, south of Cilandak, is fairly small with only one indoor arena and no paddock for horses. Despite that, it's quite popular and is fairly easy to access.

WHERE TO GO Jl. H Montong #23−Ciganjur Jagakarsa.

HOW TO GET THERE From the outer ring road, take Jl. Cilandak KKO. Follow it as it turns into Jl. Muhammad Kafi I (note that due to a one-way stretch, you'll need to detour on to Jl. Mabes Polri, then on to Jl. Paso, before getting to Jl. Muhammad Kafi I). Follow this road until you spot Jl. H Montong to the left.

WHO TO CALL 021-786-3063/021-7888-0176

ARTHAYASA EQUESTRIAN CLUB is located at the far end of Cinere. It takes some time to get here, and the traffic can be a little rough as the roads are quite narrow. That being said, this used to be *the* club for Jakarta's serious equestrians. Most of the good riding instructors have taught here, and it sits on a huge expanse of land with several paddocks for horses to graze in. There is a swimming pool and tennis court too. The place has seen better days, but still it's worth a day trip for a stroll around the grounds and a little riding.

Indonesian cross-bred horses racing at the Pulomas Horse Racing Course.

WHERE TO GO Blok Tengki, Desa Grogol–Depok.

HOW TO GET THERE See website for detailed instructions.

CHECK OUT www.arthayasa.com

HORSE RACING

Pacuan Kuda Pulomas (Pulomas Horse Racing Course), a large swath of green in east Jakarta set aside for horse racing, is the place to be on a lazy Sunday afternoon.

Chill out with good buddies, speculate on the horses in the nearby corrals and feel the thrill of half a dozen beautifully muscled beasts sprinting 1,400m around a track under a hot Jakarta sun. Most of the horses arc G3 or G4, which means they are the third or fourth generation of a local Indonesian horse that was bred with a thoroughbred from abroad. They are now referred to as a KPI (*kuda pacu Indonesia*), an Indonesian racing horse. You can get more information by picking up a racing guide at the track that features lists of horses and their stats, race start times, jockey names, stables and prize money for each race. Note: It's best to have some binoculars to watch the action from start to finish.

Races are held throughout the year, though in order to get the updated schedule or race information you will need to call ahead. The races are not held regularly, but you could just rock up on a Sunday and pray it's your lucky day.

HEADS UP

Gambling is illegal in Indonesia, and at the race track there is no formal place to bet. All money wagered is passed from hand to hand rather than through any official channel.

WHERE TO GO Pacuan Kuda Pulomas in east Jakarta, bounded by Jl. Kayu Putih and Jl. Perintis Kemerdekaan.

HOW TO GET THERE Take Busway #2 to the ASMI stop and walk or take an *ojek*.

FOR DRIVERS Take the Ir. Wiyoto Wiyono toll road to the Suprapto flyover and head east on Jl. Perintis Kemerdekaan, turn on to Jl. Pulomas Timur and then turn left on to Jl. Sirap.

CHECK OUT www.forum-sandalwood.web.id

ICE SKATING

In a country where snow and ice don't exist, there is nothing more entertaining than watching a bunch of people trying to figure skate for the very first time. The **Sky Rink** ice rink in Taman Anggrek Mall is just the place to go, with open skating for the public, private and group lessons, competitions and a hockey league that plays once a week (for the Canadians).

It's a bit small to attempt those triple axles you've seen on TV, but it's a great place to set the kids free, letting them run into walls and stumble around like newborn giraffes in high heels. It's not an activity for the self-conscious, however, since an observation area looks over the rink from one level up.

Kitted out for a game of paintball.

> ### FAST FACT
> The rink is located in Mal Taman Anggrek (Orchid Garden Mall), which was built on what was once a massive orchid garden. Now the only flowers one can find here are the cheap plastic ones for sale in the Metro Department store.

CHECK OUT www.skyrinkjakarta.com

WHERE TO GO Taman Anggrek Mall on Jl. S. Parman.

PAINTBALL

Slithering through the greasy mud, a soldier clutches his weapon of war. Sweat pools in his ears as the sniper on the hill pins him down. A solid hit in the shoulder and he is going home. Well, he's going back to the starting point, at least, to load up on more paintballs.

The **Patriot Paintball Sport** office is full of guns and war memorabilia–Vietnam War era pictures depicting grunts getting pulled out of hidden underground bunkers and big guys with big weapons.

After signing in, donning the fatigues provided and picking out your widow maker (made for paintballs, of course), you'll get an introductory course on why you shouldn't shoot others in the head at close range and other important information. Then you're let loose in a jungle-like setting and encouraged to blast away at loved ones while stealing their team flag to win the competition.

Between rounds, keep an eye out for paintball commandos who come religiously to play assassin, soldier and mercenary, as well as members of the Indonesian army who frequent the place.

Patriot Paintball Sport also has a special 'management retreat' in which mid-level managers are encouraged to drop the polite water cooler conversations and instead imagine that 'Bob from accounting' is actually a baby-killing Commie from the mountainous regions of Crackistan.

WHERE TO GO Alam Sutera Family Park, Sutera Boulevard, Alam Sutera, Serpong, Tangerang.

HOW TO GET THERE Take the Jakarta-Merak toll road to Jl. Serpong Raya, then head south as far as the Alam Sutera clocktower. Turn left on to Jl. Alam Sutera to Sutera Boulevard.

WHO TO CALL 021-539-7777

GETTING IN Open 10am to 5pm, 7 days a week.

OTHER Children ages 12 and under are not allowed to play.

RUNNING

If running and drinking beer are two activities you thoroughly enjoy, the Hash House Harriers will be right up your alley. Hashing is running made fun, because rather than just jogging around your neighborhood in circles, someone sets up a course out in nature and others must follow the clues to make it from start to finish. Once a runner has successfully completed the course, the fun begins, with a social activity called the

Guidebook author Andrew Whitmarsh running in a local neighborhood.

Co-ed teams playing Ultimate Frisbee.

'circle' where members socialize, sing drinking songs (while drinking) and new members get named. Generally runs start at 5pm on weekdays and last one hour, although the circle can go on through the evening. Weekend runs usually start at 4pm and last from one to one and a half hours.

There are several different groups that cater to men, women or both. Jakarta HHH runs on Mondays and is made up predominantly of men. The Pussy Hash, or Jakarta Hash House Harriettes, is women only. Their runs tend to be milder and they go out on Wednesdays. Batavia Hash House Harrier Hoons (or B4) runs on Thursdays. Only men are allowed except on the 4th Thursday of each month. TGIF is held on the 2nd and 4th Saturday of each month and is co-ed. Betawi H3 runs on the 1st and 3rd Saturday and 2nd and 4th Friday of each month. Finally, JAVA House Hash Harriers runs on the last Sunday of the month.

CHECK OUT www.indohash.com. Also try going through Jakarta Free Spirit (see contact information below).

HELPFUL HINT To join, just show up at one of the runs and pay up to whoever is collecting money.

JAKARTA FREE SPIRIT For those looking for more running and less drinking, this is the go-to group. It meets every Saturday at the Ragunan Zoo at 6.30am to run among the animals. The group runs a 5km loop, which anyone is welcome to join. Smaller groups run together in Pondok Indah, Kemang, Kelapa Gading, Pelita Harapan and start from the Four Seasons during the week.

For a fee, you can get on the mailing list to find out more about the runs, get discounts on stores in Jakarta and Singapore, be part of social gatherings throughout the year, join trips outside of Jakarta and be up on their 5km, 10km and marathon race schedules.

CHECK OUT www.jakartafreespirit.org

ULTIMATE FRISBEE

This sport, which employs the throwing and catching of a Frisbee, is named Ultimate because those who play it regard it as the greatest sport on earth. Note: It shares very little with the games played with one's dog on the beach. A cross between football, rugby, American football and basketball, Ultimate is played by two teams of seven on a field roughly the size of a hockey field. The basic premise is that players must pass the Frisbee from teammate to teammate until one of them catches it in the end zone.

Competitors will find themselves leaping in the air, sprinting the length of the field, throwing forehands, knocking poorly thrown discs from flight and sweating like they've never sweated before. Fast-paced, since there are no referees to slow things down, and safe, because it's non-contact, the only way to determine if it truly is the Ultimate sport is to go and try it. The main idea of the sport is 'the spirit of the game,' which means players call their own fouls and everyone is there to have fun.

WHERE TO GO Pick-up games are held every Sunday from 4pm to 6pm on the field hockey pitch at the north end of the Gelora Bung Karno Sports Complex off Jl. Gerbang Pemuda.

CHECK OUT www.ultimateindonesia.com

MUARA ANGKE

ANGKE KAPUK MANGROVE FOREST TOURISM PARK
Garden House

Pantai Indah Kapuk

Marina Housing (Timur)

Muara Angke Fish Market

Pantai Indahkapuk

Katamaran Indah

Muara Angke

PLTN PLTU Power Plant

SPORT COMPLEX

Perta Oil Vi

Cengkareng Drain

Pantai Indah Timur

Pantai Indah Barat

Mandara Permai

Pantai Indah Utara 3

Mandara Permai 4

Pantai Indah Kapuk

MUARA ANGKE WILDLIFE RESERVE

Galeria Niaga Mediterania

Pluit Karang Utara

Pluit Utara Raya

Wisma PLN

Pluit Village Mall

Pluit Indah

Ebony Golf Club

Marina Raya 2

Mandara Permai 2

Pantai Indah Utara 2

Sports Club

Taman Resor Mediterania

Pluit Karang Utara

TAMAN TIRTA LOKA

Pluit Timur Raya

W

Un

Waterbom Jakarta ★

DAMAI INDAH GOLF & COUNTRY CLUB

Bukit Golf

Pantai Indah Utara 1

Mayang Indah

Pantai Indah Utara 1

Pluit Karang Sari

Pluit Karang Permai

Prof Sediyatmo Toll Road (Airport Toll Road)

Retention Basin (Waduk)

Pluit Selatan Raya

P. Barat Penjaringan

Recreation and Sport Facilities (Proposed)

Pantai Indah Kapuk

Retention Basin (Waduk)

Pantai Indah Selatan 1

Mandara Indah 1

Mandara Indah 2

Mandara Indah 1

Carina Saya

Kom

Kamal Muara Raya (Kapuk Raya)

KAWASAN INDUSTRI

Pantai Indah Selatan 1

Pantai Indah Barat

Pantai Indah Selatan 2

Vikamas Timur

Vikamas Raya

Kapuk Muara

Teluk Gusti

Reservoir

PENJARING

Pluit Mas

Jembatan Tiga

Kebon Jahe

Toserba Jaya

Taman Grisenda

V.T.1

V.M.Tengah 9

Vila Kapuk Mas (Vikamas)

Duta Harapan Indah

Teluk Panjang

Teluk Gong Raya

Jembatan Dua

Mutiara Taman Palem

Utan

Vila Kapuk Indah

Duta Harapan Indah

Taman Permata Indah 1

Jembatan Dua

Perumnas Bumi Cengkareng Indah

Cengkareng Indah

Kapuk Raya

Taman Permata Indah 2

Kampung Gusti

Prof.Dr.Latumeten

CENGKARENG

Pedongkelan

Aneka Elok

Bumi Cengkareng Permai

Saluran Irigasi

Kapuk Pulo

Pos Polisi

Peternakan 2

Poglar

Pangeran Tubagus Angke

Taman Duta Mas

Jelambar Barat 3

Jelambar Barat 1

Pakuwon

Jembatan

Daan Mogot Estate

Bumi Cengkareng Permai

KAWASAN INDUSTRI DAN PERGUDANGAN

Jelambar Ilir

Duta Mas

Wijaya

Jelambar Barat

J.Utama 1

J.Selatan

J. Selatan

Daan Mogot Estate

Cengkareng Elok

Komplek Imigrasi

Komplek Ambon

Komplek Markas Besar Kepolisian

KAWASAN INDUSTRI

Grawisa

J.U Sakti

GROGOL PETAMBURAN

Dispenda

Saluran Mookervaart

PLN Cengkareng Indah

Jembatan Gantung Komplek Perdagangan

Daan Mogot

Komplek Departemen Agama

Asrama TNI Poglar

Perdana Utama Sakti

Komplek BNI

Perdana Kusuma

Merpati

J.Madya Timur

Gereja

Jelambar Madya

Kota Grogol Permai

B.Semeru

Kelingkit

Kembangan

Taman Kota

Vila Green Garden

Plasa Apel Gardena

Karya Barat 3

Komplek BDN

Kavling POLRI

Jelambar 6

Latumeten Station

Klingkit Permai

Kaduung

Basmol

Taman Kota

Pesing

Hadiah 1

Komplek Penerangan

Dr.Muwar

Manggis Raya

Carina Sayang

Klingkit

Kedoya Green Garden

Hero

Indosiar

Daan Mogot

Komplek Yayasan Abadi Grenvil

Jelambar

Citraland

Grogol 1

Kacang Tanah

Pulau Matarani 3

Sunrise Garden

Ratu

Tanjung Duren Barat

Grogol 2

Kya

Wo

Persada Sayang

P.Bira

P.Sepa

Ratu Melati

Kemuning

Taman Duren

Durian Barat

Tap

Taman Permata Buana

Green Garden

Surya Utama

Surya Wijaya

Taman Ratu Indah

S. Parman Central Park

Gelora B.

Kali Angke

Vila Kedoya

Kedoya Assiddiqiyah

Surya Sarana

Kepa Duri Mas

Vila Tomang Indah

Pertamina Village

Mal Taman Anggrek

Taman Permata Buana

Kedoya Garden

Puri Kedoya

Surya Gardenia

Surya Mandala

Panjang

Kepa Duri Mas

Hero

Palem Raya

Patra Raya

Tanjung Duren

Taman Permata Indah

Buana Biru Besar

Kembang Agung Utara

Kedoya Raya

Taman Ratu Indah Selatan

Kebon Jati

Duri Kepa

Tomang Toll

Buana Biru Besar

Kembang Ayu Utama

Puri Indah

Pilarmas Indah

Delta Kedoya

Kedoya Raya

Kedoya Duri

Duri Kepa

Komplek Sekneg

Puri Indah Raya

Puri Indah

Kedoya Albasa

Albasia 2

Plaza Kedoya Elok

Jakarta-Merak Toll Road

Batu Sari

ISan

KEMBANGAN

0   1km

N

Java Sea

Ancol Baru
Reclamation
(Proposed)

KAWASAN
INDUSTRI
ANCOL BARAT

ANCOL
Fantasy World

Metro
Marina

Marina

Pantai
Carnaval
Dome ★

Festival
Beach

Binaria Indah
Beach

Beach
Pool

Dutch War
Cemetery

Puri Nusa Dua

SUNDA KELAPA

Sunda Kelapa Harbor ★
Sunda
Kelapa
Fish
Market ★

PADEMANGAN

Taman Impian
Barat

Pantai Indah

Atlantis
Water
Adventure

Ocean Arena

Taman Impian
Timur

Puri Jimbaran

INDUSTRIAL ESTATE

Maritime
Museum ★

Ancol Barat

Puri Marina

KOTA AND MANGGA DUA

ECOPARK

Sea World

Pasir Putih Raya

Harbor Toll Road

Pakin

Gedong
Panjang

Lodan
Center

Karang Bolong Raya

Lodan Raya

Arts Market

R.E. Martadinata

Ancol

Griya Sunter
Pratama

Komp.
Segitiga
Senen 3

Fatahillah
Square

Bandan

Kp. Bandan Raya

Kampung Bandan

PERMATA ANCOL

Pademangan

Budi Mulia

Benyamin Sueb

Agung Utara 1

Agung
Utara 24

Tiang
Bendera

Kuni

Muka

ITC

WTC
Mangga Dua

Kalimati

Gang 22

Danau Sunter Utara

Komp.
Dakota

Kopi

Pinu Kecil

Jakarta History Museum
Jakarta Kota

Mangga Dua Raya

Electronic
Plaza

Gunung Sahari

Hidup Baru (Kalimati)

Danau Sunter Utara

Spring Hill Golf
Residence

Dukuh Golf
Jakarta

Kota

Jembatan
Batu

Bumi
Plaza

Jayakarta

Mangga
Dua
Square

Maspion
Plaza

Sunter
Muara

Pasar Pagi
Lama
(Asemka)

Gloria Market

Pangeran Jayakarta
Harco
Glodok

Indah
Jayakarta

D. Suratmo

Rajawali

Jakarta Fair
Pekan Raya
Jakarta (PRJ) ★

Victory
Market

Mangga Besar

Tangki

Snake Market

Angkasa
Pura

Bursa Mobil
Kemayoran

Mega Glodok
Kemayoran

Angkasa
Pura

TAMBORA

Temple of
Glorious
Obligation

GLODOK

Glodok

Limo

Lokasari
Plaza

Jembatan Merah

Mangga Besar

Kartini

Rajawali
Industri

Pekan Raya

Landasan Pacu
Timur

Komp.
Dakota

Kerendang
Utara

Temple of the
Goddess of
Devotion

Keadilan
Raya

Mangga
Besar

Taman
Kartini

Kemayoran
Villa

Landasan Pacu
Barat

Giant

Angkasa
Pura

Saint Mary
of Fatima
Catholic
Church

Keamanan

Mangga Besar

Hayam
Wuruk
Plaza

Taman
Sari

SAWAH
BESAR

Kemayoran

Taruna Jaya

Duri

National
Archives
Museum ★

Tanah
Sereal

Mangga Besar

M.O

Krekot
Bunder

Angkasa Raya

Tunnel

Kemayoran

KEMAYORAN

Duri

MANGGA BESAR

TAMAN SARI

Asam Reges
Automotive Spare
Parts Market

Sawah
Besar
Batu Ceper

Plaza
Globe

Ps. Baru

Garuda

Permai
Indah

Komplek
PT. Gas Negara

K.H. Zainul
Arifin

Sukarjo Wirjopranoto

Lautze

K.H. Samanhudi

Bakti

Gajah Mada

Petojo
Plaza

Harmoni
Central Busway

Istana Pasar Baru
Juanda

Pasar Baru
Juanda

Gedung
Kesenian

ITC Roxy
Mas

Petojo

K.H. Hasyim
Asyhari

Carrefour/
Duta Merlin
Petojo

Ir. H. Juanda

Dr. Sutomo

Indomart

Biak

Veteran

Pecenongan

Dr. Wahidin

Kepu Selatan

Kali Baru
Timur 3

Let. Jend. Suprapto

Balikpapan

Medan Merdeka
Utara

Istiqlal

Deplu

Senen

Galur

Rawa

Kwitang

Presidential
Palace

MONAS

Istiqlal

RSPAD
Satria
Mandala

Atrium

Pasar
Senen

Senen
Sentral

Komp.
Krajaba

Tanah Abang 2

Monas

Gambir 1

Tugu
Tani

Atrium Senen

Komplek AD

Senen

Komp. Sentiong

National
Museum

Gambir 2

Balaikota

Kwitang

Kramat

SENEN

Komp.
Tomang
Raya
Indah

Bank
Indonesia

Medan Merdeka
Selatan

Kebon
Sirih

Kebon Sirih

Gunung
Agung

Pal Putih

Sentiong

JOHAR
BARU

Textile
Museum ★

Tanah
Abang

Ramayana

K.H. Wahid
Hasyim

Sarinah

Spain

Gondangdia

Kramat Raya

Kramat Sentiong

Kramat Sentiong

Komp. Perhubu.
Udara

Kawi-
kawi
Atas

North Jakarta

North Jakarta has a grittier, working-man's neighborhood feel. With its mix of Chinese culture, Dutch architecture, shipping ports, fishing industry and seaside tourism, it is a fascinating area to explore. North Jakarta is a mishmash of economic brackets and ethnicities. It contains areas of absolute poverty where people forage for a daily pittance, while other areas, right next door, consist of megalomaniac mansions with armies of servants catering to the lavishly wealthy occupants.

Industrially and commercially speaking, north Jakarta is crucial to the city's economic pulse. There are factories and industrial parks, and hundreds of tiny fishing boats launch from the coastline every day in search of the seafood to feed the city. Larger boats come in and out hauling goods to Indonesia's other islands, while massive barges and freighters work out of the Tanjung Priok industrial port, disgorging and receiving goods.

Industrial growth in the area has been hard on the environment. Waterways have become polluted, mangrove forests have been paved over and most estuaries have been reduced to sludge. Happily, it's not all bad news: reclamation efforts are underway and the area is also home to a couple of good nature spots.

For entertainment, north Jakarta is worth dozens of visits. There are historical sites, museums, outdoor cultural performances, temples, markets, places to shop and a solid spread of dining options. That being said, there is also a high concentration of the seedier side of late night entertainment: brothels, massage parlors, gambling dens and darker nightclubs.

For those with kids, or who are kids at heart, **Ancol** is a sprawling seaside fun park. There are roller coasters in the Dufan theme park, sharks in SeaWorld, and succulent seafood at Segarra. There is the Atlantis water park, an art market with artists at their easels, and sailing boats available for hire. Don't forget your shorts: Ancol is bicycle-friendly with dedicated lanes and an excellent spot for walking. The Ancol Marina is located here for those wanting to launch off to the Thousand Islands for a weekend getaway.

Two coastal areas, the **Suaka Margasatwa Muara Angke** (Muara Angke Wildlife Reserve) and the **Angke Kapuk Mangrove Forest Tourism Park**, have been protected and restored so the mangroves can do their job in hosting marine, terrestrial and aviary life, slow the rate of erosion of Jakarta's northernmost border and serve as educational corridors for

Tourists in Fatahillah Square, the original old town square in the center of Jakarta.

Young boys diving from a bamboo pole jetty in the Java Sea.

Jakarta's youth. Look out for the three troops of monkeys consisting of around 100 individuals while enjoying an early morn-9ing bird watching session with Indonesia's nature group, Go Wild! Indonesia.

Want to go for a stroll through maritime history? Step back in time at the **Pelabuhan Sunda Kelapa** (Sunda Coconut Harbor) and gain an insight into what Jakarta looked like when it went by the name Batavia and was one of the most important seaports in the world. From Sunda Kelapa, take a small fishing boat over to **Pasar Ikan**, a fish market hundreds of years old. Climb the worn stairs of the old Dutch Watchtower and stop at the Maritime Museum where the treasures of the East Indies were once stored before being shipped off to Europe.

Taman Fatahillah (Fatahillah Square) is ground zero for a look at historical Jakarta and the days of Dutch rule. Café Batavia serves good food in a century-old restaurant overlooking the square, which once held nearly daily executions.

Go into the old City Hall where the gavel used to sound the verdicts of law, prisoners were shackled in the basement, the sick were nursed to health, and behind which thousands of Chinese were slaughtered in 1740.

Regular events and festivities are held in Fatahillah Square at the weekends, to which the historical buildings make a dramatic backdrop. There are musical festivals, art shows, outdoor theater and performances of the traditional Kuda Lumping dance with its trance-induced performers eating lightbulbs and cracking whips.

Don't miss Chinatown and all its secrets. From the wet markets to the incense-scented temples to the 24-hour pulse of Stadium, Jakarta's most historic club, **Glodok** is a neighborhood no adventurer should miss. Much of the magic lies in the narrow lanes threading through the neighborhood: wending past traditional medicine shops, tasty pork noodle eateries, cobra sellers and creaking-wheeled pedicabs laden with goods from the market.

For culinary adventures, **Jl. Mangga Besar** cooks up something dramatically different. Snake meat is the specialty, but turtle, dog, monitor lizard and bat can be eaten along this road. Interspersed with the exotic dining spots are *jamu* kiosks selling traditional health drinks to cure all ailments.

One trip to north Jakarta is not enough. It's a big area with innumerable back streets to explore and activities to sample. It can be challenging to get around and overwhelmingly crowded and pungent at times, but it's where the original soul of the city and its commerce is found and the souls of the city's founders are buried.

Walking Tour 1

MUARA ANGKE AND ANGKE KAPUK

Mangrove Forests and a Fishermen's Market: An Exploration of North Jakarta's Varied Coastline

1. **Muara Angke Fish Market**
2. **Fish Snack Center**
3. **Fish Drying Racks I**
4. **Fish Drying Racks II**
5. **Muara Angke Wildlife Reserve**
6. **Waterbom Jakarta**
7. **Angke Kapuk Mangrove Forest Tourism Park**

The two main neighborhoods west of Pluit are the *yin* and the *yang* of Jakarta, and they demonstrate the incredible way two very different human habitations can lie at one another's doorsteps. To the east, the **Muara Angke neighborhood** is a rough-and-ready fish market. Here, you can discover what an industrial fishing village feels like, as rubber boot-wearing workers trundle by pulling carts laden with frozen squid. You'll see dump trucks filled with massive blocks of ice which are unloaded on to workers' shoulders, and fishermen either heading out to sea or unloading, sorting, weighing, washing, packing, cooking or eating their catch.

Moving deeper into this kilometer-wide by kilometer-long piece of land, which is surrounded on all sides by water, takes you to the expansive seafood drying racks that cover a large part of the area. Thousands of fish, squid, prawns and other sea life are spread across hectares of land to dry in the sun before being processed as snacks and cooking ingredients.

Exploring the canals that lead to the sea brings visitors face to face with a flotilla of traditional fishing boats and the seafaring men that run them. The right price can get you on one for a trip along the coastline.

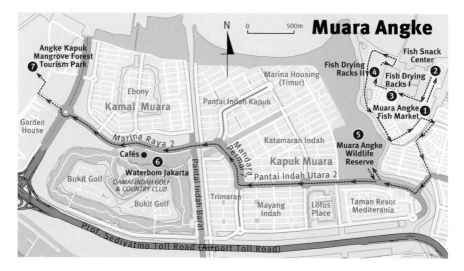

Just around the corner from the Muara Angke neighborhood is one of Jakarta's few nature reserves, the **Suaka Margasatwa Muara Angke** (Muara Angke Wildlife Reserve), which serves as a sort of buffer zone before really slamming into the upper-class neighborhood to the west. Home to a plethora of sea, land and air creatures, including nearly 100 wild monkeys, the reserve boasts a long boardwalk that stretches out into the mangrove forests, providing a glimpse into an estuary life almost lost in this rapidly industrializing city.

Heading up the road, in a westerly direction are the more exclusive, suburban neighborhoods of the ever-expanding upper class. **Waterbom Jakarta** is also located here, and it's not a bad place to zip down the waterslide or cool down with a lazy drift along the 'Wild River.' Finally, to the far west, at the edge of the upscale housing developments, is a large mangrove reclamation project, the **Angke Kapuk Mangrove Forest Tourism Park**. Stroll among the lengthy rows of newly planted trees and catch glimpses of the wildlife that call them home. Rent a small boat and guide and enjoy the sight of herons gliding effortlessly through an evening sunset.

WHO? It's all family-friendly, except for the Muara Angke Fishing Village. This low-income neighborhood is not particularly clean, it can smell and is not set up for tourism—in fact, it's an industrial area. For those looking for a pleasant day's activities, it's recommended that you skip the fishing village, and instead start at the nature reserve.

HOW LONG? Full day.

HOW FAR? 12.5km, includes walking (5km)/driving/*becak* ride.

GETTING THERE Head to Kapuk Muara and Kamal Muara, just west of Pluit. By car, take the Pluit-Tomang toll road to the Harbor toll road. Exit immediately on to Jl. Jembatan Tiga and head north; turn left on to Jl. Pluit Indah. At Jl. Pluit Barat Raya, turn right and take it to Jl. Pluit Utara Raya, turning left. By Busway, take corridor #9 to the Penjaringan stop. Continue north by *ojek*/taxi to Jl. Pluit Utara Raya; this road goes west, directly to the Muara Angke entrance.

Note: Unlike most of the other tours in this book, having a car makes this tour easier

because of the distances between places and the notable reduction in taxis and public transportation. You can still get around fine without a car, but it will require additional patience and flexibility.

OTHER Once into the Muara Angke neighborhood, don't worry too much about road names and which way you are going. Just stroll around and enjoy the adventure. Even better, rent a *becak* and have them pedal you around for half an hour; that's sightseeing in style!

Be aware that except for the standard Bluebird/Express taxis, the beat-up, no-name types that ply this area often don't use a meter. Be sure to check when getting in, and if they don't want to use the meter, bargain for a price. Even if you don't like their final price, don't get huffy, just pay up.

1 MUARA ANGKE FISH MARKET
The tour starts at the **Pasar Ikan Muara Angke** (Muara Angke Fish Market). For those coming by taxi, get dropped off just before entering the Muara Angke *kampung*, which starts after crossing the canal bridge from Jl. Pluit Karang Utara to Jl. Muara Angke. There are a number of boats in the water here, as well as a sign in the shape of a boat reading:

Cockles for sale in the Muara Angke market.

A worker boiling squid at the rough-and-ready Muara Angke Fish Market.

Pemukiman–Nelayan (Fishermen's Settlement). For those arriving by car, it's best to park near the bridge and begin your explorations on foot. Note: The area can look overwhelmingly dirty, chaotic and uninviting. Give it some time and it will become less crowded and more enjoyable the farther you get.

HEADS UP

Some of the streets along here may be flooded in the rainy season. Be sure to wear appropriate footwear, such as sports sandals, old trainers or even flipflops.

After crossing the bridge, take an immediate right to check out the cool fishing boats. People can charter these boats to chug around the Java Sea, cruise around the Muara Angke Nature Reserve or visit some of the Thousand Islands, including Pulau Onrust and Pulau Rumput (see p. 188). The fee depends on your bargaining skills, but plan to pay at least Rp500,000, as fuel doesn't come cheap these days. Most of the boats here are working boats, however, and not intended for tourists, so don't expect life jackets and a complimentary bottle of water.

Continue on past the boats and take a right on Jl. Pendaratan Ikan. Follow this road, checking out and chatting with the seafood sellers, all the way to its terminus at the sea. On the right is a giant warehouse where mass amounts of seafood are delivered, weighed, sorted and distributed. On the left is more of the same. Just wander about, take pictures and perhaps even pick up dinner. Keep an eye out for the trucks laden with giant slabs of ice and watch them unload the perspiring, rectangular blocks using long, metal hooks.

2 FISH SNACK CENTER

Also along Jl. Pendaratan Ikan is a long stretch of *otak-otak* sellers. This tasty snack is made from steamed fish wrapped in a banana leaf and grilled over charcoal. It's a specialty from Sulawesi, but many other regions have their own variations. Past these vendors, on the left, is the **Pusat Jajanan Serba Ikan** (Fish Snack Center), which caters to those looking for a fresh seafood dinner. Near here is the largest concentration of fresh seafood sellers in the area, most of whom display their collections on tables, in Styrofoam coolers or in large, three-legged bowls. Catches include crabs, clams, lobsters (including females loaded with eggs), squid, shrimp, mussels, snails and a large variety of fish, from snapper to sardines. This is a great place for photographs, but be sure to smile and ask before taking a person's photo. As with all markets, especially fish markets, the action is hottest when it's cool–early in the morning. Try to get here around 6am, if possible.

FAST FACT

According to local legend, the name Muara Angke may come from Tubagus Angke, a warlord from the kingdom of Banten. Other derivations include the Hokkien word *ang* for 'red,' referring to when the nearby river ran this color after the Dutch slaughter of the Chinese in 1740. The word *muara* means estuary.

---

③, ④ FISH DRYING RACKS I AND II

After reaching the end of the road, turn back and watch out for Jl. Pelelangan on the right, which is just before the fire station. Turn right and walk up the road, passing a football field and some apartment blocks. On the right are shrimp ponds. On the left you'll spot the vast **Fish Drying Racks**, each covered with splayed-out fish that have been soaked in salt water and left to dry under the baking sun.

Wander up and down between the racks, play hide-and-go-seek with the local kids, talk with the workers and try to estimate how

many kilos of seafood they have racked up. If it starts to drizzle, they will quickly unravel tarps to keep their precious stores dry. The long bamboo tables here are only the tip of the iceberg. Pushing up and into this neighborhood will reveal hundreds of the same. (Take a look at a Google Earth map of the place to get a better sense of the scale.)

Another thing to look out for are the boiling vats of salt water filled with squid that sit above brick, wood-fired ovens. Workers repeatedly dump in buckets of these tentacled creatures, boil them for 15 minutes, scoop them out with sieves and load them on to wooden carts to be hauled away. The job is a hot and sweaty one, but the *dangdut* soundtrack keeps workers' hips rotating and gives them something to sing along to.

HEADS UP

The fish drying done here was once all natural. In recent years, however, some unscrupulous business people started using formaldehyde rather than salt to help preserve the fish. A recent crackdown has helped to curb the practice, but it certainly hasn't ended.

Back on the road, continue straight and follow the road to the right as it turns. Up on the right is another vast sea of salted and

Fishing boats crammed cheek to jowl along the Muara Angke Canal.

dried seafood–a photographer's delight. Stroll among the tables and take it all in while still staying out of the way.

You can continue walking from here, but a ride on a *becak* at this point is highly advisable. There should be a number of them plying this route, so wave one down, point forward and say *Jalan jalan*, which means he'll just pedal around, most likely sticking to the main road. That road will soon turn left and follow the sea wall which edges the Java Sea. This is a favorite spot for local kids to strip down and leap off the docks into the water. The *becak* driver will stop anytime he is asked, so don't be shy about having him pull over if there are things to be seen or photographed.

The road will again hook to the left and go upstream, along the **Kali Muara Angke** (Muara Angke Canal), which reveals the very poor side of a fishing family's life. Watch for the large groups of women and children shucking clams or working at other money-making tasks. On the right are fishing boats, which usually pull out around 7pm and do not return until early morning. It's possible to join these guys on an overnight fishing trip for a big adventure, and a deal. If this seems a bit over the top, an hour-long or half-day jaunt on one of these boats can be arranged, either just around the area, up the coast, or even to some of the nearby islands. There is no set price, so bargaining is necessary.

The road will eventually turn left on to Jl. Muara Angke. Pass a school on the left and travel through the small **Muara Angke Market** before reaching the bridge where the tour began.

5 MUARA ANGKE WILDLIFE RESERVE

After crossing the bridge over the canal that takes you out of Muara Angke, take a taxi or *ojek* or drive your car along Jl. Pluit Karang Barat to Jl. Mandara Permai and turn right. Take this road to the roundabout and head west on Jl. Pantai Indah Utara 2. Just up ahead on the other side of the road is the entrance to the Muara Angke Nature Reserve, marked by the large wooden sign **Pusat Pendidikan Konservasi dan Lingkungan Margasatwa Muara Angke** (Muara Angke Conservation Education Center and Wildlife Reserve).

A few years ago, the mangrove forests and wetlands at **Suaka Margasatwa Muara Angke** (Muara Angke Wildlife Reserve) were

Boardwalk at Muara Angke Wildlife Reserve.

mostly an afterthought, abandoned to ruin and decay. The conservation group Jakarta Green Monster has since adopted the reserve. They have helped facilitate the construction of new buildings and have joined with the Department of Forestry to build a wonderful boardwalk that winds its way through the mangroves. Jakarta Green Monster also leads educational tours, conducts species identification and holds occasional volunteer clean-up days to rid the area of garbage. The group's ongoing rehabilitation programs work to protect the plants, animals, fish and insects that call the mangroves home.

Unfortunately, despite the time and effort that was put into the nature reserve's creation, it has since been given only cursory attention. Things are already falling apart: the boardwalk is pockmarked, a few planks are missing and vegetation is slowly gripping the path. Still, the reserve offers a fantastic trip into nature, allowing visitors to see at least nine types of mangroves, various species of snakes and frogs, more than 90 types of birds and three troops of long-tailed macaques.

Stroll to the end of the lengthy boardwalk and sit quietly for an hour taking in the sounds and sights of wildlife. When you've finished, visit the small educational center near the entrance (generally opened by request). Note: Someone will most likely ask to see a letter of permission to enter the center. This letter can only be obtained from the University of Indonesia, in the far south of the city. If you don't have a letter, a small amount of rupiah will gain you access.

CHECK OUT www.jgm.or.id

GETTING IN Open 8am to 4pm daily.

6 WATERBOM JAKARTA

Now it's time for lunch. For drivers, take Jl.
Pantai Indah Utara 2 west until it intersects
with a roundabout. Turn right and then left
at the next roundabout. Cross over the large
canal on Jl. Marina Raya 2 and stop at one of
the cafés lining the road on the right. You'll
be in the Kamal Muara/Pantai Indah Kapuk
neighborhood, across from the Damai Indah
Golf and Country Club. Those without a car
can hop on an *angkot* and ride it until they
see the golf course. It should cost a couple
of thousand rupiah per passenger.

Stroll along the nice stretch of cafés. Most
offer local food, with quite a few specializing
in pork and ribs. Indoor and outdoor seating
is available, and most stock cold beer.

With lunch complete, it's time for some
bikini bottom fun. Just down the street from
the golf club is **Waterbom Jakarta**. After
buying entrance tickets, grab a rubber pad
and launch down the steep, slippery slides,
but be careful not to scream too loud or
you'll get a mouthful of water. Not into the
thrill rides? Grab an inner tube and float
along the lazy river that meanders its way
around the grounds. Kids have their own
special section, where Dr Seuss meets Willy
Wonka in a weird world of giant dumping
buckets, waterfalls, water sprays and lots
of stuff to clamber on.

WHERE TO GO Jl. Pantai Indah Barat
No. 1–Pantai Indah Kapuk.

CHECK OUT www.waterbom-jakarta.com

Most of the development in this neighborhood consists of large, gaudy mansions and
wide boulevards that are relatively free of
traffic. That makes it great for bicycling, so
come back some time with bikes and tool
around for a bit.

7 ANGKE KAPUK MANGROVE FOREST TOURISM PARK

To wrap up the day, head over to the **Taman
Wisata Hutan Bakau Angke Kapuk**
(Angke Kapuk Mangrove Forest Tourism
Park). To get there, head west on Jl. Marina
Raya 2 and turn right once you reach the
giant roundabout. Up on the left is the man-
grove park.

The Ministry of Forestry and a private
company teamed up to create this 100-
hectare rehabilitated mangrove forest, which

A bird at Angke Kapuk Mangrove Tourism Park.

doubles as a recreation and tourism area.
With it comes a rare opportunity to escape
into nature without having to leave city limits.

Although the park is quite new, and therefore consists mostly of young, freshly planted
mangroves, it is already flush with a wonderful array of wildlife, including monitor lizards, many types of fish, shrimp, crabs,
snakes and birds. By walking out along the
dirt berms and simple bamboo bridges that
separate different sections of the mangroves,
you can watch the different bird varieties
glide along looking for tasty morsels.

The park provides information on how the
mangroves work to buffer the sea from storm
surges, inhibit erosion of coastal areas and
provide food and shelter for marine life. It
also offers visitors the opportunity to support
the mangrove gardens by buying a couple of
plants from their nursery and planting them
right there on location. For those who want a
closer look at the mangroves, another option
is to take a reasonably priced motorized boat
tour with a guide.

If one afternoon isn't enough, there are
various types of overpriced accommodation
available, including little cabins, which offer
a night of escape from the grit and gridlock
of the city. On the surrounding grounds are
a wide range of small fruit plants, including
mangoes, starfruit, chili, forest apples, rose
apples and oranges.

WHERE TO GO Angke Kapuk, Pantai Indah
Kapuk–Kamal Muara.

OTHER The entrance fee is not much, but
photographers should prepare for sticker
shock. The park expects Rp200,000 to take
pictures, otherwise the camera must be
left behind.

Walking Tour 2

ANCOL

A Day at the Beach and Jakarta's Fantasy World

1. **Fantasy World**
2. **Marina Jaya Ancol**
3. **Festival Beach**
4. **Gondola Station**
5. **Gondola Station**
6. **Putri Duyung Resort**
7. **Atlantis Water Adventures**
8. **Art Market**
9. **Outbondholic**
10. **Bikaholic**
11. **Ecopark**
12. **Gondola Station**
13. **Ocean Arena**
14. **SeaWorld**
15. **Bandar Djakarta Restaurant**
16. **Binaria Indah Beach**
17. **Beach Pool**
18. **Le Bridge**
19. **Bike Beach Carnaval**
20. **Segarra Restaurant**
21. **Pantai Carnaval Dome**

grounds with bands generally playing live music from early afternoon until night on the weekends. For those who love being where the action is, Ancol is particularly exciting during big holidays, such as Independence Day or New Year's Day, but be warned, the traffic on these days can be grizzly.

Weekdays or early weekend mornings are a good time to go for a jog or bike ride, either along the promenade or along the dedicated bike lanes.

This walk goes to most of Ancol's main attractions, big and small. It is therefore

The 57-hectare Ancol Bay City has enough to keep children and adults busy for many a Jakarta weekend. Those looking to escape can find a quiet place at **Pantai Carnaval** (Bike Beach Carnaval), a spot on the eastern edge of Ancol that is perfect for some reading or uninterrupted sunbathing. Meanwhile, thrill-seekers and adrenaline junkies can get their kicks at the **Dunia Fantasi** (Fantasy World), where roller coaster riding and plummeting action abounds or they can get soaked at **Atlantis Water Adventures**.

At the **Pasar Seni** (Art Market), visitors can search for the perfect painting or sculpture for the living room, while for music lovers, stages are spread throughout the more of a showcase walk for people who want to know where everything is and stretch their legs while doing it. For most visitors, picking a couple of activities and taking the whole day to do them is the best way forward. Pairing up something like **SeaWorld** and a sailboat ride with a sea-food dinner could take a good five to six hours alone.

Be aware that the people at Ancol are always coming up with something new. Even for people who have been here already it's worth exploring recent developments.

WHO? The walk itself is quite long, and is therefore geared toward adults. Those with kids may only want to walk short sections, taking more time to stop and play along the way. An excellent alternative is to go by bicycle since it allows for some serious cruising.

HOW LONG? Full day–depending on the number of attractions stopped at along the way.

HOW FAR? 6.7km.

GETTING THERE: Take Busway #5 which drops passengers inside Ancol. By car, come in via the Harbor Toll Road. There is plenty of parking once inside.

CHECK OUT www.ancol.com and www.seaworldindonesia.com

GETTING AROUND Bicycle rentals, including tandems, are available for a very reasonable hourly rate from a number of different Rodalink stalls located throughout the park. They are generally open weekends and holidays only. Bicycle lanes have been set out across the complex, adding an extra sense of safety and security. But don't be surprised to find inconsiderate car and motorbike drivers blocking the paths. There are plenty of taxis lazing about, as well as *ojek* drivers ready to zip people across short distances.

GETTING STARTED Most people enter through **Pintu Gerbang Utama** (North Gate) which consists of two iconic side-by-side orange and pink arches held fast with a web of guide wires. Parking lots are spread throughout the complex, but the closest one

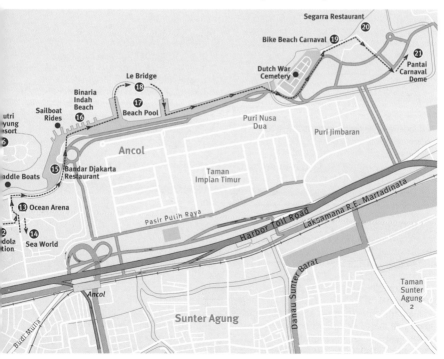

This roller coaster at Fantasy World is located in the middle of lush vegetation.

to the amusement park is the first lot to the left of the North Gate. Those coming by taxi can get dropped off at the amusement park's ticket box, which sits behind a large statue of Dufan's floppy-nosed mascot. Busway passengers are let off in the parking lot directly across from Dufan.

HEADS UP

Jaya Bowling is a massive bowling alley with two claims to fame: it's both the largest in Indonesia as well as the training center for Indonesia's National Bowling team. It's located just outside the North Gate, accessed by Jl. Lodan. Keep an eye out for it in case the mood to knock down some pins should strike before entering Ancol.

1 FANTASY WORLD

The entrance to **Dunia Fantasi** (Fantasy World) sits at the end of the esplanade behind a pedestrian roundabout. A great place to start for everyone, no matter their age, the amusement park has the usual spread of roller coasters, swing rides, bumper cars and other contraptions meant to make riders lose their lunches. Lines are generally not too long and there's enough variety to keep you entertained throughout the day.

A must-try is **Istana Boneka** (Palace of the Dolls), a floating trip through an intriguingly weird wonderland much like Disney's 'It's a Small World' ride.

2 MARINA JAYA ANCOL

Head left from the roundabout, past a Starbucks. At the three-way intersection, turn right and cross the street, Jl. Marina. On the left is the **Marina Jaya Ancol**, which extends north toward the pier. This is where the majority of boats and ferries depart for the Thousand Islands (see p. 188.) Watch for the anchor at the next intersection, which leads straight to the Marina Office. The office has information on boat trips to the islands, seaplane and sailboat rentals as well as canoes, paddleboats and fishing equipment.

3 FESTIVAL BEACH

Turning right on to Jl. Pantai Indah, next up is **Pantai Festival** (Festival Beach), on the left. This is one of the most popular beaches at Ancol and is absolutely swarmed with fully dressed women, naked kids and guys in undershirts, all frolicking around in knee-deep water with every cheap, inflatable toy China ever produced. Don't expect to lie out peacefully and get a solitary suntan here on the weekends—but weekdays are much quieter.

Ancol Marina, from where most boats and ferries depart for the Thousand Islands.

[4], [5] GONDOLA STATION

Head to the water's edge and follow the promenade to the **Stasiun Gondola** (Gondola Station), a cable car that makes easy travel for those looking to get a bird's-eye view of Ancol. There is just one route—from Pantai Festival to the Art Market, or vice versa.

HEADS UP

Watch for the signs that say 'Dilarang Mandi—Pantai Curam.' They are warning people away from areas where the sand drops off steeply just past the shoreline.

Across from the roundabout on Jl. Pantai Indah, just past the Gondola Station, is the first spot where you can rent bicycles. Continuing along the seashore, the next attraction is the **Mercure Hotel**, which offers nice rooms to crash in for those who are not yet ready to go home. The nearby **Copacabana Fitness Center and Spa** is potentially worth a visit, though note it's geared more toward men looking for a happy ending massage. Behind the Mercure sits the **Neptunus Sailing Club**, which offers laser and optimist sailboat rentals as well as wind-surfing lessons.

[6] PUTRI DUYUNG RESORT

Just past the sailing club is a place to rent jet skis. If riding one of these is not your cup of tea, push on to the Gondola Tower, turn right and walk along the road. This road turns to the right and then joins the main road. Hook left and on the left-hand side is **Putri Duyung Resort** (Mermaid Resort), a nice but pricey resort for staying overnight. With a beachside restaurant that serves up a decent-sized plate of seafood and rooms lining both the sea and a little bay, it's a great spot to pretend to be on holiday. They have standard hotel rooms but also some very funky cabins. The resort grounds are rather splendid, so even without a booking it's worth a stroll through the compound.

Past Putri Duyung on the left is an inlet that is bordered by a sandy strip with benches, playground equipment, lots of trees and plants and a curious three-pronged monument.

[7] ATLANTIS WATER ADVENTURES

Across the street, just before the monument, find the entrance to **Atlantis Water Adventures**. This place has all the slips, slides and paddling pools you would expect from a water park. Play water basketball, catch a wave in the Poseidon Wave Pool, duck into a sea of colored plastic balls or dunk friends under a waterfall.

An overview of Atlantis Water Adventures from the cable car.

8 ART MARKET

Continue walking, with the water park on your right. Follow the road as it hooks to the right, eventually crossing it to enter **Pasar Seni** (Art Market). The market is an open-air gem, comprising a plethora of talented artists painting, carving, daydreaming of their next great masterpiece and displaying their wares. Pick through the pieces, chat to the artisans, bargain a little and support a starving artist. Not everything is great, but there is quite a lot of both fabulous and unique art to be found. At the center of the market is a stage where you can check out afternoon and evening music performances while drinking from a young coconut and tucking into a bowl of noodles. Also worth exploring is the **North Art Space**, which is a gallery as

well as a music, dance and art school.

Sunday is a great time to be at the Ancol complex. Community members gather at the Sunday Market, home to everything from a fish market to live entertainment.

9 OUTBONDHOLIC

Just past the art school, on the southern end, is **Outbondholic**. Whereas most outbound courses in Indonesia are geared toward middle-aged moms and little kids, with usually only a flying fox and a cargo net to scramble around on, Outbondholic offers some real challenges. Based on a French design, with multiple routes and separate kid and adult areas, the course even has an extreme route that pushes contenders to complete it at speed.

⑩ BIKAHOLIC

Across the street from Outbondholic is **Bikaholic**, a new spot for bicyclists with balls. There is a large half pipe for BMX enthusiasts and multiple dirt racetracks that start from elevated ramps. Here, bikers can sprint over the jumps, up and around banked curves and down flights of stairs. Bicycles are also available for rent here, although they can't be used on the Bikaholic courses.

⑪ ECOPARK

To the right of Bikaholic is the new **Ecopark**, which was still being built at the time of publication. The park is part of Ancol's two-pronged green/blue concept, which seeks to educate Jakarta's citizens on environmental issues by creating a green corridor through the Ancol complex, as well as cleaning up the water and making it more visitor-friendly. The Ecopark will include diverse fauna and flora and eco-based attractions, such as a discovery center, forest camping, a skywalk, fishing, and jungle and adventure trails.

⑬ OCEAN ARENA

From the future Ecopark site, go back through the Art Market and exit to the right. Walk past the roundabout and the second Gondola Station will be on the right. This is a good time to hop on for a round-trip ride, especially if the line is short. Continue walking straight until the road T-junctions. Straight ahead is **Gelanggang Samudra** (Ocean Arena). The site includes a 4D theater, an animal variety show (which some may be uncomfortable with), a dolphin show, a sea lion show and a water stunt show.

⑭ SEAWORLD

Turning right at Ocean Arena leads to **SeaWorld**. This is a very well-done attraction with large underwater worlds, one of which can be viewed through a see-through tunnel. It has three large aquariums, a giant piranha tank, a dugong tank, a shark aquarium and crocodiles. Activities abound as well, including tank scuba diving, a feet fish spa and a touch pool. Looking for an exotic wedding location? SeaWorld offers the opportunity to say 'I do' surrounded by a tank full of exotic fish. Go on and take the plunge!

⑮ BANDAR DJAKARTA RESTAURANT

To continue with the walking tour, turn left from SeaWorld and follow the road back to the inlet. Cross the main road and walk along the man-made beach, where paddleboats are available for rental. Next, continue to follow the path to the east end of the inlet, where the **Rumah Makan Bandar Djakarta** (Bandar Djakarta Restaurant) is located. Hidden behind Seaside Suki Restaurant, Bandar Djakarta is probably the most famous place to eat in Ancol, because customers get to pick out their own seafood from a display out front. Sit along the water and enjoy the pleasant view.

⑯ BINARIA INDAH BEACH; ⑰ BEACH POOL

When that's done, continue past the restaurant, crossing in front of Pizza Hut and turning left on to **Binaria Indah Beach** (Beautiful Beach). There is a long expanse of playground equipment here that borders the lengthy promenade along the water's edge.

Sailboat rides are the special attraction, with the choice of a personal charter or a public ride operated by a trained professional. Sometimes the sailboat offers can be rather bothersome as there are so many guys continually trying to get people on to their boats. Just say *Sudah*, which means 'already' and point behind you, and they should generally wander off.

Otherwise, follow the path as it makes a sharp left-hand turn at the café area and A&W Restaurant. Turn right here and then enter the boardwalk which stretches out across a small man-made bay and swimming area called the **Beach Pool**.

⑱ LE BRIDGE

Stop for a drink at **Le Bridge** while soaking in the fresh sea air and noting all the photographers who come out to capture shots of cute couples with wind in their hair. Despite the crowds of people playing in the water, it is quite polluted with run-off from the city's canals, and swimming here is not advised. Note that the grubby water reportedly clears up around 3pm.

Further along the boardwalk is the **Backstage Beach Concert Café**. Behind it the promenade continues. A McDonalds sits off to the right, but there are far better Indonesian eateries at Ancol. The promenade eventually terminates at a spot where people can pay to fish from little thatched huts that sit out on the water. At this point, head to the right and continue until reaching the cemetery.

The recently renovated 300-sq m **Dutch War Cemetery−Ereveld** is filled with roughly 2,000 victims of conflict. It contains both men and women, most of whom were said to have been beheaded at this spot due to their resistance against the Japanese in World War II. Surrounded by a wicked security wall topped with long shards of gleaming glass, the cemetery is filled with long stark rows of brilliant white crosses set in a well-manicured lawn. Unfortunately, there is one catch−members of the public are not generally allowed to enter, only family members of the deceased. It never hurts to try though as the gate is usually unlocked and open.

19 BIKE BEACH CARNAVAL

From the cemetery the path continues parallel to the road and passes a large, golden gong on the right. The way is pleasant and shaded, and it eventually turns left and undulates before hitting the short stretch of **Pantai Carnaval**, also known as Bike Beach Carnaval. This beach is the quieter, more laid-back little brother to the packed and kid-crazy Pantai Festival.

You can sunbathe here without being stepped on or hassled.

20 SEGARRA RESTAURANT

Once at the beach, follow the path which runs parallel to the sea, until it ends at **Segarra** restaurant.

Segarra, which means 'sea' in Sanskrit, is a wonderful place for those who want to escape the city and pretend they're having an evening out in Bali. Sit on sofas just meters from the water's edge, enjoy the clean, white sand and watch the pleasant sunset over the Thousand Islands as sailboats bob in the foreground. The good food and decent mixed drinks make it worth hanging out for a while.

21 PANTAI CARNAVAL DOME

For those with a need to rock out, the **Pantai Carnaval Dome** is a mid-sized concert venue that often showcases local and touring bands and is located just across the field from Segarra. Check the local papers for the next big show.

When it's time to get home, and if it's not too late, a free shuttle bus delivers visitors back to the main drag. There is also a spot to rent bicycles here if other options for getting back to the main entrance fail.

GOING SAILING IN ANCOL

Ancol offers loads of colorful, wooden sailboats that can be rented for 15-minute increments and come complete with a captain and deckhands. If one can put a price on peace and quiet, then this activity comes cheap. Hop on board and let the crew do the rest. Imagine waves slapping against the hull, the sail flapping in the breeze and the warm sunshine pooling on the deck. The crusty old captain is likely to engage in a bit of show and tell, such as handing around a plastic cup with a tiny octopus inside that he's scooped up from the water.

Go for a short jaunt around the bay, or even head out to the nearest island and take a swim and a stroll before heading back to shore. Boats can hold at least 10 people with room to spread out, so pack a picnic complete with wine and fancy cheese and just enjoy the pleasant cruise. There are plenty of boats to choose

Sailing boats are available for rent.

from, so for a more authentic Indonesian experience hop on a vessel already packed with half a dozen happy-go-lucky families.

Boats are available 24 hours a day, seven days a week, and are located along the entire stretch of Ancol beach. In the morning, when there is little wind, captains have to use the boat's engines, so it's better to wait until the afternoon. Generally the price is set, but if bargaining does become an issue remember that paying an extra Rp10,000 is a much bigger deal to them than it is to you—so don't be too tight with the cash. The captains generally have a wealth of knowledge about life on the sea, and striking up a conversation with them is highly recommended.

Walking Tour 3

SUNDA KELAPA HARBOR

A Walk through the Ancient Seafaring History of Old Jakarta and a Still-functioning Port

1. **Watchtower**
2. **Maritime Museum**
3. **Fish Market**
4. **Tourist Information**
5. **Sunda Kelapa Harbor**
6. **Batavia Marina**

Sunda Kelapa, in the far reaches of north Jakarta, is the place to see old-fashioned, Bugis-style wooden ships. Lined up in nice stately order, the large boats are a blast from the past but still a crucial part of modern-day society. Lithe, well-muscled men who could have been pirates a hundred years ago now run up and down planks, carrying loads to toss into holds. Little boats, like cleaner fish, ply the waters between the big ships looking for passengers to scoop up and motor about for a behind-the-scenes look.

The area just inland from the port is historically important, since a great number of battles were fought here. At stake were the giant stores of spice, timber, metal and other valuable goods that were kept at what is now the **Museum Bahari** (Maritime Museum), a fairly well-preserved building which gives you a good sense of the past. Of course, all the residents needed feeding, as did those out at the Thousand Islands, so the **Pasar Ikan** (Fish Market) arose to meet demand. It's fascinating to wend through the tiny alleyways of the neighborhood adjacent to the fish market, with its cramped and close quarters packed with small children darting from home to home.

For two centuries, the area around the **Menara Syahbandar** (Watchtower) was the center of Batavia and its commercial hub. In fact, it wasn't long after its establishment that

it became the region's dominant trading center, beating out other large port towns, such as Makassar and Banten.

A modern addition to the area, but one done in great taste, is the **Batavia Marina**. Just a flying fish skip away, it offers respite from the heat in the form of ice cream and cold drinks. For those who like mixing with the locals, diving into the surrounding neighborhood is bound to deliver some unique encounters.

WHO? Anyone can do this tour–although it's not particularly child-friendly.

Sunda Kelapa
Batavia Marina 6
0   200m
N
Sunda Kelapa
Sunda Kelapa Harbor 5
Tourist Information 4
Luar Batang
Fish Market 3
Ujung Japat
Lodan Raya
Maritime Museum 2
Watchtower 1
Krapu
Pakin
Tongkol

HOW LONG? Anywhere from two hours to half a day.

HOW FAR? 2km.

GETTING THERE The tour begins at the confluence of Jl. Pakin and Jl. Pasar Ikan, directly across the street from Jl. Kakap.

GETTING STARTED The Menara Syahbandar, along with its four cannons out front, is visible just down the road on the right. Those who arrive before the Watchtower is open should ask for the man with the key. If you stand there long enough looking confused, he may well show up in search of some 'coffee money,' which means a few thousand rupiah for unlocking the door.

1 WATCHTOWER

Ascending the **Menara Syahbandar** (Watchtower) is an excellent way to get a bird's-eye view of the surrounding area. Built in 1839, on top of the old city wall, it replaced the flagpole that had been there for centuries. Climb eight flights of stairs, checking out the pictures along the way, to enjoy the breeze on the tower's top while looking out across the port over the old VOC Shipyard, or Galangan. Imagine a time when those posted here signaled incoming ships and took meteorological readings. Climb up through the tiny door to access the roof. Here, you'll find a modern flagpole and a great 360-degree view of the area.

FAST FACT

Most of the area to the north of the Watchtower was shallow sea in the early 1500s.

Leaving the Watchtower, turn right and follow the road as it hooks to the left and sweeps in front of the Museum Bahari. Note the shops across the street from the museum that sell drums, guitars, tambourines, nautical equipment and knick-knacks made from seashells.

2 MARITIME MUSEUM

The **Museum Bahari** (Maritime Museum) is one of the better museums in the city. It's housed in a complex of old VOC Dutch warehouses, some dating back to 1652, that once stocked nutmeg, pepper, coffee, tea and cloth

Climb the Watchtower for a bird's-eye view.

marked for passage to Asian and European markets. Between the warehouses and the nearby city wall, stocks of copper and tin were kept until ready for loading on to ships destined for European ports.

The museum itself is fairly large, cool and well maintained. Life-size replicas of boats and canoes, dioramas depicting north Jakarta's history, fishing gear and pieces from various lighthouses set the historical scene. Step outside for some good pictures of the old, repainted building with its large wooden doors and century-old cannons. Note that the wall out front is one of the few small sections of the original city wall that still remains from the 17th century, making it one of the most historical artifacts of all.

CHECK OUT www.museumbahari.org

GETTING IN Open 9am to 3pm, Tuesday to Sunday.

3 FISH MARKET

Continue along the road as it hooks right, and when it splits head to the right to Pasar Ikan.

Pasar Ikan (Fish Market) is best visited in the wee hours of the morning. Arrive too

The Maritime Museum is in an old warehouse.

Tourists rent bicycles and hats to explore the traditional pinisi ships at Sunda Kelapa.

late and it will be pretty much deserted.

From tiny sardines to giant groupers, the market unveils the secrets of the deep blue sea. Buy a fresh fish and eat it for lunch or just wander around and marvel at the selection. The neighborhood to the north of Pasar Ikan is Luar Batang, which means 'outside the log.' It got its name because at one time a great log was used to close the nearby Ciliwung River at night.

Continue along the road in front of the fish market warehouse until you reach the sea wall. Turn left and walk along to the end of the alley, where anchors and chains are sold. To get a glimpse at the homes of those who live around here, continue to follow the sea wall into the *kampung* and wander the narrow alleyways. Although it's easy to become a bit disoriented here, you can't get too lost because the area is bounded on all sides by the sea. The friendly residents will point the way out should you really get turned around.

4 TOURIST INFORMATION

For those who don't head into the *kampung*, take a left at the anchor and chain sellers and follow the road as it hooks around to the left. Then take the first right, which leads back to Jl. Pasar Ikan. Take this road back past the Watchtower to Jl. Pakin. Next, turn left on

Jl. Pakin and cross over the canal. Follow the road as it turns left and then go straight, under the archway and into Sunda Kelapa Harbor. Watch for the **Pusat Informasi Wisatawan** (Tourist Information Booth) up and to the right, but don't worry if it's not immediately obvious because the guys here hire themselves out as guides and will find you before you find them. The Booth has bathrooms if nature is calling.

5 SUNDA KELAPA HARBOR

In business now for roughly 900 years, the **Pelabuhan Sunda Kelapa** (Sunda Coconut Harbor) has witnessed some of the greatest and most historically important times in Indonesian history. Throughout the ages, cargo as diverse as pepper, animals, gold, slaves and rhino horns were picked up and dropped off at this port, although lately it sees shipments of much more ordinary things, such as timber and cement.

The Bugis and Makassar people, who hail from Sulawesi, own most of the large picturesque boats seen here. Stopping to chat with a few of them will provide a better insight into life on the seas and will introduce you to the unique cadences of the Bugis.

The main attraction is watching the boats being loaded by dozens of lithe men carrying

Luxury boats moored at the new Batavia Marina.

dusty, heavy loads while scurrying up a thin plank to then toss whatever they're carrying into the hold. These guys are working incredibly hard for incredibly little, but so it's been since time immemorial. Sadly, in regards to tourism, the loading of boats in this manner is beginning to disappear as more often cranes are being used instead.

While standing about shooting photos, ask nicely and you might be allowed to clamber on board for a picture. In fact, captains of boats have been known to invite guests to come on deck, explore the cabins and check out the captain's quarters. If given this opportunity, just be respectful and don't get in the way of any workers as they dash to and fro, and keep your eyes open for a monkey chained up on board as they are often kept as pets.

It's up to you how far down the line of ships you walk, admiring them as you pass. It's likely that along the way a guy will offer you a quick ride in a skiff, his boat bobbing between the looming hulks of the big wooden ships. Take this opportunity. It's quite interesting to see the ships from a different angle and to check out the ongoing repairs and repainting. Board the little craft by climbing over the wall and down a little ladder. Ask the seaman to motor the boat over to the Luar Batang neighborhood. He'll wait for you while you explore

this fishing village on foot, before ferrying you back to where you boarded.

⑥ BATAVIA MARINA

Back on land at the harbor, note that just past the Information Booth is Jl. Baruna Raya, and some signs for **Batavia Marina**. For those with the time and energy, it's another 10-minute walk to get to this new building. Have a bite to eat or just enjoy a cocktail or cool drink while resting up, then ask to visit their small lookout tower for a better view of the harbor. The staff are very proud of the place and will be happy to give a small tour and explain some of the finer details. Note that much of the furniture, adornments and paneling were constructed out of salvaged wood from the sea.

Once things are wrapped up at the marina, the friendly staff can call a taxi to take you home. Or, for those looking for additional adventures, Fatahillah Square is quite nearby. To go there, walk back to the boats and find an *ojek sepeda* or bicycle taxi. These are not *becak*, where a person sits in front, but rather a standard bicycle on which you sit on a little padded seat behind the driver. Hang on tight as they weave in and out of traffic, breaking all sorts of rules along the way. And with that, the tour is complete.

Walking Tour 4

KOTA AND MANGGA DUA

The Old Walled City of Jakarta and the Original Town Square

1. **Fatahillah Square**
2. **Shadow Puppet Museum**
3. **Fine Arts and Ceramics Museum**
4. **Jakarta History Museum**
5. **Café Batavia**
6. **Toko Merah Building**
7. **Chicken Market Bridge**
8. **Raja Kuring Restaurant**
9. **VOC Shipyard**
10. **Portuguese Church**
11. **Mangga Dua Mall**
12. **Mangga Dua Plaza Elektronika**
13. **Mangga Dua Morning Market**
14. **International Trade Center**
15. **Grand Boutique Center**
16. **WTC Mangga Dua**
17. **Mangga Dua Square**

It can be hard to imagine a time when Kota was nearly the entire city of Jakarta. That is the very reason, though, that the area is considered such a historical goldmine. Go back a few hundred years to when Kota was surrounded by a defensive wall and moat to keep the ruling government safe inside while the riff-raff and would-be plunderers were held at bay on the outside. Imagine the energy and excitement the Europeans felt as they explored and exploited a new land, their wealth rolling in and power growing. For the Asian community as well, there was plenty of money to be made if one was in the right position to do it. Others found themselves slaving away for a pittance.

The heart of Kota, which means 'fortified place' in Sanskrit, is **Taman Fatahillah** (Fatahillah Square). A number of historically vital buildings surround it, including the **City Hall of Batavia**. Many are now museums. While the square itself is plain, it is driven by the energy it draws from the crowds of local and foreign tourists, the special events, the cultural performances and the throngs of young, cool kids who come to hang out and be seen.

While the area has massive potential to become the pride and joy of the city, at the moment it is still fairly grungy. The leaders with the ability to transform it into something truly special still lack the communication and coordination to do so. That being said, there is something special about pedaling around on a forest green **Dutch-era bicycle** wearing a woven explorer's hat and posing in front of the cannons once used to repel would-be invaders. Once it's time for a break, stepping into the cool confines of **Café Batavia** for a cocktail will do wonders for the soul.

Be aware that it can become extremely hot during the day and there is little shade, so come well prepared and start early. Sundays are very busy: swarms of young school children armed with English 'surveys' look to practice their English and snap pictures with visitors. The first half dozen students may be cute, but after that it can get old. Feel free to say no, but stay pleasant about it.

WHO? This tour is for everyone. It's short enough that a whole family can do it and it doesn't require you to step too far out of your comfort zone.

HOW LONG? If this tour is done strictly as a walk, without stopping along the way, it will take less than an hour. If a number of the museums are explored, a leisurely lunch is eaten and the opportunity to wheel around on a rented bicycle is taken, it could take all day.

Promenading in front of the old City Hall of Batavia in Fatahillah Square.

HOW FAR? 3.5km to the VOC Building and back. It's 4.5km if the Portuguese Church is included.

AN ADDITIONAL NOTE This walking tour can easily be combined with the Sunda Kelapa walking tour.

GETTING THERE Take Busway #1 to its terminus at Kota. Those driving can come via Jl. Gajah Mada or the Harbor toll road. Both traffic and parking can be challenging in the Kota area, so taxis or the Busway are recommended. From the Busway, exit on the Bank Mandiri side–watch for the signs. If coming by taxi, ask to be dropped off at the Bank Mandiri Museum.

GETTING STARTED Upon exiting the Busway, follow the direction of traffic toward the **Bank Mandiri Museum** just ahead on the left. Continue along to enter the **Bank of Indonesia Museum**, which is just past the Bank Mandiri Museum.

Both bank museums are good escapes from the heat and traffic, but they are still ultimately museums about banks, so don't plan your whole day around them. They do provide interesting insights into the past, however, and are certainly worth a stroll around. The Bank of Indonesia Museum has gone the extra step of presenting some of its

information via multimedia, and is therefore a bit more interesting for kids.

GETTING IN Open 9am to 4pm, Tuesday to Sunday.

Next, carefully cross the busy road on the right and proceed straight, passing between the large concrete balls installed to keep the traffic out. Continue on to Taman Fatahillah.

1 FATAHILLAH SQUARE
Taman Fatahillah (Fatahillah Square) was named after the commander of the Cirebon forces who, in 1526, surrounded Sunda Kelapa, as Jakarta was then known, and burned it down. He is considered the founder of Jakarta since he then rebuilt the city, naming it Jayakarta. The Portuguese during this time steered clear of Fatahillah, who had developed a deep hatred for them after they took over his hometown in north Sumatra. Fatahillah so disliked the Portuguese that when 30 of them swam to the shore of Jayakarta after their boat was shipwrecked, he had his soldiers beat and kill them all.

In the center of the square sits the replica of an octagonal fountain that was first built in 1743. Water from this fountain once flowed from the Ciliwung River in Glodok via an underground brick pipe. Until around 1650, the water was fairly drinkable, but soon after

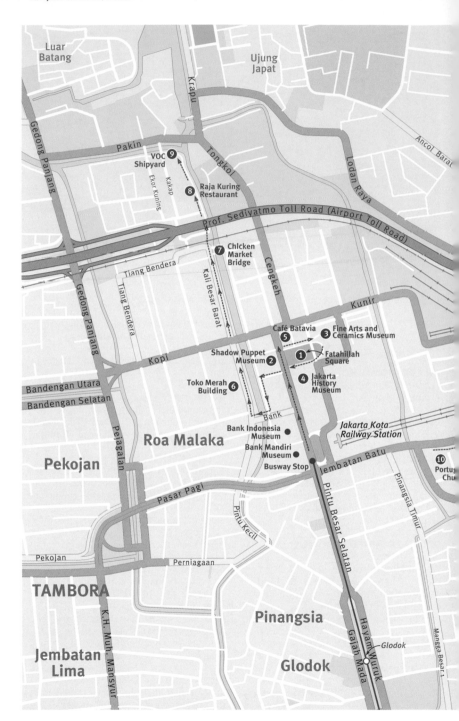

Kota and Mangga Dua

A tattooed street performer doing snake stunts at Fatahillah Square.

it became intolerable: polluted by trash, human waste and hospital offal. Unfortunately, a peek inside will afford a similar view even today.

> ### *FAST FACT*
> The Chinese and Dutch used to drink from the same polluted river, but the Chinese got sick much less. The Dutch wanted to know why. They decided it was all the tea the Chinese drank, so they began chewing tea leaves for their supposed medicinal properties. Little did they know it was the boiled water the Chinese used for tea, rather than the leaves, that was saving the day.

Historically, the square was a joyous location, as it was the sight of public markets and all-night feasts and festivals up through the 18th century. It had a dark side, too, as a place where countless tortures and punishments were meted out. On the eastern side of the square sat a sawhorse with a sharpened back. Prisoners would be forced to sit there for days with weights dangling from their feet, until the device slowly sliced them in two. Executions by guillotine, gallows or sword were held on certain days each month, and were overseen from the second floor of

the courthouse by the judges who ordered the sentences. Slaves hated bearing witness to the killings the most, since they made up the highest number of victims.

Other types of torture included branding, whipping or impalement, with the accused left to die slow, terrible deaths while straddling sharpened metal stakes. Chaining a person to the ground before dropping a heavy wheel on him was not uncommon, nor was stretching a prisoner until he confessed, cutting off his ear, putting him in a cage to face ridicule or forcing him to wear an iron necklace.

THE TWO-WHEELED TOUR The square boasts a plethora of bicycles for rent, most of which are ancient, all-steel, Dutch-era cruisers. Rent one to tool around Fatahillah Square or go big and hire a guide to take you round the sites. Some guides will also provide two-seater bicycles for those who don't feel confident pedaling on their own. Each bike comes with an explorer's sun hat and a ring-ting-tinging bell.

The usual route includes the Maritime Museum, the Watchtower, the Fish Market, Sunda Kelapa Port and the Chicken Market Bridge, all of which are just north of Kota. At each spot the guide will extol his knowledge of the historical facts and figures, although generally this will be in Indonesian as most don't speak English. For additional sites, check out the guide's brochure. A highly recommended route–though it involves a jaunt up narrow, traffic-clogged lanes–is the one past the temples in Chinatown and the old St. Maria de Fatima Catholic Church (for more on these, see p. 76, Glodok).

Settle on a price before pushing off, but don't bargain too hard as these guys are living a fairly tough life, with many spending the night sleeping rough in the Square. Note that additional locations add to the price.

HEADS UP

Guides may not provide much assistance while cycling across busy roads. Most will make a token wave at the traffic, leaving you to follow quickly behind or fend for yourself. Crossing streets, riding against traffic and going up jammed-up alleyways may seem tricky, especially if you depart from the usual route. But the guides have been weaving in and out of Jakarta traffic for years, so it's normal for them.

---

② SHADOW PUPPET MUSEUM

Standing in the Square, you'll find the **Museum Wayang** (Shadow Puppet Museum) to the left. This building was built in 1912, became the City Museum in 1939, and in 1975 took on its current function. It was actually erected on the foundations of two now defunct churches, the Old Dutch Reformed Church and the New Dutch Church. Funnily enough, the first of these churches was knocked down because a specially ordered church organ was found too big to fit inside. Rather than remodel, architects decided to bulldoze the place and build a bigger church. The second church was wrecked beyond repair by an earthquake. Members of the congregation took this as a sign that perhaps the location was not the best place for a church.

Just one hour at the Museum Wayang provides a wealth of knowledge and insight about Indonesia's famed puppets, among others. Located over two floors, and with artifacts from around the world, including a set of Punch and Judy puppets from Great Britain, the museum is a pleasant stroll through the peculiar world of puppetry. There are string puppets from India and Guignol puppets from France, as well as

Chinese and Polish puppets.

The Indonesian puppets are made from a variety of materials, including buffalo hide, bamboo and even grass, sticks and leaves. There are life-sized puppets that a person can wear, as well as a wide selection of masks from all across Java, Madura and Bali. Gamelan music figures heavily in puppet performances, so there are numerous displays of all the instruments used.

GETTING IN Open 9am to 3pm, Tuesday to Sunday.

ADDITIONAL INFORMATION The museum hosts a puppet show every 2nd, 3rd and 4th Sunday of the month from 10am to 2pm (subject to change). Be warned, though, your children may not sit merrily clapping their hands throughout the show as the pacing and content of these traditional performances are not child-oriented. Visitors can drop in and then leave at their leisure.

③ FINE ARTS AND CERAMICS MUSEUM

After leaving the Museum Wayang, cross both the square and Jl. Pos Kota to get to the **Senirupa dan Keramic Museum** (Fine Arts and Ceramics Museum). While this sounds splendid, unfortunately the building's architecture is its greatest draw. Built in 1870, it was originally the Supreme Court of Justice. Once inside, there *are* fine arts and there *are* ceramics to be seen, but they are limited to about 400 fairly unexciting pieces. Some of the paintings are quite nice, though, and the spiraling wrought-iron staircases that lead to the second floor are quaint.

People often come here for photo shoots, and these can be much more entertaining than the museum itself. The building also

Maritime exhibit in the Bank of Indonesia Museum.

houses the Earthenware Studio, where visitors can make their own ceramics, and a library for those who want to brush up on their art history.

GETTING IN Open 9am to 3pm, Tuesday to Sunday.

4 JAKARTA HISTORY MUSEUM

After the ceramics museum, re-enter Fatahillah Square and head left to check out the **Museum Sejarah Jakarta** (Jakarta History Museum). It is a beautiful old building that keeps a close guard over the Square. It served as the City Hall of Batavia from 1710 until 1913, and of all the buildings from the VOC (Dutch East India Company) era, it is the largest still in existence. Once a prison compound, police and military offices and a city hall, the building finally became a museum in 1974. Many rooms are devoted to old wooden furniture of limited interest to the general public, but there is a range of newer displays that are worth checking out, many of which have English translations.

Take a moment to imagine nearly 200 years' worth of activity here: people going to court, doing business, attending church services, registering marriages, working for orphan protection–or being thrown in prison, whipped, tortured and put to death. In fact, often more than 300 prisoners could be held here at one time. Most were chained up in the basement, generally suffering and often eventually dying, just waiting for a day with the judge. Often prisoners were locked away for nothing more serious than petty theft, while the mentally ill, with nowhere else to go, found themselves bolted to the walls right along with the law breakers.

One particularly famous prisoner, held in the east wing on the second floor, was the Javanese hero Prince Diponegoro, who started a holy war against the Dutch in central Java that lasted from 1825 to 1830. He was later shipped off to Makassar, Sulawesi.

J. P. Coen, the founding father of Batavia, was buried here before being transferred to the nearby Dutch cemetery, where the Museum Wayang now sits. The two-term Governor General ruled Batavia with an especially heavy hand, then succumbed to cholera in 1629.

Spend a few moments in the pleasant courtyard at the back of the museum. There will be crowds of teenyboppers taking

pictures with their mobile phones, but try to block them out and imagine what the place was like when it served as the scene of the 1740 Chinese massacre. Riots had broken out in the streets on October 9th, and the Chinese were being held accountable. Although the Chinese prisoners and hospital patients at the City Hall couldn't have had anything to do with the chaos, all were brought into the courtyard and murdered, one by one: no court, no judge, no accountability.

The centerpiece of the courtyard is the **Si Jaguar Cannon**, which was brought over by the Dutch in 1641. The clenched fist at the rear of the cannon is said to represent cohabitation, and some women have taken this to mean it will increase fertility. With so many women riding and grinding on the cannon like some kind of sexually infused iron bucking bronco, museum officials decided to relocate it from the Square, where it originally sat, to the back of the museum. Despite the move, women still find the cannon and ride it, ignoring the sign that implores them to stay off it.

Before leaving the museum, note the octagonal tower on its roof. It held a bell that rang once in the early morning, when death-row inmates were brought before the court to be identified. It rang a second time when they were taken to the Square, and then rang a third time when executions began. Until mysteriously disappearing in 1957, a statue portraying the female figure of Lady Justice also used to grace the roof of the building.

FAST FACT

In 1629, a young woman called Sarah Specx was staying at the home of the Governor General, J. P. Coen. Being the wayward 13-year-old that she was, she let her soldier beau stay over too late one night and was caught. Coen first suggested the couple be sewn up together in a sack and tossed into the sea. Next, he considered death by hanging. He finally settled on beheading the luckless male lover in Fatahillah Square while the young woman was stripped half-naked and whipped at the entrance to the City Hall.

GETTING IN Open 9am to 3pm, Tuesday to Sunday.

5 CAFÉ BATAVIA

After leaving the Jakarta History Museum, head straight across Fatahillah Square to **Café Batavia**, one of the oldest houses from the era when Jakarta was known as Batavia. The lower half of the building was built in 1810, and the upper section was added in the 1930s. It's an absolutely wonderful place for a meal or a cool drink on a hot afternoon. Take the time to look at the hundreds of movie star pictures that adorn the walls on both the top and bottom floors.

Sit at a table upstairs to enjoy a tasty bowl of *bubur ayam* (chicken porridge), a local breakfast dish, while enjoying the view through the large windows of the action in the square and wallowing in the grandeur of such a fine historical setting. For those with teenage sons, be sure to give them a five-minute time limit in the bathroom, since the risqué photographs there may be very distracting for virgin eyes.

CHECK OUT www.cafebatavia.com

With refreshments taken care of, re-cross the square, exiting via Jl. Kali Besar Timur 5, which is off to the right. This leads to Jl. Kali Besar Timur. Cross the road to walk alongside the canal, which may be a tad smelly. Straight ahead and to the left is a tall, red brick building called Toko Merah. To get there, turn left and follow the canal. At the bridge, cross the canal, turn right and follow the canal on the other side. Toko Merah is on the left. Feel free to cross the street for a close up, although entrance is not allowed.

6 TOKO MERAH BUILDING

Toko Merah (Red Shop) was built in 1730, during a time when Kota was a happening neighborhood. History holds that this building was once the former residence of a number of Dutch governors and an academy for marines. It was also used by private companies. During World War II, the Japanese kept their medical equipment here—that is, after murdering the Dutch who had been working in the building.

7 CHICKEN MARKET BRIDGE

Continue along the **Kali Besar** (Great Canal), passing the **Batavia Hotel** off to the left, and stop at the 17th century **Jembatan Pasar Ayam** (Chicken Market Bridge). While at one time it was a working drawbridge, it is now a

The historical red building, Toko Merah.

restored historical landmark. It's a good example of Dutch architecture, and with some imagination you might be able to visualize a time when ships still plied the waters here. In fact, in 1632 the Dutch straightened the river beneath the bridge so that small boats could go upstream to aid trade and transport. Originally, there were three bridges, though now only this one remains.

Early in the morning, a group of spandex-clad housewives exercise to clubbing music here, along with a body-beat leader who uses the bridge as her power-pump platform. They may be photo shy, so go easy on the picture taking.

For many people, this much of the tour is enough for one day. For those wanting to explore further, there are two options. One is to continue on up to the Sunda Kelapa Port to start a second walking tour. Another is to head back to the Busway station and from there check out a historical church, as well as some of the area's infamous shopping options.

OPTION #1

After the Chicken Market Bridge, walk straight, following the canal by crossing

Colonial-style buildings bordering the canal exhibit many features of Dutch architecture.

the road and passing under a double set of railroad tracks and then an underpass.

8 RAJA KURING RESTAURANT

Continue along the canal, noting the **Restoran Raja Kuring** (Raja Kuring Restaurant, www.rajakuring.com) on the left and later the large statue of an anchor on the right.

9 VOC SHIPYARD

Next is the **Bekas Galangan Kapal VOC** (VOC Shipyard) building on the left, which appears after hooking left at a T-junction. Look for the sign on the wall to confirm it is the VOC Shipyard. Then turn right and go under the archway and over the canal. Cross the main road, Jl. Pakin, and head to the right just a tad. This is the start of the Sunda Kelapa Port tour.

For a quick rest first, and to get off the streets for a bit, pop into the café at the VOC Shipyard. There is a peaceful courtyard there, where visitors can sip a cool drink. There is also a tiny art shop to poke around in.

10 PORTUGUESE CHURCH
OPTION #2

Backtrack to the main intersection of Jl. Jembatan Batu and Jl. Pintu Besar Selatan, just past the Bank Mandiri Museum. Cross the intersection and turn left, heading east up Jl. Jembatan Batu.

After crossing the canal, turn right up Jl. Pangeran Jayakarta and cross the street to find the **Gereja Portugis** (Portuguese Church). Dating back to 1695, this is the oldest building in Jakarta which still retains its original function; even most of the furniture is original.

The street runs through what was once one of the most fashionable neighborhoods in Jakarta due to the expansive mansions and their equally expansive surrounding gardens built there. The cemetery, which surrounded the church at the time, was filled rapidly in the late 1700s as life in Batavia had become quite unhealthy, due to a combination of a malaria outbreak as well as extremely unsanitary living conditions. In one year alone, nearly 2,400 unfortunate souls, or roughly 15 percent of the city's population, were buried in the cemetery. Note that the true name of the church is Gereja Sion, but few people refer to it as such these days.

> ### FAST FACT
> The Dutch had various means to protect their health during this time, though not all were scientifically founded. Many thought that starting the day with a tumbler of gin would help—combined with the assistance of non-stop smoking during the day, often of cigars.

11 MANGGA DUA MALL, 12 MANGGA DUA PLAZA ELEKTRONIKA, 13 MANGGA DUA MORNING MARKET, 14 INTERNATIONAL TRADE CENTER, 15 GRAND BOUTIQUE CENTER

From the church, go back out to Jl. Mangga Dua Raya and check out any number of the mega malls along this strip. Many Jakarta residents will list shopping and going to the mall among their top hobbies, and Mangga Dua is a famous hot spot. Walking along the right-hand side of the road, check out **Mangga Dua Mall** and later **Mangga Dua Plaza Elektronika**. On the other side of the street are **Pasar Pagi Mangga Dua**, **International Trade Center** and **Grand Boutique Center**.

16 WTC MANGGA DUA, 17 MANGGA DUA SQUARE

At the end of the road, where Jl. Mangga Dua Raya hits Jl. Gunung Sahari, is the megalithic **WTC Mangga Dua**, which offers unlimited discount shopping, and if that is still not enough, to the right is **Mangga Dua Square**, an equally mind-blowing large shopping monstrosity. Come with money, come with time and come with a moving truck to take away all those purchases.

CHECK OUT www.wtcm2.com

OTHER WAYS TO EXPLORE KOTA Join local Indonesian group Jelajah Budaya who are passionate about both conserving and exploring Kota, its museums and other such areas.

CHECK OUT www.jelajahbudaya.blogspot.com

Contact Ronny at **Jakarta Hidden Tours**. He leads tours around Fatahillah Square, to the museums and the port, and provides a unique perspective on the people and places. Get ready for an atypical tourist experience in which you will be led off the beaten track. He also offers 'slum tours' which are detailed on his website.

CHECK OUT www.jakartahiddentour.wordpress.com

Walking Tour 5

GLODOK AND MANGGA BESAR
An Exploration of Jakarta's Old Chinatown: Its Markets and Temples

1. **Victory Market**
2. **Temple of the Goddess of Devotion**
3. **Ting Ting Shop**
4. **Saint Mary of Fatima Catholic Church**
5. **Temple of Glorious Obligation**
6. **Gloria Market**
7. **National Archives Museum**
8. **Snake Market**

Unlike many of the world's Chinatowns, Jakarta's version is not a well-publicized tourist attraction and the city administration has done little to make it a visitor destination. That makes wandering the streets a much more local experience, though, as relatively little has been created just to appeal to what a tourist would hope or want to see in a Chinatown. What this means is that visitors to the area can rub shoulders with real people in real shops without the illusion that this has all been re-created just to please them.

The Glodok neighborhood originally sat outside the city walls of Batavia, and it was where the Chinese settled after the Dutch launched a terrible, unwarranted massacre of their people in 1750. They were able to live and trade freely here until May 1998, when riots erupted, sparked by opposition to then President Suharto's rule, as well as high prices on commodities and rising unemployment. Ethnic Chinese, who were accused of

The entrance to Glodok's Chinese-dominated Pasar Kemenangan wet market area.

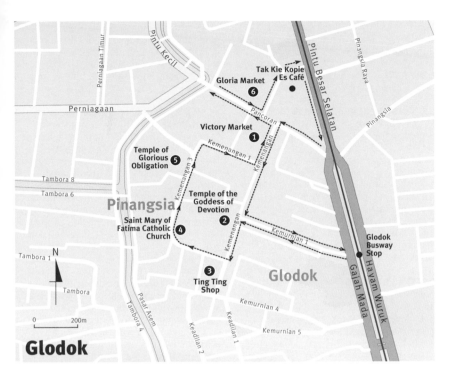

accumulating too much of the nation's wealth, were made targets of wanton violence. Many of the shopping plazas and department stores that were destroyed by mass looting and arson have been rebuilt, but the area has still not fully recovered. As evidence, visitors can still see shells of burned-out shops along Jl. Gajah Mada.

More than a decade later, the area is back in business–and business is thriving. Unfortunately many of the original shopkeepers fled abroad, where they felt more secure, and never returned, allowing for many newcomers to move in and replace them.

Go from the ordinary to the extraordinary at **Pasar Petak Sembilan** (Victory Market), a wet market with an unsettling but must-see array of raw food options. Along the way, be sure to explore the little shops selling dried snacks, incense, offering oil and other temple related goods. The area is also a great place to people-watch and observe the brass tacks of bartering. Stop by **Vihara Jin De Yuan** (Temple of the Goddess of Devotion), a fine Buddhist temple filled with massive candles and clouds of incense smoke. Then head over to the **Gereja Katolik Santa Maria de**

Fatima (Saint Mary of Fatima Catholic Church). The proximity of the two places of worship is a good indication of the many religions practiced in Jakarta. At this point, it's time to try some of the amazing array of small eateries Chinatown offers. Get a bowl of pork noodles or gamble on one of the curious snacks at the many streetside stalls.

Glodok boasts an abundance of entertainment options, including karaoke bars, nightclubs, hotel pubs and restaurants. One of the most unusual streets in Jakarta shows its true colors at dusk, when the **Pasar Ular** (Snake Market) gets going. And time spent in Jakarta would not be complete without a visit to the infamous **Stadium** nightclub. Shoppers in search of electronic goods will be delighted at the incredible choices and the lowest prices in the city.

WHO? The walk is suitable for almost anyone, although the wet market might make some feel a bit uncomfortable.

HOW LONG? A straight walk with little stopping will take around an hour, but you should take time to explore. If you stop to eat and chit-chat, the tour will take between two and three hours.

HOW FAR? 1.75km for the walk around Glodok alone.

GETTING THERE Traffic around Glodok can be challenging, so arriving by Busway or taxi is recommended. Drivers may find parking at Galeria Glodok, just north of the Glodok Busway stop, or along Jl. Pancoran. Busway passengers should get off at the Glodok stop and cross the street to the left. On the opposite side of the road are a number of large industrial shopping malls such as Harco Glodok, Plaza Pinangsia and Hayam Wuruk Indah, which sell air compressors, chainsaws and rubber gaskets, along with loads of various electronic goods.

GETTING STARTED Directly across from where the walk starts is a building labeled 'Rajamas Hotel', while off to the right is the colorful LTC Glodok. As you enter Jl. Kemurnian 1 (Purity Street), look for the vendors grinding up coconuts or chopping up chickens to the left, as well as parked snake

Satay seller on Jl. Kemenangan III.

meat food carts to either side. Continue along this street, which looks a bit off-putting at first but gets better along the way, until it ends at Jl. Kemenangan and Pasar Kemenangan, an intriguing Chinese wet market.

1 VICTORY MARKET
Pasar Petak Sembilan (Victory Market) is one of the coolest sites in the city. Packed with shoppers from the far reaches of Jakarta, all in search of the freshest, tastiest and cheapest deals, the narrow lanes are thick with bargain hunters looking to fill their kitchens with the best ingredients they can find. As it's a wet market, standard fare here are headless snakes, writhing eels and large turtles, all in tanks, buckets and boxes, with fresh fish still swimming or laid out on slabs as well.

Skinned and splayed-out frogs, with their pink fleshy muscles, line the walls of stalls, while some of their luckier brethren are still alive but bundled together around the waist, each trying to hop in a different direction, so collectively going nowhere. Cockle shells, clams and oysters are all set out–washed, shucked, shelled or still intact–shoppers can have them any way they like. This market is not for the squeamish, since blood and guts abound. Watch as a man with his tub of eels whips one out, lays it wriggling on a stump of wood, drives a nail through the head to hold it down, runs a thin blade along its body and then thumbs out the guts in one quick, slick motion. Off comes the head and the whole thing is over with before it even got started.

The market is not just about the animals, though. There are loads of fruit and vegetable stalls as well as surrounding shops with an equally vivid, though less grim, array of goods. Browse among paper lanterns, traditional medicines, giant bags of brightly colored snacks and dried goods, temple offerings and the usual collection of socks, shirts and sandals.

2 TEMPLE OF THE GODDESS OF DEVOTION
Turn left and walk a few meters. On the right is a small archway, the first of three that lead to a series of Buddhist temples. Vendors often sell flowers here, which people buy and lay as offerings in the temples. Next to the tiny canal nearby is a chicken killing field. Arrive at the right time and be rewarded with the sight of a flurry of knives ending lives. Before

A visit to the Victory Market is not for the faint-hearted.

passing though the archway here, look to see if there is a seller around with a large cage stuffed with more than 100 twittering little birds. He sells them for Rp2,000 each to devotees to release in front of the temple. By releasing these birds, a person releases their bad luck and increases the chance of a long life. The perfect number to buy according to tradition is 108.

Inside the courtyard and to the right is the **Vihara Jin De Yuan** (Temple of the Goddess of Devotion). Originally named Temple of Golden Virtue, the name change was forced during the Suharto era. This temple was constructed in the mid-17th century and stands out, in part, because of the curvature of the large, colorful roof as well as the pearl-encrusted dragons, lotus flowers and phoenixes decorating its detailed exterior. Note the *kilin*, a one-horned, ox-tailed, horse-hooved, fish-scaled, unicorn-like creature decorating the front of the temple. It represents goodness, purity and peace. Off to the left is a dragon, while to the right is a bird of paradise; they come as a standard pair.

Although it is a Buddhist sanctuary where monks once lived, it also contains certain Taoist elements. Note the two 18th century stone lions, called *boa-gu shi*. In the middle of the courtyard, under a pagoda, is a giant

brass incense burner which is continually stuffed with incense stick offerings billowing out great clouds of smoke. Enter the temple, often overwhelmingly thick with incense smoke, and weave among the big bundles of incense, the large, two-meter-tall, 250-kilo red candles, and 18 golden Buddhas. Notice the bowls of oil that people are adding to; oil represents light, so adding an offering here can lighten up one's work and home life. Head toward the back to find the main goddess Kwam Im, whose job it is to help people, no matter their ill.

Pass through one of the temple side doors and walk around the outer courtyard to see some of the idols, including the God of Earth, the God of City Protection and the God of Wealth. People bring bundles of incense and give three lit pieces to each god. Others may offer fruit and most, at some point, will burn square pieces of thin paper which represent money in one of many large furnaces as an offering to the gods.

Leave the main temple, go straight under the archway and into the larger courtyard where the beggars tend to hang out. Generally, each morning they are ordered to line up in an orderly fashion to receive their daily alms of Rp2,000. Enter the first of the three smaller, more modern temples to the right.

The mid-17th century Vihara Jin De Yuan or Temple of the Goddess of Devotion.

These are **Xuan-tan Gong**, for the God of Wealth and also reportedly for health; **Di-cang-wang Miao**, dedicated to the King of the Underworld and a good one to pray to if one has bad karma, and **Hui-ze Miao**, for the gods of the Hokkien clan and for family.

Inside the first temple, take a moment to quietly observe some of the rituals taking place here. Or try one yourself. Begin by holding a wooden container with long, thin, numbered sticks. State your name, address, age, the current date and what you are praying for. Shake the container and eventually one stick falls out. Stick it in an incense bowl. Next, pray over two small, half-oval wood blocks, shake them and toss them into the air. If the blocks land facing in an acceptable direction (check with a temple attendant), the number on the stick is then checked and a small fortune, typed out on a piece of paper, is brought out. This practice is done for in-sight into the future.

The temples are particularly busy around Chinese New Year, on the days of the new and full moons when people pray for protection and prosperity, and between December 1st and 22nd when people give thanks for the good luck they've had that year. Tourists are welcome to enter any of the temples and take photographs, but be extremely courteous and don't invade people's privacy.

3 TING TING SHOP

Exit the temples via the large archway, turn right and follow the road as it hooks right. Just a few meters up, at Jl. Kemenangan III #34, is the **Toko Ting Ting** (Ting Ting shop), run by English-speaking Lukman. Pop into his shop and check out all the paper offerings he has for sale. These offerings are paper representations of modern-day goods. People send them to their ancestors in the afterworld by burning them in the furnaces at the temples. You can buy a paper car, motorcycle, tuxedo, mobile phone and even loads of cash. One, in particular, is the 1,000,000,000,000,000 bill (one quadrillion dollars), which people hope has strong purchasing power in another dimension.

> ### FAST FACT
> If you see something gold in the shop, it's meant for the gods. If it's silver, it's meant for ancestors. The color red represents luck.

Continue on. As the road turns right, there is a crook in the road and a nice new arch-way with a small altar on the left side of the road. The altar is dedicated to Aum A Hum, the Earth God. To make an offering, tap the altar floor three times to call the god and let

A religious relief set in a wall at the Saint Mary of Fatima Catholic Church.

him know you are there to pray. An interesting message written on the altar says 'Warning–anyone who tries to profit from this temple will suffer from an accident, curse or disaster.'

4 SAINT MARY OF FATIMA CATHOLIC CHURCH
Feel free to stroll up the incredibly cute little lane under the archway, Jl. Kemenangan I, before returning and continuing along Jl. Kemenangan III, keeping to the right to be safe from passing motorbikes. On the right is the **Gereja Katolik Santa Maria de Fatima** (Saint Mary of Fatima Catholic Church).

This church, also known as **Gereja Toasebio** (Big Chinese Church), was originally a house built in the typical Chinese architectural style of the early 19th century. It was converted into a church in 1970. At the front of the site are two lions, one female and one male, which serve as guardians of the church and represent the glory and nobility of those living within. Note the flower and fruit adornments that represent peace and prosperity. If someone is around to let visitors in, check out the interior, which is a curious mixture of temple and church. If you are unable to get through the door, take a moment to climb the seven tiny steps of **Bukit Maria de Fatima** (St. Mary of Fatima Hill).

5 TEMPLE OF GLORIOUS OBLIGATION
Leaving the church, turn right and continue along the road. Watch for a street vendor selling *kue bantal*, a stodgy little fried pillow-cake breakfast snack, for a few thousand rupiah. Up on the left sits the wonderful little **Vihara Dharma Jaya Toasebio** (Temple of Glorious Obligation), which harkens back to the 1750s. Pass through the entrance gates painted with hatchet-carrying guards and note the lanterns and giant swirling incense hanging from the ceiling. In the far back is the god Cheng Goan Cheng Kun, a type of war god with a penchant for alcohol, which explains the cans of Guinness on the altar. Note his guard dogs below him. They don't like booze but people do offer them chunks

Paper offerings inside Vihara Jin De Yuan.

A group of two-meter-tall, 250-kilo giant candles inside Vihara Jin De Yuan.

of meat and cakes. Head to the back left area to see a serious display of burning candles. Here, you can write the name of a family member or even their company, post it on the candle and pray for them.

After exiting the temple, turn left and continue up the road. Rather than hook left however, go straight up the small alley. Follow the alley as it zigzags and then straightens. Later it will be a narrow lane to the left, but continue going straight. Along the way are tables selling Chinese knick-knacks, snacks, massage implements, jewelry, incense, frogs, turtles and much more. The alley ends at

Caged 'lucky birds' at Vihara Jin De Yuan.

Jl. Kemenangan, where heading to the right leads back to the large temple compound where the tour started.

Go left instead and up the street until you reach the red and white shop on the right with three golden Chinese characters on it. Take the small alley just before it on the right to check out a very full-on section of the wet market. After following this alley to the end, backtrack out and turn right, continuing along Jl. Kemenangan until it ends on the busy sidewalk of Jl. Pancoran.

Turn left here and walk up the road, noting all the traditional medicine shops. Just before **Toko Obat Soo**, Jl. Pancoran 1-7 will appear, a lane packed with all sorts of goodies. Take a quick jaunt to its end and back again, then continue along Jl. Pancoran, with all its snacks, dried foods, toys, jewelry, pets, kitchenware and more, until the sidewalk ends at the **Kali Krukut** (Krukut Canal). Make sure to buy some *mochi* along the way—little cakes made from glutinous rice and stuffed with sweet filling.

6 GLORIA MARKET

Cross the road on the right, turn right and walk along the shops here, passing in front of what was once **Pasar Gloria** (Gloria Market). This was recently burned down and was demolished, but is now being rebuilt.

The National Archives Museum is housed in a beautiful building with green surroundings.

Just before the Fortuna Hotel is a long, famous alley of food stalls. This is the top spot for a bowl of noodles and a refreshing drink. Try the *bakmi ayam* (chicken noodles) and a *kopi es* (iced coffee) at **Tak Kie Kopi Es Café** on the right side of the alley. The café opened in the 1920s, though it was only a stall in its early days. Coffee is what they do best, but turtle soup is their claim to fame, and it often sells out by midday. A short way past Tak Kie, also on the right, is **Soto Betawi Afung** where the best bet is the *soto Betawi* (Betawi soup) and *soto mie* (noodle soup). Be wary of the other menu options, which include *babat* (stomach), *urat* (muscle), *kikil* (foot skin) and *paru* (lungs).

For food adventurists looking for something on the wild side, look for the specialty dish *sekba*, a dish made from pig guts.

> ### HEADS UP
> Visitors might think twice before trying the turtle soup (*pie tim*), since it is sometimes made from protected species.

After eating, continue a short way up the road until it splits at a three-way junction. Turn right and continue until you reach the main road of Jl. Pintu Besar Selatan.

From here there are two choices. The first is to turn left and walk up the road to a gathering of portrait artists and street vendors selling everything from oil lamps and rare coins to small daggers called *keris*. Continue past them to get to Kota Tua (Old City), where the Kota walking tour begins at the Bank Mandiri Museum.

The second option is to turn right and circle back to Glodok, also perhaps passing some portrait artists. Upon reaching the corner where Jl. Pancoran begins, turn right and continue up the sidewalk back to the Fortune Hotel and the food hawkers. Along the way, watch for a guy selling cobras from a street cart. He should be happy to pull one out and show it off. He also sells cobra oils, pills and dried meat.

At this point, the tour is complete. For those looking for more, return to Jl. Kemenangan, go back through the wet market and return to the Busway. Jump on the Busway and ride it south to the Mangga Besar stop. Exit to the left and walk along the road until you reach Gedung Arsip Nasional.

7 NATIONAL ARCHIVES MUSEUM

The beauty of the **Museum Gedung Arsip Nasional** (National Archives Museum) is its architecture, green lawn and peaceful courtyard behind the main building rather than its sparse collection. Built in 1760, the house is located in what was then considered the countryside, and was originally a residence staffed by more than 100 local and foreign slaves. Later, it became an orphanage and eventually the National Archives from 1926 to 1979. Unfortunately, the building began to deteriorate so badly that the archives were moved to south Jakarta until the building was restored again in 1998 and the precious archives could be returned.

FAST FACT

By the end of the 17th century, slaves comprised half of Jakarta's population. Around 500,000 slaves in total were traded during the Dutch VOC era. In the early 1800s, a Balinese woman could be bought for $150 due to both her work ethic and legendary beauty, while a man from the same island could be had for as little as $10. Many slaves became the wives or concubines of Dutch men, who occasionally sold off these women and the children they bore before returning home to Holland.

WHERE TO GO Jl. Gajah Mada #111

CHECK OUT www.gedungarsip.com

GETTING THERE DIRECTLY Take the #1 Busway to the Mangga Besar stop. By car, drive north on Jl. Gajah Mada. There is plenty of parking in front of the museum.

8 SNAKE MARKET

Next, it's time to head to the snake market. Getting there by foot from the National Archives Museum is a fair trek, but it can be done by walking north up Jl. Gajah Mada and then heading up Jl. Mangga Besar until the snake vendors start popping up. Otherwise, just hop in a taxi or find an *ojek*.

Located in the sweaty, pulsing heart of Jakarta, **Pasar Ular** (Snake Market) is the place to dine on freshly sautéed cobra or barbequed python. In the evening, the street abounds with stacked cages of slithering serpents and snake-based products. Shoppers can purchase snake's bile (*empedu*), ointment (*salep*) or oil (*minyak*). There are a number of *warungs* that also serve monkey (*monyet*), and one that specializes

Mangga Besar

in different types of soup, including turtle, rabbit and dog (*mokoyong*).

If exotic meat is off your menu, try one of the men's stamina-enhancing drinks. Unlike traditional *jamu* (herbal tonics), these drinks come from powder sachets with descriptions that claim to 'enhance the stamina of strong, durable, mighty men.' One particular version is Kuku Bima, a famous brand seen on buses throughout the city boasting the ability to prevent premature ejaculation and promote the libido.

Once you've selected your poison, the vendor will mix the powder with a raw duck egg, honey, cheap wine and thick, goopy galangal syrup. Hammer it down, chase it with warm orange juice and feel the manliness build and burble.

Istana Raja Kobra (King Kobra Palace) offers indoor dining and the chance to pore over a varied menu. Ask for the Palace by name, or watch for its dilapidated cobra and Komodo dragon façade.

One starts by drinking the snake's blood mixed with some alcohol and then dines on the meat afterward. Other choices include bat, monkey, flying fox, turtle and monitor lizard, which is better as a soup since the meat is a bit tough.

The main attraction at the King Kobra Palace is watching the staff kill the snake. They let customers observe the process as they deftly whack off the snake's head, drain its blood, squeeze its bile into a cup and skin it. Suppliers say snakes are not in short supply in Indonesia, but since they are wonderful predators of mice, rats and other pests, some might choose to just have a stroll around the restaurant for a look-see rather than exacting a death sentence on one of the reptiles.

Snakes for sale from street vendors.

WHO TO CALL 021 629 6087

DANCE IN A TRANCE Although Jakarta boasts a number of excellent and upscale dance venues, such as X2, Blowfish and Dragonfly, the most legendary is **Stadium**. On the weekends, the venue doesn't stop. Many party-goers enter on a Friday night and don't emerge again until Monday, just in time to head to work. The place is also notorious for shady characters and illegal substances, so leave your valuables at home and decide carefully what you want to indulge in.

WHERE TO GO Jl. Hayam Wuruk 111.

GETTING THERE DIRECTLY Take Busway #1 to Mangga Besar or take a taxi.

CHECK OUT www.stadiumjakarta.com

GUIDED TOURS FOR PHOTOGRAPHERS Photographers who want to see the city and improve their skills, should join up with **Melbourne** and his wife Maria. The couple lead photo safaris into various neighborhoods in the city, with Glodok being a specialty. Melbourne has a reputation for being one of the finest photographers in town and gives workshops on photography skills as well as Photoshop.

CHECK OUT www.phototoursindonesia.com

FACT OR FICTION

The blood and bile of poisonous snakes reputedly cures impotency, asthma, eczema and heart disease. Monkey and cobra meat cures skin diseases, while snake powder provides energy and prevents skin diseases and kidney problems. Turtle oil can stimulate penis growth, soften the skin and enlarge women's breasts.

GETTING THERE DIRECTLY Take Busway #1 to the Mangga Besar stop. The King Kobra Palace and Snake Market are located on Jl. Mangga Besar #93C.

Central Jakarta

Coursing through central Jakarta is the city's main thoroughfare, Jl. Sudirman, flanked by wide sidewalks, trees, shopping malls, skyscrapers, driving ranges and sports grounds. The city center is cosmopolitan and, unlike north Jakarta, feels as though it was planned.

Central Jakarta is the playground of Jakarta's élite class, politicians, embassy staff and international aid workers, but it is also home to the hundreds of thousands of working-class citizens who make up the backbone of the service industry, office staff and street-level commerce.

The area is easy to explore by foot, bicycle, *bajaj*, bus or taxi. The umbrella-like boughs of the old trees provide some sidewalk shade, the distances between places of interest are often quite short and their locations are relatively easy to find.

Culturally speaking, central Jakarta packs it in with the **Gedung Kesenian** (Arts Building) performance arts house, the **Taman Ismail Marzuki** cultural center and the Cikini-based **Institut Kesenian Jakarta** (Jakarta Institute of Fine Arts), which offers weekly performances in its many theaters and a more cutting-edge artistic spirit. For history buffs, the best museum in town is the **Museum Gajah** (Elephant Museum). The museum is packed with artifacts from across Indonesia's history and archipelago, and has a more modern wing next door exploring the evolution of Indonesia's languages, tools and customs.

Central Jakarta is a haven for shopaholics. Spot the rich and famous in the highfalutin **Plaza Indonesia**. Over the road is **Grand Indonesia**, a gargantuan, self-proclaimed shopping town. **Ratu Plaza** is the center for

Central Jakarta at night at the Bundaran HI traffic circle.

A panoramic cityscape of Indonesia's capital city, Jakarta, at sunset.

electronics; **Plaza Senayan** and **Senayan City** face each other off as rival luxury malls, and **Sarinah Mall** is of shopping history noted for being the city's first department store. Not all shopping has to be mall-based though. Walk along **Jl. Surabaya** for local gifts and souvenirs or stroll through the covered promenade of **Pasar Baru Market** seeking out spices and textiles. Head over to the **Pasar Rawabening** (Gemstone Market) for a shiny rock or explore the menagerie of animals at the **Pasar Burung** (Bird Market).

Sports and nature lovers are in luck also. The city center holds more green and exercise friendly spots than at first glance. The **Menteng** walk alone passes through seven parks, including the little-known **Taman Situ Lembang** (Situ Lembang Park), with its lemon drop-shaped pond. The **Monas** has several shady, leafy paths wending their way around the giant central obelisk, and is the venue for monthly sporting events, including 5km and 10km fun walks and races. Feel real grass underfoot at the Dutch **Menteng Pulo Cemetery** while strolling amongst the meticulous rows of brilliant white grave markers.

Senayan is home to the **Gelora Bung Karno Stadium** at which nearly every conceivable sport is practiced or played. Jakarta's main football stadium sits at the heart of the complex, with the surrounding land a patchwork of sports fields, including rugby and baseball fields, hockey pitches, tennis and basketball courts, jogging tracks and an Olympic-sized swimming pool. The **Jakarta Convention Center** is located here, holding events each week of the year while the nearby indoor tennis stadium is a hot spot for live

music, hosting international acts. To add a splash of color, a lengthy nursery runs green tendrils along nearly half of the sports complex perimeter.

Sports spill into the streets on Sunday mornings when the Jl. Sudirman-Jl. Thamrin main drag is closed to cars. The thoroughfare becomes a festival of runners, cyclists, rollerbladers, speed walkers, badminton players and families with tots on trikes. Drinks and snacks vendors pitch their kiosks, musicians play live music, bike clubs congregate, and people paddle in the Bundaran HI fountain.

For those in search of a different adventure, don't miss the **Aries Shooting Club** where a would-be Dirty Harry gets to blast away at paper bad guys. Try a **blind massage** or **fire therapy** in Bendungan Hilir, or make your own *batik* at the **Museum Textil** (Textile Museum).

Many of the city's best secrets are behind the arrow-straight roads and gleaming business towers. Here, in the thrumming hearts of the rarely visited *kampung* neighborhoods, the rules of the city are swapped for the customs of village life. Serpentine paths thread between houses packed and stacked together. Here are the thousands of *kosts* (boarding houses) for the city's workers, as well as endless tiny eateries, internet and telephone spots and places to get the laundry done. This is where life whirrs and women sing along to songs of the *dangdut* queens and kings.

Geographically speaking, central Jakarta is by far the smallest of the five official districts and yet, activity-wise, it's definitely the richest.

Walking Tour 6

MONAS AND PASAR BARU
Central Jakarta's Treasure Trove of Historical and Cultural Sites

1. **Memorial Park Museum**
2. **National Museum**
3. **Arjuna Monument**
4. **Monas and Freedom Square**
5. **Freedom Palace**
6. **Diponegoro Statue**
7. **Freedom Hall Museum**
8. **Gambir Train Station**
9. **Ciliwung Canal**
10. **Istiqlal Mosque**
11. **Cathedral Church**
12. **Lapangan Banteng Park**
13. **Arts Building**
14. **Pasar Baru Market**
15. **Gurdwara Sikh Temple**
16. **Sai Baba Center**
17. **Pancasila Building**
18. **Immanuel Church**
19. **National Art Gallery**
20. **Ikada Statue**
21. **National Library**

If there is one recognizable icon in Jakarta, it's the Monas. This centrally located, flame-tipped marble statue marks the center of the city, perhaps not geographically, but certainly in relation to business and government.

All the neighborhoods surrounding the Monas monument and its park contain stories of glory years past. In the 19th century, small orchards and grand estates occupied the land, and it wasn't until the latter half of the 20th century that the area around the Monas became a popular destination for the general public, with the creation of the Jakarta Fair Grounds and a recreation park (both since relocated).

Historical buildings are now museums that display the art, history and famous figures familiar to the country's school-children. Many of the original, massive mansions, including one owned by Sir Stamford Raffles, the governor of Java in the early 1800s, have been converted into government offices.

The historical elements of this walk quickly become apparent with the spooky, centuries-old tombs of the **Museum Taman Prasasti** (Memorial Park Museum). Next comes the **Museum Nasional** (National Museum), which showcases the history of Indonesia and its people, followed by the towering **Monas**, designed in part to resemble the mortars and pestles of a million kitchens across the city. The tour continues to the massive **Masjid Istiqlal** (Istiqlal Mosque), which sits across the street from the **Gereja Katedral** (Cathedral Church), the proximity of which is often referred to as symbolic of the pluralism that marks this multi-religious nation. You then cut through **Taman Lapangan Banteng** (Buffalo Field Park) and head over to **Pasar Baru** (New Market), Jakarta's original site to shop, before wending over to the **Galeri Nasional Indonesia** (National Art Gallery) and finally back to the Monas, just in time to catch the twice-weekly laser light shows.

This walk is attractive for many reasons. It keeps to relatively undisturbed sidewalks, most attractions along the route have been fairly well maintained and the pleasant landscaping and abundance of shade trees provide wonderful respite from the sun.

WHO? Anyone can do this walk and it is family-friendly.

HOW LONG? A half to a full day.

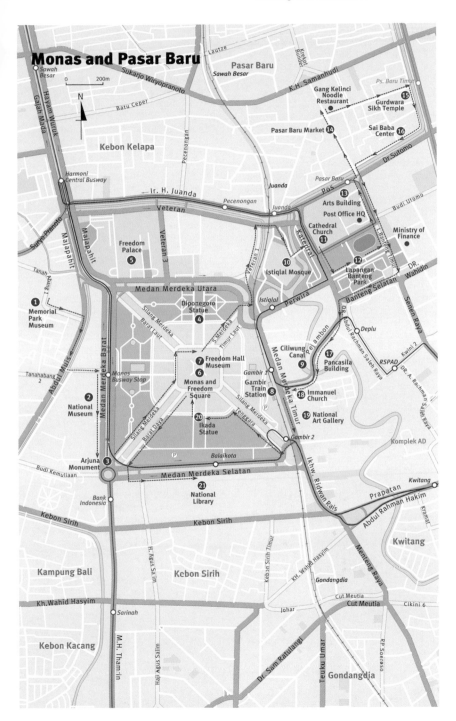

HOW FAR? 10km.

GETTING STARTED Begin on Jl. Tanah Abang 1 at the Taman Prasasti Museum. By Busway, take corridor #1 to the Monas stop, follow Jl. Museum to Jl. Abdul Muis, turn right and follow the road up to Jl. Tanah Abang on the left. By car, come via Jl. Thamrin to Jl. Medan Merdeka Barat. There is parking in front of the museum.

1 MEMORIAL PARK MUSEUM

The **Museum Taman Prasasti** (Memorial Park Museum) is more about the cemetery than the museum. The graveyard not only contains the headstones of Dutch citizens who died during the Japanese occupation, but some date back to the early 1700s. Due to the terrible state of health and sanitation in the early 1800s, a hearse made trips here twice daily from the hospital with bodies arriving on small boats via the nearby **Kali Krukut** (Krukut Canal). Most of the graveyard was closed down in 1976 as a parking lot was deemed more important.

To enter the cemetery, push open the giant wooden doors that guard the entrance (sometimes they're already open), and wander around graves adorned with worn statues of angels, sleeping children and small turrets. Come early in the day for fabulous photos and bring a gothic model to really make the shoot. Head to the near left corner of the cemetery to visit the small museum, which has dioramas portraying the different burials offered in Indonesia. As a matter of interest, Sir Stamford Raffles' first wife, Olivia Marianne, is buried in this graveyard.

2 NATIONAL MUSEUM

Exit the museum and follow the road to Jl. Abdul Muis. There is a good sidewalk here and the median has a lovely flower garden in it. The tip of the Monas should be visible ahead. Cross the road at the three-way intersection and turn right, following the canal. At the next stoplight, turn left on to Jl. Museum. Walk on the right-hand side of the road to enjoy the sidewalk and flowerbeds. Turn right at the end of the road to enter the National Museum.

The **Museum Nasional** (National Museum) opened in 1868 with the intention of highlighting the many cultures and crafts found throughout the surrounding islands. This is a great museum and one of the only ones in town in which you can wander around happily for hours. Exhibits of interest

The National Museum is packed with artifacts showing Indonesia's history and culture.

The Monas laser light show combines choreographed fountain shows with lights and music.

are giant maps, models of indigenous homes, handicrafts and well-stocked wood, stone and ceramic sections. Artifacts from the Jakarta region date back to the 15th century BC. A treasury upstairs displays gold and other precious objects.

An exhibition hall connected to the central museum by a walkway often hosts traveling exhibits. A modern, well-done addition on the upper floors offers visitors a walk through Indonesia's history, showing how languages, tools and behaviors have evolved over time. There are some nice displays here, so be sure not to miss them.

While self-guided tours are relaxing and can be done at your own pace, the guided tours that are provided by members of the Indonesian Heritage Society are highly recommended. With 14 different languages available and tours given at least three times per week at 1.5 hours each, there's no excuse for missing out.

There is small bronze elephant on a white pedestal out front of the museum, presented by the King of Siam (now Thailand) in 1871 during a state visit, hence the museum's nickname, **Museum Gajah** (Elephant Museum). There are also two large Dutch cannons, one from 1676 and the other from 1696, and six smaller ones.

GETTING IN: 9am to 4pm, Tuesday to Friday; 8am to 5pm, Saturday and Sunday.

CHECK OUT: www.museumnasional.or.id

3 ARJUNA MONUMENT

Leave the National Museum and cross Jl. Medan Merdeka Barat, passing in front of the Busway stop. Turn right and walk along the sidewalk to the **Arjuna Monument** in the center of the road. The statue depicts Krishna driving a chariot with the archer Arjuna just behind him. Note the imposing castle-like Bank of Indonesia building in the background. From here, enter the Monas.

4 MONAS AND FREEDOM SQUARE

The **Monas** gets its name from Mo in Monumen and Nas in Nasional, as in **Monumen Nasional** (National Monument). Also referred to as **Medan Merdeka** (Freedom Square), it is roughly 1 sq km and is best identified by the recognizably erect obelisk that oversees the city like a modern-day lighthouse. Looking into the past, this plot of land was called Buffelsveld (Buffalo Field) in the 17th century. As the name implies, cattle and buffalo were grazed here while brick makers used it to ply their trade. Later, in 1809, it became a training field, and in 1810 a French colonel was executed here. The same year saw roads built around the square and Sir Stamford Raffles took up residence on the nearby Jl. Veteran. In 1818, the name was changed to the more noble King's Square.

Although large swaths of the 80-hectare area are cobbled and lack vegetation, there are multitudes of paths to stroll along which go past fountains, along wide lawns and in amongst the shade of the trees. For those in search of other families who are enjoying a park, this is by far the most likely place to find them. Notably, nowhere in the city are there more benches.

It's very active here on most weekends, with running and sporting events, political rallies, concerts and more. For the athletes, there is a volleyball court (bring your own net), four futsal courts and a basketball court. This is an excellent location to ride a bicycle, throw a Frisbee or practice juggling. More leisurely activities include hanging out and people-watching, though kite flying is by far the most popular. Additionally, check out the 75 white-spotted, light brown deer that roam a 12-hectare section of the southeast corner of the park.

HEADS UP

For those here on a rainy weekend, have no fear, the umbrella boys are out in force. For a few thousand rupiah, an opportunist with a monster umbrella will happily provide protection until the storm is over. These entrepreneurs can be found at many of the city's office buildings, malls and tourist sites.

Return in the evening as the weather is cooler and many families and friends come to have small picnics, lounge about chatting, drink cups of coffee from roving coffee sellers and play with glow-in-the-dark toys sold by vendors. There is a one-hour **laser light show** every Saturday and Monday night which begins somewhere between 7pm and 7.30pm. It's well worth watching as it combines choreographed fountain shows with music, lights and various 'stories'. It's a wonderful atmosphere, especially for kids.

To enter the Monas, pass through the gates on the corner. To the right, on the other side of the fence, are souvenir stands, snack stalls, toilets and a boxing ring, in which the police occasionally train. A free **Tourist Train** starts here and takes passengers on a three-minute ride to the other side of the Monas. Continue straight, pass an exercise station and turn left at the paved junction. Follow the wide path here, noting the pigeon mansions and small forest of *palem raja* (king palm) trees to the left. Behind them are paths that lead back into the trees where a man-made stream boasts fish and fountains, little bridges and a water wheel. There are bathrooms there too.

5 FREEDOM PALACE

Continue straight to the pond with three tiers of amphitheater-style seating and a bust of national hero **Mohammad Husni Thamrin**, President Sukarno's right-hand man. This is the pond where the laser light show happens. Keep following the path past more birdhouses to the paved tentacle that leads to the northwest and out of the square. Walk up it and out the gates to peek at the **Istana Merdeka** (Freedom Palace), the official lodging of the President, off to the right. The armed guards aren't too friendly to voyeuristic tourists, so don't aim your camera in their direction.

6 DIPONEGORO STATUE; 7 FREEDOM HALL MUSEUM

Return to the main square and head east to the **Diponegoro Statue**, an 18th century rebel leader depicted riding his horse. Take the underground tunnel here that leads to **Ruang Kemerdekaan** (Freedom Hall Museum). At the end of the tunnel, buy a ticket and check out the dioramas of Indonesia's history in the museum. Wander among the statues and friezes in the inner courtyard surrounding the monument and then assess the length of the queue for the 11-person elevator which takes tourists to the top of the Monas; it's the only way up, there are no stairs. When there are a hundred or more people in line, this can mean a long wait. Those that do make it up, though, are rewarded with fine, if not hazy, views of the city. Lines should be manageable most days except for weekends and public holidays.

The 117m-tall Monas is made of Italian marble and was built by Italian workers. The 25m flame on top is covered in 35kg of gold leaf. It is open from 8.30am to 5pm daily.

Go back through the tunnel, and after exiting pause to get your picture taken with the Monas in the background. A number of photographers offer this service and it's an economical but fun souvenir. Next, head straight and to the left, towards the gates at the square's northeast corner. Before exiting out, note the sports courts off to the right, as well as Stasiun Gambir.

8 GAMBIR TRAIN STATION

Stasiun Gambir (Gambir Train Station) is the departure point for cities across Java, including Semerang, Yogyakarta, Solo and Surabaya. More importantly, it's the kicking off point to a couple of nearby cities everyone should visit–Bogor and Bandung (see p. 194, Bogor). A trip to the latter boasts excellent views, especially during the rainy season when vegetation and rice fields are lush.

With tickets easy to get, little hassle from shifty guys in leather jackets and fairly clean facilities, it's a comfortable and easily accessible leaping off point for any weekend warrior. For those who want to try a shorter jaunt, take the train to Kota and back. Train classes include *eksekutif* (with air-con) or *bisnis* (no air-con). For the longer trips, the *eksekutif* option is recommended but for the shorter jaunts to Bandung or closer, the *bisnis* option is just fine.

CHECK OUT www.kereta-api.co.id

WHO TO CALL 021-842-777 or 021-352-3790 for information on schedules and 021-692-9194 for general information.

Exit the Monas, head left and cross the street to the same side as the elevated railroad tracks. Follow the tracks as they lead up Jl. Veteran 1. Cross to the left side of Jl. Veteran 1 to walk along the strip of restaurants here.

Dapur Babah Elite (#18-19) has a must-see interior as well as a wonderful mix of Chinese, Dutch and Javanese food. For something more budget-friendly, try **Pondok Wong Palembang** (#12A), which serves a tasty *pempek kapal selam* (submarine fishcake). Try the *otak-otak* (banana leaf-wrapped fish cake) and *kangkung* (water spinach), and wash it down with a chocolate-laced *jus alpokat* (avocado juice). Then indulge your sweet tooth at **Ragusa Es Italia** (#10), a landmark since 1947, and a good spot for a banana split or some durian ice cream.

FAST FACT
Pempek is made of fish and sago and dipped in a delicious sauce. There are many varieties, but the *pempek kapal selam* is reputed to be the most nutritious and the tastiest, perhaps because of the egg ensconced in the dough.

---

9 CILIWUNG CANAL
With ice cream cone in hand, cross the street to the canal side and continue straight, hooking to the right as the road turns. The Juanda

train and Busway stations are on the left as you cross over the **Kali Ciliwung**, the most famous river in Jakarta. In the 16th and 17th centuries, this waterway supplied Portuguese and Dutch ships with fresh drinking supplies, though its current brackish condition makes that difficult to imagine. Past the river on the right is the entrance to the Istiqlal Mosque through two giant, silver gates. If they are locked, just continue a little farther to the next set of gates. The Cathedral Church is visible on the left.

10 ISTIQLAL MOSQUE
Indonesia's largest and grandest house of worship, the **Masjid Istiqlal** (Istiqlal Mosque), is a unique setting for a religious experience. It's purported to be the largest of its kind in Southeast Asia and the third largest in the world, holding up to 200,000 people. President Sukarno inaugurated the project but President Suharto was in power when it was finished. One of the most notable guests was Bill Clinton in 1995 while President Susilo Bambang Yudhoyono is said to come four times a year, schedule permitting. It contains the largest drum in Indonesia.

The mosque sits on 9.5 hectares of land and was designed by a Christian architect from north Sumatra. It took 17 years to build and uses German steel and Indonesian marble. The larger dome, 45m in diameter to signify the year 1945 when Indonesia declared independence, comes from Germany. The smaller dome, 8m in diameter, represents August, the month of independence. The 17m between the ceiling and the symbol of the star and moon on the roof represents the 17th of August, Independence Day.

There are five floors, which represent the five pillars of Islam. People of all religions and nationalities are welcome to enter and walk around the mosque, but note that only Muslims may actually step on to and pray in the main prayer area. The building is meant to symbolize tolerance and, in fact, on Christmas and Sundays, Christians headed to the next door Cathedral Church use their parking lot.

FAST FACT
The word Istiqlal in Arabic means freedom.

Before entering the mosque, remove your shoes and head past security to the informa-

Istiqlal Mosque, the largest mosque in Southeast Asia, can hold up to 200,000 worshippers.

tion office. All female visitors will be given a light robe to wear before being guided through the mosque. Self-guided tours are not allowed. There should be a guide around that can give a tour in English. It's all right to take pictures and, in fact, the noon prayers on Fridays make for excellent shots. After the tour, a donation will be expected, based on whatever you feel like giving. Exit the mosque, cross the street and enter the Gereja Katedral.

11 CATHEDRAL CHURCH

Gereja Katedral (Cathedral Church) is a stunning work of architecture both inside and out. Enter the front gates and stroll toward the back left side of the church grounds to find **Gua Maria** (Maria's Cave). The devout come here to sit on stone benches, pray, light candles and look upon a statue of St. Mary set in a tall stone wall covered with vines. Nearby is a small canteen, bookshop, lending library and rooms for choir practice.

The Cathedral Church was established after the original church, built in the early 1800s by the Jesuit Ordo, collapsed due to poor construction. Created in the neo-Gothic style, it was officially opened in 1901 after a fair bit of effort. Easily seen from afar, the church sports twin spires, one called the Ivory Tower, which represents Saint Maria's purity, and the other

the David Fortress Tower, which guards against the powers of darkness.

The church has become a very important landmark as well as a stopping place on Sunday mornings. People of all faiths are welcome to attend services (generally in Indonesian) and enjoy a performance by the choir. The wooden pews can accommodate up to 800. Before or after the sermon, check out the 14 paintings depicting Christ's crucifixion and watch as birds flit in and out of the booming hall. The confessional is in the back.

Head upstairs to the upper balcony to check out the **Cathedral Museum** with its small but interesting collection of items, such as garments, books and paintings from Pope Paul VI's visit in 1970 and Pope John Paul II's visit in 1989.

CHECK OUT www.katedraljakarta.or.id

12 LAPANGAN BANTENG PARK

Leave the Cathedral and go left on Jl. Katedral. Cross Jl. Banteng Utara, pass the football fields to the left and enter **Taman Lapangan Banteng** (Buffalo Field Park), a nice green space greatly underutilized by the general public. The park is known for the towering **Patung Pembebasan Irian Barat** (Irian Jaya Liberation Monument), which depicts a wild-haired man breaking free of

Cathedral Church, with its twin towers, is notable for its stunning neo-Gothic architecture.

his shackles in commemoration of the liberation of Papua from the Dutch in 1963.

In the mid-17th century, the area was wild forest and swampland. Rhinos, wild boar and crocodiles roamed here and tigers occasionally ate the locals. Later, it became grazing grounds for cattle, a coffee plantation and a site for markets. It has gone through several different names, including Lion's Field and Waterloo Square. Back in its heyday in the 19th century, the field was the center of social life, with Jakarta residents coming to be seen, often on horseback. The spot has often served a military purpose of some sort, and men in uniform still inhabit one corner of the park. Now, you find paths to stroll on, an amphitheater, loads of brightly colored stump chairs, football fields and more than enough space to throw a Frisbee.

After exploring the park, exit from where you entered and cross the street toward the **Departemen Keuangan** (Ministry of Finance), built in 1828. Turn left here and walk along Jl. Lapangan Benteng Timur. On the left, across the road, is the **Kantor Pos Pusat** (Central Post Office), followed by a long row of portrait artists.

13 ARTS BUILDING
Beside the post office is **Gedung Kesenian** (Arts Building), a hot spot for concerts, theater productions, dance performances and more. Set in a nearly 200-year-old building, it was originally called the City Theater. The first production, in 1821, was Shakespeare's *Othello*. Watch newspaper listings for the latest performances.

CHECK OUT www.artsindonesia.com and click on the link to Gedung Kesenian.

From Gedung Kesenian, cross Jl. Pos/Dr. Sutomo using the Busway pedestrian bridge to reach Pasar Baru (spelled Passer Baroe on the sign). To the left of the market entrance is **Galeri Fotojurnalistik Antara**, known for its excellent photo exhibitions. Return to the market entrance.

CHECK OUT www.gfja.org/index.php

14 PASAR BARU MARKET
Pasar Baru (New Market) is said to be the oldest market in the city, although it has recently been renovated. It's a semi-covered street sandwiched between rows of shops and provides a rare outdoor pedestrian shopping experience.

Once home to mainly Indian traders, the market now sells T-shirts, jeans and shoes. Fortunately, there are still some Indian shops selling fabric, textiles, clothes, jewelry and

A vendor wheels his bicycle past a fruit stall in the Pasar Baru Market.

Indian spices for curry nights at the homestead. Look out for the dueling shopkeepers promoting their goods by talking loudly and incessantly into cranked-up microphones.

Wander around the market watching for Jl. Kelinci Raya on the right, which leads past the ever-popular **Bakmi Gang Kelinci** (www.bakmigangkelinci.com), where hungry walkers can grab a bowl of *bakmi swekiau* (dumpling and noodle soup). Along this road is an **Indian Mini Mart** and an interesting **rock and mineral shop** at #16A.

15 GURDWARA SIKH TEMPLE; 16 SAI BABA CENTER

Keep following Jl. Kelinci to its end at the canal. Pay a few thousand rupiah here to take the 10-second ferry ride across the canal and back, just for fun. Then turn right and follow the road as it parallels the waterway and hooks right, before finally returning to the Pasar Baru entrance. Watch for the **Gurdwara Sikh Temple** (#10) and **Sai Baba Center** (#26), where devotees to the Indian Guru Sai Baba gather. Both places are open to members of the public.

When you've finished at Pasar Baru, return to Buffalo Field Park. Cross the park and turn left. Walk to the intersection with a small grass divider and watch out for a brown sign reading 'Gereja Immanuel.' Follow this sign

by walking along Jl. Pejambon to Gedung Pancasila.

17 PANCASILA BUILDING

Built in 1819, **Gedung Pancasila** (Pancasila Building) was where President Sukarno delivered his most famous speech, on June 1st, 1945. In it, he announced Indonesia's five founding principles, the Pancasila: belief in one God, a just and civilized humanity, unity, democracy and social justice for all. The word Pancasila comes from the Sanskrit terms *panca* (five) and *sila* (principles). Visitors may enter the front garden here, but are prohibited from entering the building.

18 IMMANUEL CHURCH

Farther up Jl. Pejambon is **Gereja Immanuel** (Immanuel Church), which was built in 1834 and was originally called the Willemskerk Church after the Dutch King Willem I. Surrounded by more than a dozen impressive columns and capped by a dome, the church is definitely worth checking out. The interior is much smaller than it looks from the outside, although it can seat 700 people. The church has a worn feel, but its massive organ, built in 1843 and containing more than 1,000 pipes, deserves appreciation. Weddings take place here on most weekends.

The Immanuel Church, surrounded by imposing columns, houses an impressive organ.

After the church, walk to the end of the road where it meets Jl. Medan Merdeka Timur. The Gambir Train Station is directly across the street. Turn left and walk with traffic to the pedestrian bridge. On the left is the Galeri Nasional Indonesia.

19 NATIONAL ART GALLERY

The **Galeri Nasional Indonesia** (National Art Gallery) is a collection of fine buildings harking back to 1817. A number of them originally served as mansions for wealthy aristocrats. The gallery now has nearly 1,800 works of art by both local and foreign artists. A collection of paintings, sculptures and art installations are displayed in a building in the far left of the complex. Signs in Indonesian and English do their best to elucidate on the subject of art.

The central building and exhibition halls at the gallery often display the works of more prominent artists as well as local artists. Before coming, check ahead to make sure something special is happening or the place may feel a bit empty.

CHECK OUT www.galeri-nasional.or.id

Upon leaving the National Art Gallery, cross the pedestrian bridge, turn left and follow the sidewalk as it curves to the right past the Gambir II Busway stop. Enter the Monas grounds and head to the left to see the deer in their enclosure. To the right are some pebble-studded **reflexology walks**. Take off your shoes and massage your tired soles by trying to walk from one end to the other without making a squeak.

20 IKADA STATUE

Walk over to the **Patung Ikada** (Ikada Statue). These five firm-bottomed guys are raising a flag for the environment. Exit the Monas grounds through the gates you first entered. Cross the main intersection to the left and turn left to walk up Jl. Medan Merdeka Selatan. Up ahead on the right is the Layanan Perpustakaan Nasional.

21 NATIONAL LIBRARY

The **Layanan Perpustakaan Nasional** (National Library) was commissioned in 2007 by Vice President Jusuf Kalla. It's fairly well-stocked for an Indonesian library but ultimately still meager. There are both English and Indonesian titles, a reference section with encyclopedias, a children's section, magazines and sections on religion, philosophy, history, art and sports. There is a multimedia room with computers; also photocopiers, clean bathrooms and plenty of couches and chairs to chill out on.

Walking Tour 7

KEBON SIRIH AND THAMRIN

A Walk through Jakarta's Downtown Districts of Upscale Boutiques and Backpacker Backstreets

1. Welcome Statue
2. Plaza Indonesia /Grand Hyatt Jakarta
3. EX Plaza
4. Hotel Indonesia Kempinski
5. Grand Indonesia
6. Thamrin City
7. Theresia Church
8. Sarinah Mall
9. BSM Culinary Zone
10. Kopitiam Oey Café
11. Mak Erot Treatment Center

Although Jakarta doesn't have an official downtown area, you could say that the Bundaran HI traffic circle marks the center of the city. The area around the traffic circle is flush with grand places to spend money, fancy four- and five-star hotels for discerning guests, high-end restaurants, happening clubs and wallet-melting watering holes for those with extra cash to spend. The landmark building here, and the spot where the tour starts, is **Plaza Indonesia**, where diamond-studded shoppers and the city's best dressed come to see and be seen. The mall has competition from the newer **Grand Indonesia**,

Mobile siomay seller along Jl. Sudirman on a car-free Sunday morning.

The Welcome Statue at the Bundaran HI roundabout marks the center of Jakarta city.

a goliath upscale mall with New York- and Amsterdam-themed corridors.

From here you head north along Jakarta's premiere thoroughfare, **Jl. Thamrin**, passing by the **Sarinah Mall**, Jakarta's first shopping center. This strip of road is a breeze to walk along as the wide sidewalks are not cluttered with food carts, sidewalk salesmen, motor-cycle taxis and the hordes of various other characters that generally render sidewalks unusable (though far more interesting).

From Sarinah, the tour turns down the narrow **Kawasan Kuliner BSM**, a food hawkers' market, and carries on to the de-lightful **Kopitiam Oey** for a cup of a coffee in a cute little café. Then it's on to the tiny lanes of the Kebon Sirih neighborhood before winding up at the city's notorious backpacker hub, **Jl. Jaksa**. Have a quick beer and a cheap lunch before returning to the narrow streets of Kebon Sirih to catch a glimpse of life off the beaten track. Finally, pop over to the one-of-a-kind **Dyna Pub** before returning to Plaza Indonesia by taking one of the rumbling *Kopaja* buses a short stretch.

WHO? Anyone can do this walk, although the thread-like, potentially claustrophobic lanes of Kebon Sirih may push your comfort zone a bit.

HOW LONG? Two hours for the walk alone. Bar time and shopping not included.

HOW FAR? 3km if you take the bus back, 3.75km if you complete the whole tour on foot.

GETTING THERE For drivers, park at Plaza Indonesia and head to the front of the Grand Hyatt, facing the roundabout. Busway pas-sengers can take corridor #1 and get off at the Bundaran HI stop.

GETTING STARTED The walking tour begins at the traffic circle, which has gained popu-larity among cyclists who gather here on car-free Sunday mornings, protestors who stage rallies around the fountain, and lovers who embrace and take pictures of them-selves surrounded by the bright lights and big buildings. For diners and guests in the surrounding malls and hotels, the view of the traffic circle, especially at night, is some-how a calming one.

1 WELCOME STATUE
In the center of the fountain is a 30-meter-tall statue of a boy and girl holding flowers. Officially called **Patung Selamat Datang** (Welcome Statue), it was commissioned by President Sukarno in 1962 to welcome athletes and visitors to the Asian Games.

A regular sight here is the entrepreneur-ial teenage boys on bicycles laden with hot water thermoses, plastic cups and ribbons

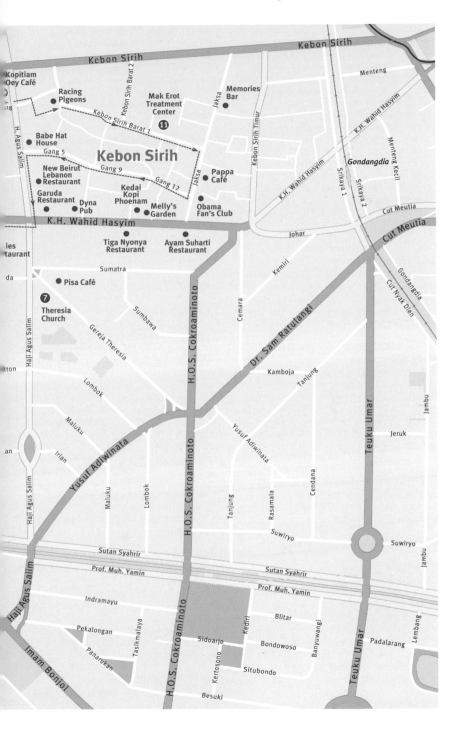

Kebon Sirih

Kebon Sirih

Kopitiam
Oey Café

Racing
Pigeons

Kebon Sirih Barat 2

Mak Erot
Treatment
Center

11

Jaksa

Memories
Bar

Menteng

Kebon Sirih Barat 1

K.H. Wahid Hasyim

Menteng Kecil

H. Agus Salim

Babe Hat
House

Gang 5

Kebon Sirih

Kebon Sirih Timur

Gondangdia

New Beirut
Lebanon
Restaurant

Gang 9

Gang 12

Jaksa

Pappa
Café

K.H. Wahid Hasyim

Srikaya 1

Srikaya 2

Garuda
Restaurant

Dyna
Pub

Kedai
Kopi
Phoenam

Melly's
Garden

Obama
Fan's Club

Cut Meutia

K.H. Wahid Hasyim

Johar

Cut Meutia

ies
taurant

Tiga Nyonya
Restaurant

Ayam Suharti
Restaurant

Kemiri

Gondangdia

da

Sumatra

Cut Nyak Dien

Pisa Café

Cemara

7

Theresia
Church

Sumbawa

Dr. Sam Ratulangi

ton

Gereja Theresia

Kamboja

Tanjung

Teuku Umar

Jambu

Lombok

H.O.S. Cokroaminoto

Yusuf Adiwinata

Jeruk

Maluku

an

Irian

Yusuf Adiwinata

Maluku

Lombok

Tanjung

Rasamala

Cendana

Suwiryo

Haji Agus Salim

Sutan Syahrir

Suwiryo

Jambu

Prof. Muh. Yamin

Sutan Syahrir

Prof. Muh. Yamin

Indramayu

Blitar

Lembang

H.O.S. Cokroaminoto

Banyuwangi

Pekalongan

Kediri

Bondowoso

Padalarang

Haji Agus Salim

Tasikmalaya

Sidoarjo

Teuku Umar

Imam Bonjol

Panarukan

Kertosono

Situbondo

Besuki

of drink sachets. Known as *kopi keliling*, which loosely translates to 'coffee on the go,' the cycling vendors ply their trade throughout the downtown area. Other types of bicycles appear at the traffic circle on Sunday mornings, when **Jl. Sudirman** and **Jl. Thamrin**, from the Senayan roundabout to the Monas, are closed off to give cyclists, joggers, walkers and skaters the chance to cruise the open street with impunity. Collectors of classic Dutch bikes, called *sepeda onthel*, park their bicycles in long, stately rows while gathering to chat, while gangs of fixed-gear fanatics, the latest trend sweeping Jakarta, populate the roundabout fountain area. For more on riding a *sepeda onthel*, see p. 66, Kota.

Note: The stretch of road from the Monas to the Senayan roundabout closes every Sunday morning from 5am to 8am, though vehicles are allowed on some stretches. In addition to these times, twice a month the road is closed to cars until mid-afternoon, usually on every second and last Sunday of the month.

② PLAZA INDONESIA/GRAND HYATT JAKARTA

Plaza Indonesia sits in the middle of the Jl. Sudirman-Thamrin thoroughfare and offers upscale shopping opportunities to those whose credit card is the color of a precious metal. It's at this landmark building that the ultra rich come to be seen spending their vast wealth on handbags and fancy pens. If guests are coming to town, they can be put up in the **Grand Hyatt Jakarta**, which shares the building with the mall. Best in the evening, **Cork and Screw** provides good views through the large wall of windows. Have the steak and a glass of red wine.

CHECK OUT www.plazaindonesia.com

③ EX PLAZA

If wealthy parents are at Plaza Indonesia, their wealthy children are next door at **EX Plaza**, which is connected via a walkway. This hip mall has all the latest trends and coolest fashions for those who are twenty something (or want to look that age). Bands and DJs often set up here to rock out for the MTV-generation kids who pack the shopping corridors.

CHECK OUT www.e-xgeneration.com

④ HOTEL INDONESIA KEMPINSKI

Directly south of Plaza Indonesia is the **Hotel Indonesia Kempinski** (formerly Hotel Indonesia). For bookworms and pub quiz enthusiasts, this is where protagonist Guy Hamilton stayed in *The Year of Living Dangerously*, a quasi-famous novel about an Australian journalist covering the overthrow of President Sukarno.

To the east of **Hotel Indonesia Kempinski** is the **Mandarin Oriental**, an important marker because just behind it is **Face Bar** (#85 Kusuma Atmaja, Imam Bonjol), a three-floor venue with Indian, Thai and Moroccan cuisine and a gathering place for journalists happy to knock back some of the best drinks in town. Although the service here is reliably lackluster, don't miss the chance to try their excellent Singapore Slings and Caipiroskas.

CHECK OUT www.facebars.com/en/jakarta

⑤ GRAND INDONESIA

West of the traffic circle is the eight-story **Grand Indonesia**, which is split into east and west wings and is best navigated by GPS.

This mall has quickly become a favorite place for family outings thanks to its incredible array of shops, themed corridors, fountain shows and comfortable food courts.

Head down to the Lower Ground Floor (LG) in the East Mall to check out the **Jakarta Art District**, which houses some good contemporary art. **Social House**, on the first floor, offers excellent views over the roundabout fountain if you get there before the crowds (and you are a smoker). The tasty breakfast menu provides a good reward after the walking tour; reservations are recommended. Another place with good views is **Spinelli Coffee Company** on the second floor of the West Mall.

CHECK OUT www.grand-indonesia.com

⑥ THAMRIN CITY

Just to the right of Grand Indonesia is the megalithic **Thamrin City**, a working-class mall and wholesale center similar to the Tanah Abang Market. Although the space is largely empty of tenants, it does stock well-priced *batik* and budget clothes.

⑦ THERESIA CHURCH

To get back on the walk, head up Jl. Sudirman from the traffic circle and cross over the

An Indonesian Peranakan restaurant located in a former colonial residence.

Busway footbridge toward the Pullman Jakarta Indonesia. Walk against the traffic here, taking note of the fortress-like Japanese Embassy across the street, just in front of the oddly shaped EX Plaza. At the corner of Jl. Sunda is the French Embassy, and to the right here and at the end of the block is **Gereja Theresia** (Theresia Church), built in 1934 to accommodate Catholics who needed somewhere convenient to worship in a quickly expanding city. Across the street from the church is **Café Pisa**, a good pizza venue with outdoor seating, live music and a great ice cream shop.

8 SARINAH MALL

Just past Jl. Sunda is the legendary **Mal Sarinah** (Sarinah Mall), which got a facelift recently after US President Barack Obama mentioned the 48-year-old mall on TV while reminiscing about his childhood in Jakarta. The highlight here is the extensive collection of Indonesian art and souvenirs, similar to the one in Pasaraya Grande in Blok M. **Chilies**, a well-established US restaurant chain, serves American-sized portions of Tex-Mex food and very cold beer.

FAST FACT

Sarinah Mall was named after President Sukarno's childhood governess.

Continue walking along Jl. Thamrin, crossing over Jl. K. H. Wahid Hasyim. Head up to the Sari Pan Pacific Hotel, but look across the street for the Jaya Building. Just behind it is the **Jaya Pub**, one of the more unique bars in town. Opened in the 1970s, the Jaya Pub has fared well in a city of constant change. From the walk up the old wooden steps to a spot at one of the oversized, dark wood booths, this is the type of place grizzled old cowboys come to die or just sink their brains in booze. If it's a busy night, live bands rock the house, so plunk down and toot the horns strung above the booths in appreciation of the music. The best thing here is the non-PC décor, which will offend a person and make them laugh simultaneously.

9 BSM CULINARY ZONE

Back on the tour, walk past the Sari Pan Pacific until reaching the six metal posts in the sidewalk. This is Jl. Kampung Lima where the **Kawasan Kuliner BSM** (BSM Culinary Zone) is located. With its dozens of hawker stands, it's a nice covered space for cheap and tasty food from around the region. Note: The hawker area caters to local office workers, so it closes fairly early and is not open on the weekends.

After reaching the end of the hawker street, turn left on **Jl. Agus Salim** (Jl. Sabang). The evenings are best here, as *warungs* spring up on the sidewalks and the many restaurants get busy. A quirky little spot is the **Babe Hat House**, which was opened in 1999 by a guy going by the name Babe, which is the word for 'dad' in Betawi. Usually decked out in suspenders, this older fellow will show customers around his tiny shop, pointing out not only the wide range of hats—from berets to bowlers, cowboy hats to top hats—but also the canes, pipes and bow ties to complete an outfit.

10 KOPITIAM OEY CAFÉ
Almost at the end of the road is a small coffee shop on the left, **Kopitiam Oey Café** (#18).

This cool wi-fi connected café was created with the aim of providing a relaxing respite from the city's rush and crush while adding a solid dash of nostalgia to the atmosphere. The posters and ornaments are vintage style, with even the menu using the old Dutchified way of spelling. You can almost hear the Chinese coffee traders shouting out *ka fe tien* as they arrive at port.

Scrub up in the city's smallest bathroom before unfolding a menu of delights. Order a *roti canai kari ayam* (chicken curry with flatbread), some Dutch croquettes or *sego ireng* (traditional blackened rice with egg and chicken). The café has a good selection of coffees and teas, but for those with a sweet tooth, the *wiener mélange* (Viennese blend) is a must; it's an espresso with a dollop of ice cream on top. It's non-smoking inside and opens at 7am.

CHECK OUT www.kopitiamoey.com

Cross the street and turn right, backtracking down Jl. Sabang until you reach Jl. Kampung Lima, a narrow lane on the left that is a continuation of the food hawker lane followed earlier. Walk up this lane, which has small drainage canals on both sides and graffiti art on the left. Turn right at the first tiny lane and follow it until it emerges at a three-way intersection. You will be passing through a very compact neighborhood here, so it's best to say *Permisi* (Excuse me) before you squeeze past people and walk through their conversations.

On the left of the three-way confluence (possibly behind closed gates) is a large collection of competitive racing pigeons. To see the birds, ask for their owner, Agus, who doesn't speak more than a few words

of English but is happy to show off the assortment of colorful houses where the birds shack up two by two. This is important because it is a fact that if the female pigeon is held back, the male pigeon ultimately returns to the trainer. The birds know where they live based on the color and smell of the house, and they personalize their own 'houses' with bits of sticks and leaves. Agus has around 50 pairs of birds, with names such as Jaguar, and he takes them out to various spots around the city to compete weekly.

11 MAK EROT TREATMENT CENTER
From the intersection, follow the road to the left and then take a quick right on to Jl. Kebon Sirih Barat I. Pass the Bintang Kejora Hostel and Madrasa Ibtidaiyah Alhuda on the right until you see the **Pengobatan Mak Erot** (Mak Erot Treatment Center).

Named after the now-deceased Mak Erot, the 100+-year-old woman who first devised the mystical cure she's known by, the center specializes in bringing joy and satisfaction to couples suffering from consummation challenges. A man may choose to either increase the diameter, length, strength, endurance and power of his penis, or he can get preventative treatment against future ills. Women can have their vaginas tightened or breasts enlarged. Parents bring their overweight boys who can no longer see their penises. Treatments may require a massage of the affected body part, but often they only call for magically rendered food and drink. Although it doesn't come cheap, it's an arousing experience, and makes for an excellent email to friends.

WHO TO CALL 0813 1140 6646/0815 1980 2001

WHO TO EMAIL info_makerot@yahoo.com

Walk past Mak Erot's to where the street terminates at Jl. Jaksa and where the scantily stocked Jaksa Bookshop can be found.

A gathering place for backpackers, English teachers, journalists, vagabonds and a shady, jumbled mix of others, **Jl. Jaksa** is a ramshackle road lined with bars, hostels, used-book nooks, travel agents, day spas and souvenir shops. During the day, it's a real scrub hole and relatively uninteresting, but it comes alive at night as folks gather for cheap eats, cold beers and promiscuously dressed local girls (and boys who look like girls). The unfortunate state of the road now belies little about its relative glory days of yore. Feel free to detour from the tour a bit and stroll up and down the street, heading up any one of the numerous side lanes which branch off. One of the more notable bars is the grammatically challenged **Obama Fan's Club**, a recent addition to the strip.

CHECK OUT www.jalanjaksa.com

After a short look around, walk past the legendary **Pappa Café**, which has been on Jl. Jaksa since the prehistoric period. This place hasn't seen a paint job since it opened and in general is fairly grungy, but ultimately they have an extensive menu of affordable food and drinks and the clientele are an extremely mixed bag which can make for some unique encounters.

Then turn right up the narrow Jl. Kebon Sirih Barat I Gang 12. While walking, look out and up for the green and cream-colored minaret with its brassy orange top. Pass the mosque on the right and notice all the old women perched along the road, chatting, spitting and staring into space while children run up and down the lane, darting in and out of tiny alleyways and doorways. You'll likely see food vendors hawking fried snacks and boiled meatballs (*bakso*), while teenagers cram into the tiny **Wartel Mega Toba Gang XII** on the left, a place to play video games and check Facebook.

As the path continues, you'll notice it's bounded on both sides by tall, barbed wire-topped walls and a gutter on each side. Once this lane spills out on to the main road of Jl. Agus Salim, turn left and walk straight, watching for the **New Beirut Lebanon Restaurant** (#57), one of the city's few Middle Eastern restaurants. Continue on to the four-way intersection.

To the left are **Dyna Pub** (#116 Jl. Wahid Hasyim) and **Melly's Garden** (#84, IBEC Building, Jl. Wahid Hasyim), two laid-back bars with a broad range of clientele, affordable drinks and great ambience. To keep on the tour, turn right, walk past the *bajajs* and Sarinah Mall and turn left at Jl. Thamrin. For those with a sense of adventure, hop on a #640 Metro Mini, pay the Rp2,000 fare and ride it until you reach Plaza Indonesia. With that, the tour has gone full circle.

DANGDUT DETOUR For some local late-night entertainment, head south of the Bundaran HI traffic circle to the heart of *dangdut* land.

Dangdut music originated in the late 1960s, and comprises a mixture of Malay, Arabic and Indian music. It is generally performed by a female entertainer dressed in anything from a plastic mini-skirt to a flapper dress. She sings and dances, either slow and sultry or with hips swinging. Accompanying her is a well-stocked band of four to ten musicians, including the all-important bamboo flute as accompaniment. If you are lucky, you will witness a move known as *negebor* (drilling). Inul Daratista, a famous *dangdut* dancer and singer, popularized *negebor*, with her overtly sexual hip thrusts and swirls which were found effective for setting men's loins on fire (check it out on YouTube).

The dance floors at most *dangdut* clubs are often occupied by middle-aged men with mustaches, large bellies and striped shirts trying to bust a move. In contrast to the suggestive dancing of the singers, the women on the dance floor swing about like a leaf stirred by a light breeze, while men hold their arms at right angles and swing their forearms with both hands in the thumbs-up position, a move called *joget*.

The music varies depending on the singer, the time and the levels of intoxication. Give it some time. The later the night gets, the better it all becomes. Lonely men looking for company can find it for a small fee, but there is also plenty of space for couples and rowdy groups of friends. Don't be surprised to find the singers and *dangdut* hosts coming over to welcome you, shake your hand and say hi. For those looking for a very 'local' way to spend the evening, it can't get much more authentic than this.

DANGDUT CLUBS Lonestar, Puspita or Asmoro on Jl. Blora.

GETTING THERE Driving or walking, head south on Jl. Sudirman away from Plaza Indonesia, and turn left on to Jl. Blora, just before the canal, or take Busway #1 to the Tosari stop.

ALSO TRY The Iguana Bar in the Menteng Hotel (Jl. Soeroso #28), a 15-minute taxi ride away.

Walking Tour 8

MENTENG
A Pleasant Walk through Leafy Parks and Fashionable Neighborhoods to Jakarta's Antique Street

Menteng is well known for a multitude of reasons, including its architecturally unique homes with real yards, streets with usable sidewalks lined with massive trees, shaded avenues and well-maintained neighborhood parks. Pedestrians and cyclists are a common sight and folks from across the city come to dine in posh eateries or socialize over breakfast at a city-famous *bubur ayam kaki lima* (chicken porridge food cart).

The original inhabitants of this wonderfully eclectic neighborhood were Europeans escaping the malarial infestation and generally deplorable conditions of Kota in the 1800s. In the 1920s, a Dutch architect drafted plans for what became the wide boulevards and central square of Menteng, intending for the area to become a 'garden city.' All properties were required to reserve at least 30 percent of their space for yards, so they would be in harmony with nature.

As Menteng is one of the historical and architectural gems of Jakarta, it's not surprising that it is prime real estate for a large number of embassies (and their staff). Many of the city's élite and a great number of powerful business people and politicians have also claimed some of the best houses and properties in the neighborhood. For those who want to explore the area, it's especially pleasant on holidays and early mornings.

Taking this walk may be one of the most rewarding experiences in Jakarta. It passes through seven lovely parks, including

Taman Suropati (Suropati Park), with its string orchestra performances, and the little-known **Taman Situ Lembang** (Situ Lembang Park), which encompasses a cute, teardrop-shaped pond. For a spot of presidential history, check out **US President Barack Obama's childhood school, SDN Menteng 01**. Later, sharpen your bargaining powers during a slow stroll along the well-stocked **Pusat Barang Antik**, a large number of antique stalls located along Jl. Surabaya. Most of the tour sticks to sidewalks, making walking easy. The route is generally shaded with large, leafy trees and most of the roads have relatively light traffic depending on the time of day. Go slow, enjoy the architecture, snack along the way and don't forget to bring a book of Walt Whitman's poetry for park bench reading.

WHO? This is a fairly long but pleasant walk that can be done by anyone.

HOW LONG? At a leisurely pace, this walk should take around two to three hours. For those likely to get caught up in the treasures on Jl. Surabaya, it could take half a day.

HOW FAR? 5.5km.

GETTING THERE Busway passengers should take corridor #1 and get off at the Bundaran HI stop. Drivers can park at **Plaza Indonesia** on Jl. Thamrin.

GETTING STARTED Start by crossing over Jl. Thamrin (using the Busway bridge) and walk with the traffic. Swing left, keeping **Pullman Jakarta Indonesia** on the left and the big

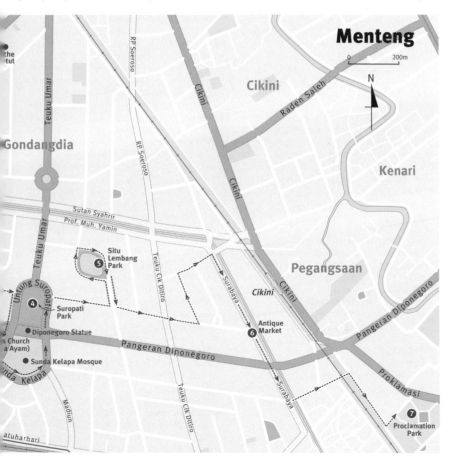

roundabout on the right. Proceed up Jl. Sultan Syahir and turn right at the first intersection.

☐ **JL. PANARUKAN PARK I/II**

Continue along this road, Jl. Agus Salim, looking out for two restaurants on the right–first **Seribu Rasa** (try the *mie Jawa* and *ketan durian Malaka*) and then **Dirty Duck**. Just across the street is Jl. Pekalongan. Head up this street, which borders the **Thai Embassy**. The consulate has made its mark on the nearby park, **Taman Jl. Panarukan I** (Jl. Panarukan Park I), by renovating it, installing two white elephant statues in the center, and inlaying ceramic elephants in the path around the inner circle.

Further along Jl. Panarukan is the second park, **Taman Jl. Panarukan II** (Jl. Panarukan Park II). It is larger than the first and has playground equipment, a small winding path for jogging (if you don't mind doing a hundred laps) and benches under ivy-covered trellises. Continue along Jl. Panarukan until it intersects with the busy Jl. Cokroaminoto. Cross the street and turn left, walking until you reach Jl. Sidoarjo, which is across the street from the Raya al-Hakim Mosque, and turn right on to Jl. Sidoarjo.

In the late evening, Jl. Sidoarjo becomes one of the hottest **hawker stalls** in Jakarta (from 4.30pm to 3am daily). The later it gets, the busier. Have a seat anywhere and be plied with offers of spicy noodles or a solid variety of other tasty dishes, and wash it down with beer or *teh botol*.

FAST FACT

Food hawkers in Menteng, as in all parts of Indonesia, work from *kaki limas*. *Kaki* means foot and *lima* is the number five—three feet for the cart and two for the seller. They are not only a wonderful example of entrepreneurship, but also an excellent way to sample cheap food from all over the country.

☐ **MENTENG PARK**

Back on the tour, continue a short way on Jl. Sidoarjo to **Taman Menteng** (Menteng Park) on the left. Before it was a park, the space was home to a football stadium where the local, bright orange uniform-wearing Persija football team played. The stadium was built in 1921 and its demolition, demanded by former Governor Sutiyoso's administration, became a contentious issue among preservationists. It also caused problems for the then homeless Persija, which eventually found a new stadium in Lebak Bulus in south Jakarta.

Regardless of its past, the 30-hectare Taman Menteng is now a rewarding place to stroll around while checking out some skateboard action or watching a game of football on one of the mini-courts. The lawn here is limited, and what they do have is off-limits, but nonetheless it is a park with paths and fountains. It's an extremely popular place for formal and informal photo shoots too, so don't be surprised by the large number of sweethearts and teenyboppers posing. There are also a few greenhouse-looking structures, which are rarely used buildings intended for art exhibitions and special events. Toilets are located near the parking garage.

☐ **KODOK PARK AND SDN MENTENG 01**

Right next to Taman Menteng is a postage stamp-sized park, **Taman Kodok** (Frog Park). It boasts four frog statues in the middle, two sweet flowerbeds, benches and more ivy-covered trellises. Leave here along Jl. Kertosono, which soon dead-ends at Jl. Besuki. To the right and across the street is **US President Obama's childhood school, SDN Menteng 01**. Inside the gates is the controversial 110-cm bronze statue of Obama as a ten-year-old child, which was originally located in Menteng Park, but moved here after some protested that statues should be of Indonesian heroes. Just across the street from the school is **Miranda**, an indoor/outdoor restaurant with occasional live lounge music. Next, turn left and follow Jl. Besuki until it runs into Jl. Untung Suropati, which circles Taman Suropati.

☐ **SUROPATI PARK**

Taman Suropati (Suropati Park), originally called Burgemeester Bishopplein (which means Mayor Bishop Square in Dutch), but now named after an escaped rebel Balinese slave, is a well-groomed park free of garbage and graffiti. Peppered with benches, garbage cans, fountains and pigeon houses, it's a great place for a stroll, picnic, good read or quick nap. The trees are labeled for easy identification and small paths wind their way around the space. On Sunday mornings, the site hosts a small string orchestra of youths who practice and occasionally perform while informal groups of musicians get together

A fire-eating performer entertains visitors in Suropati Park.

and jam. Artists set up painting stations at times and sell their wares. Throughout the year, the park hosts performing arts, such as the *kuda lumping* dance as well as art installations and photography exhibits.

Take note of the various abstract statues, with the best being the **Patung Diponegoro** (Statue of Prince Diponegoro) just outside the park, famed for his fight against Dutch colonial rule.

Next, cross Jl. Imam Bonjol and look out for the Protestant **Gereja Paulus** (St. Paul's Church) on the right, nicknamed Gereja Ayam Paulus (Paul's Chicken Church) because of the metal chicken on its steeple. Follow the curving Jl. Cimahi as it turns into Jl. Sunda Kelapa. The mosque, **Masjid Sunda Kelapa**, will be on the left. Keep circling to Jl. Madiun and back to Suropati Park by recrossing Jl. Imam Bonjol.

HEADS UP

Watch out for the food sellers peddling *gorengan* (fried foods). Generally safe to eat and taken to go (wrapped in a bit of paper), choices often include tofu, sweet potatoes, tempeh, cassava, sago, vermicelli spring rolls, veggie cakes and more. They are super cheap and super tasty.

5 SITU LEMBANG PARK

Leave Taman Suropati via Jl. Syamsurizal, heading along this road until the first intersection with Jl. Lembang. Turn left and take this street to **Taman Situ Lembang** (Situ Lembang Park), a park created by the Dutch in 1926 to act as a small reservoir by capturing water from nearby springs. Take the time to clamber about on the playground equipment, go fishing (if you happen to have a pole), read a book on a bench, splash in the pond with the neighborhood kids, check out the chained-up monkeys in the trees, use the bathroom and then exit back out.

When Jl. Lembang comes out on to Jl. Syamsurizal, turn left and continue along what will become Jl. Pasuruan. At Jl. Bandung turn left, follow it to the three-way intersection and turn right on Jl. Cilacap. Take this street to Jl. Surabaya.

6 ANTIQUE MARKET

Pusat Barang Antik (Antique Market) is along Jl. Surabaya, a one-way stretch of road lined on one side with loads of small shops. Check out the usual wooden bric-a-brac, such as figurines and wind chimes, mixed in with a smorgasbord of unique pieces, such as brass Buddha images and diving helmets, fine china and delicate chandeliers, glamorous jewels, old coins and long-forgotten

'Suami-Istri' at a shop along Jl. Surabaya.

music records. One can lose quite a few hours, as well as rupiah, at these shops, but it's a fun way to treasure hunt through stalls reeking of mystery and intrigue. Bargaining is a must, and stories of the items' origins should be taken with a pinch of salt. The hottest items are generally the masks, statues, carvings and furniture.

Stay on Jl. Surabaya until reaching Jl. Kimangun Sarkoro (also referred to as Jl. Gubeng) and turn left. Pass under the railroad tracks and turn right on Jl. Penataran. Take this road past Gedung Perintis Kemerdekaan. Then turn left and enter Taman Proklamasi.

7 PROCLAMATION PARK

Taman Proklamasi (Proclamation Park) is located where Indonesia's first president Sukarno once lived. The house was eventually torn down, but the park was then created to commemorate Indonesia's struggle for independence. There is a statue of Sukarno and his vice president, Mohammad Hatta, as well as a bronze replica of the proclamation of independence. The park attracts guys of all ages playing pick-up games of football, parents with toddling kids, a handful of kite flyers and kids on bicycles. There are some good grassy spots and plenty of shade trees.

ADDITIONAL DIVERSIONS Menteng holds too many great spots to include in just one tour. Some additional surprises include the pet fish market, puppy market street, the Italian and German cultural centers and a cheesy *dangdut* dive bar. **Taman Sumenep**, the aquarium fish market, has all the crustaceans, turtles and tadpoles, snakes and goldfish you could want. It also has a large supply of fish tanks, pumps, rocks, water wheels and bubble blowers. The market stretches along a mini-canal, so start at one end and meander to the other while enjoying the variety of creatures. Pick out a friendly little turtle to take home and marvel at the tanks of luminescent coral set out under black light. If you're in need of luck, consider buying a couple of rich gold, orange, or red and white speckled *koi*, a type of carp that promises to bring big fortunes according to Chinese superstition, and symbolizes friendship or love to the Japanese.

> ### HEADS UP
> Although the large chunks of coral may be beautiful, there is no guarantee that they haven't been torn from a reef illegally. To protect Indonesia's fragile underwater ecosystem, be 100 percent sure that any purchase isn't coming at a substantial price to the environment.

WHERE TO GO Jl. Sumenep.

GETTING IN Open 9am to 6pm daily.

A five-minute stroll from the fish market is the streetside **Pasar Anjing dan Kucing** (Puppy Market), an informal setup of puppy sellers each with their own set of stacked cages filled with cute, cuddly puppies. The sellers can handle the dogs a bit gruffly, but the little yappers still seem well cared for and healthy. The dogs come from all over Indonesia, some as far away as Bali and Kalimantan, but most are bred and raised in Bandung. Interestingly enough, if you don't want to actually buy and own a dog, you can rent one here and then return it.

WHERE TO GO Jl. Latuharhari and Jl. Cimahi.

GETTING THERE Take Busway #6 to the Latuharhari stop. The fish market is just around the corner from the bus stop. To reach the puppy market, go under the overpass and follow Jl. Latuharhari. If driving, park in front of the fish market or along the streets where the puppies are sold.

The **Italian Institute of Culture** offers Italian language classes in well-appointed classrooms as well as music, dance and other cultural events. Upstairs is a nice but small library of mostly Italian language books and multimedia for rent, as well as a café with Italian food, beer and wine. There are some pleasant spots to sit outside, although the institute's unfortunate location so near a busy street doesn't allow much peace and quiet. The center sits just five minutes away from the fish and puppy markets, and can be reached easily by walking.

WHERE TO GO Jl. Cokroaminoto 117.

CHECK OUT www.itacultjkt.or.id

The German cultural center, the **Pusat Kebudayaan Jerman** (Goethe Institute), offers a wide range of German language courses in its numerous modern-looking classrooms. As one of the top go-to cultural centers in the city, it has a very active arts program and frequently holds well-attended public events, including art, fashion, film, music, photography, dance, theater and more. The offerings are definitely worth indulging in and the inner courtyards are good places for chilling out. The pleasant library is well lit and stocks a good range of language, kids, cultural, art and photography books. It is definitely worth a browse. There is a café but don't expect much German food beyond the sausages.

WHERE TO GO Jl. Sam Ratulangi 9-15.

CHECK OUT www.goethe.de

Looking for some live *dangdut* music? Head to **The Iguana Bar**, not the classiest joint in town but an interesting place to get your groove shoes going. Things usually heat up late in the evening, and while some of the dancers are not that talented, and can be fairly promiscuous, the experience itself is worth a try.

WHERE TO GO The Menteng Hotel on Jl. Soeroso #28.

CHECK OUT www.mentenghotel.com

THE CANAL WALK For those looking to get off the beaten path, seeking a little adventure and interested in following an actual riverside path, try doing the following walk, which begins in Menteng and ends in the adjacent neighborhood of Kebon Melati. The walk follows a cobbled, ramshackle walkway which runs parallel to the Malang Canal, the train tracks, Jl. Latuharhari and Jl. Kendal.

Along the way are eucalyptus trees and benches. The grass is occasionally maintained and the area kept fairly clean of garbage. If you get there early, before the water quality degrades, you can spot **fish** darting in the water and **small monitor lizards** that call the place home. It's a good chance to see life along the train tracks, while still staying a certain distance apart from it, if you haven't had the opportunity to before. Notice the **men fishing** for dinner and plastic cups to recycle. Chat with the ladies that gather in small gaggles, and take note of the now-defunct **Canal Taxi** stops that were built in 2007 for what was supposed to be the future of public transportation.

GETTING THERE The starting point is directly across the canal from the Pasar Rumput Busway stop (Busway corridor #4) on the Menteng side. Look for the sign 'Jalur Hijau Tepian Air Banjir Kanal Barat,' which arcs over the starting point.

GETTING STARTED Follow the path west for about 10 minutes, until reaching the overpass from Kuningan to Menteng. Just before the overpass, you'll notice the **puppies** being sold on the right-hand side of the road. Continue under the underpass and get back on the canal path. A detour to the right takes you to the **pet fish and aquarium market**. Otherwise continue along the canal for another 10 minutes until reaching the Dukuh Atas train stop and Jl. Sudirman. Go up the stairs to Jl. Sudirman and turn right and right again, entering the train station. Go down the escalator and turn left, following the station platform until it ends. Turn left up a tiny space with dirt steps, which leads back to the canal again. Follow the canal side until it ends at Jl. Mas Mansyur. This should take another 15 minutes.

For those who still want more, cross under the Jl. Mas Mansyur overpass and enter the **Karet Bivak Cemetery** for a wonderful hour strolling amongst the graves in the grassy, goat-trimmed grounds.

Walking Tour 9

CIKINI
Coffee, Culture and the Arts

1. **Bakoel Koffie**
2. **Taman Ismail Marzuki**
3. **Planetarium**
4. **Galeri Cipta II**
5. **Galeri Cipta III**
6. **Cinema XXI**
7. **Graha Bhakti Budaya Auditorium**
8. **Jakarta Institute of Fine Arts**
9. **Cikini Swimming Pool**
10. **Martha Tilaar Center**
11. **Junior High School**
12. **Jl. Raden Saleh to Cikini Station**

Wall mural behind Taman Ismail Marzuki.

Cikini is a small neighborhood known for its artistic lean, great coffee and good food. It also prides itself on educational and creative facilities. It's easily accessible from the Menteng area, and is a cool place for cool people to steep their minds in life's more eclectic side.

Starting with a row of restaurants and coffee shops, most of which are tucked away in nooks with barely visible advertising, the tour includes the tasty brews of **Bakoel Koffie** and the mouth-watering dishes of **Vietopia**.

Soon after is Jakarta's artistic heart, **Taman Ismail Marzuki**, where the essence of what it means to be an artist remains vividly alive. Attending a dance performance, poetry reading, or just wandering around the **Institut Kesenian Jakarta** (Jakarta Institute of Fine Arts) provides excellent inspiration for aspiring oil painters or sculpting hobbyists.

Take a refreshing dip in the **Kolam Renang Cikini** (Cikini Swimming Pool) before moving on to a sublime massage at the **Martha Tilaar Center**. From there the tour gets historical, going past a school near and dear to the Sukarno family, the **Oasis Restaurant**, with its red-carpet reception, and the former house of famed painter **Raden Saleh**.

For those who still have a spring in their step, a final dash down the street goes via the Cikini train station and the nearby flower market.

WHO? The tour can be done by anyone.

HOW LONG? The whole tour could take a few hours or it could easily take all day. It's best to come early, but not so early that nothing is open—say around 10am.

HOW FAR? 3.8km all the way to the park, or 3.1km to Cikini Market.

GETTING THERE Jl. Cikini is a one-way street, so the best way to get there is to go up Jl. RP Soeroso (also one-way) and start at the intersection where Jl. Cikini starts. There is parking along the street here. Unfortunately, there is not a Busway stop nearby.

GETTING STARTED The tour starts at the Padang restaurant **Citra Bundo** at the top of Jl. Cikini. For those who've never eaten Padang food, this is a good place to learn the ropes. Sit down at a table and the staff will load it with a multitude of small plates, such as *rendang*, tasty chunks of beef cooked in

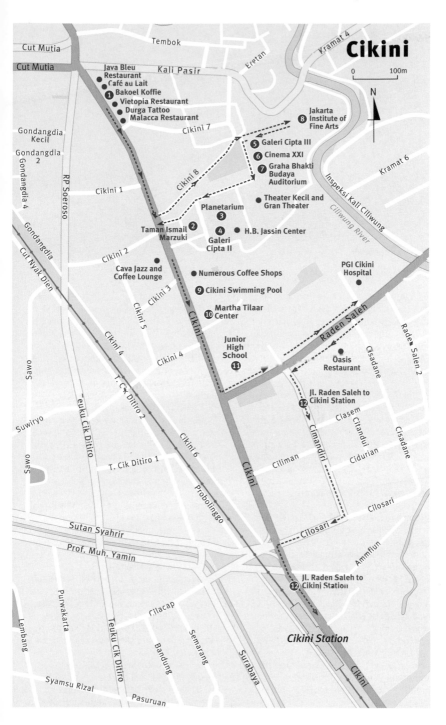

One of the many student murals on the walls at Taman Ismail Marzuki.

coconut milk. If it's too early to eat, keep moving, but note the sign for **Java Bleu**, a cute, comfy restaurant serving French dishes and found at the top of a long flight of stairs. Just past this spot, at #17, is **Tjikini**, which attracts a cool crowd and serves tasty treats and drinks throughout the day.

1 BAKOEL KOFFIE
Further down the shophouse strip is a wonderful local café, **Bakoel Koffie** at #25. It has indoor/outdoor seating and a funky spirit, drawing a diverse crowd of artists and revolutionaries, university students and Westerners with flair.

CHECK OUT www.bakoelkoffie.com

Vietopia is located just past Bakoel Koffie and serves the best Vietnamese food in town. Get a bowl of *pho* and experience bliss. Afterward, pop in to **Durga Tattoo** at #37B and score a 'hand-tapped' piece of skin art based on a Dayak design (www.durgatattoo. com). Rounding off the options here is the recently opened **Malacca**, an upstairs café/ restaurant/bar which is still looking for its crowd.

2 TAMAN ISMAIL MARZUKI
Cruise farther up the road, past the pet shop and string of bakeries, until reaching **Taman Ismail Marzuki**, better known as TIM.
Once the site of Jakarta's first zoo, the nine-hectare TIM opened in the late 1960s and currently serves as the heart of Jakarta's experimental arts scene, allowing creative minds to exhibit their talents in art, poetry, dance and music. TIM also hosts traditional *gamelan* orchestra performances and puppet shows, making it a cultural gem in a city that often puts little value on art.

3 PLANETARIUM
From the street, TIM may look underwhelming, but there is plenty to charm and interest you both indoors and out back. One of the first buildings in the complex is the **Planetarium**, which was built in 1969 and has displays that don't appear to have changed since then. It's still worth poking around in, particularly if any of the three large telescopes are open to the public. If time permits, check out one of the hour-long Planetarium Shows in the **Star Theater**.

4 GALERI CIPTA II
To the right of the Planetarium is **Galeri Cipta II**, which often has excellent art exhibitions. Across from the gallery is a little souvenir shop and a fire station. Watch for the bust of Ismail Marzuki (1914–58), a composer of patriotic songs who became a national hero.

5 GALERI CIPTA III
Walk toward the back of the complex, noting all the tasty food stalls to the left

of the parking lot; the first one has the unfortunate name of **Pondok Penus**. The outdoor *warungs* farther on are more popular than these and offer excellent fare at rock-bottom prices. At the far side of the parking lot is **Galeri Cipta III**, a hot spot for art, exhibitions, talks and politically subversive discussions.

6 CINEMA XXI 7 GRAHA BHAKTI BUDAYA AUDITORIUM

Next door is **Cinema XXI**, which screens mainly Indonesian films. To the right of the cinema are some nice bathrooms and then the 800-seat **Graha Bhakti Budaya Auditorium**, which hosts some wonderful theater productions, dance performances and music concerts. There is also a small Indonesian indoor/outdoor bookstore on the ground floor.

The gleaming glass and metal building to the far right of the cinema houses the excellent **Theater Kecil dan Gran Theater**, for more performing arts. Between the Theater Kecil and the Planetarium, up a narrow lane, is the **H. B. Jassin Center**, which houses more than 50,000 works of Indonesian literature, making it one of the largest libraries in Jakarta.

8 JAKARTA INSTITUTE OF FINE ARTS

For some deep digging, follow the street to the left of Galeri Cipta II as it leads to the **Institut Kesenian Jakarta** (Jakarta Institute of Fine Arts). Here is the greatest outdoor collection of mural art anywhere in the city. Not only does it cover the long snaking outer wall, but also nearly every building, bench, door and surface. The coolest art kids study here, and they often take advantage of the courtyard theaters for concerts, performances and poetry readings.

Follow the faux cave wall to the left, passing through the gates of the institute and watching for the beginnings of the murals. Be sure to inspect the small details and linger over the little things while looking for artists to talk to. Although it's an area constantly in flux, a visitor could come across cool wooden benches, a metal hand, a cardboard spider, a crate of shoes, metal sculptures, strangely decorated bicycles and all kinds of other wonderful surprises.

Go inside the pottery room and look around at the rock 'n roll world of clay creation. In the back is the wood shop and a small bike fix-it area. It's an excellent place to just stroll about. Then follow the outer wall until the murals cease, near a spiraling

Mural art done by a student at the Jakarta Institute of Fine Arts.

metal staircase. Head into the courtyard here and wander around, gazing at more of the wonderful wall paintings.

Eventually, exit the way you came in, but be sure to head to the left and check out the amphitheater, where there are often cultural performances or lively evening rehearsals.

Note that most of what is seen and heard at TIM and the accompanying art institute will be in Indonesian, so it's best to either bring an Indonesian friend or try to search out an English speaker who can provide the inside scoop. Better yet, grab a guide to the Indonesian language and get some practice.

The biggest challenge is knowing when and what is happening at Taman Ismail Marzuki, but watching the newspaper and regularly checking its Facebook page and website are the best bets.

CHECK OUT www.tamanismailmarzuki.com and www.ikj.ac.id (the Art Institute)

9 CIKINI SWIMMING POOL

Exit the TIM complex back on to Jl. Cikini and walk with the traffic. Note the **Cava Jazz and Coffee Lounge** across the street at #38, a wonderful place to get some peace and quiet while reading or surfing the internet. Try the duct latte or chili coffee.

Next up on the left is the very affordable **Hotel Formule 1**. The draw here is not so much the hotel as the comfy coffee shops and cafés and, more importantly, the **Kolam Renang Cikini** (Cikini Swimming Pool). It's big, it's beautiful, it's clean and it's open to the public. Go on, make a splash.

10 MARTHA TILAAR CENTER

Just a bit farther on is the queen bee of spas—the **Martha Tilaar Center**. The fine ladies who work here offer indulgent treatments that are well worth the cost. Get a facial, hot stone massage, Balinese coconut body treatment or try a round of acupuncture. The spa

KEROKAN—A TRADITIONAL CURE FOR A COLD

Waking up with a fever or cold is a real pain, but rather than search the medicine box for relief, head down to the spa. It may seem a strange place to go for healing, but it's the place to find the *kerokan* cure, an ancient Javanese form of therapy. First, the patient strips to the waist and then leans forward in their chair. An attendant then spreads eucalyptus oil over a section of the patient's upper back before taking a coin and dragging it diagonally and with force across the bare skin.

It's pleasant the first 10 times, but as the attendant keeps scraping along the same line it starts to burn. Oil, scrape, scrape, scrape; oil, scrape, scrape, scrape. This goes on until the top layer of skin is removed. Next, lines are dragged along each side of the spine, neck and upper arms. Patients can opt to have their chest scraped as well, but after glancing in the mirror and seeing the long red welts surfacing, may well decide they've had enough. Then again, if a person is sick, perhaps the more the better.

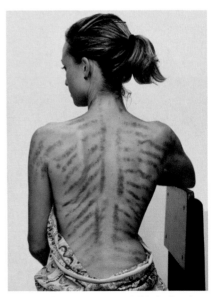

Scratches from kerokan are visible for four days.

The belief behind *kerokan* is that increased blood flow to the skin increases the body's ability to defend itself against sickness, while the stimulated nerve endings signal the brain to ramp up its attention to certain organs that may be afflicted, such as the lungs.

The Martha Tilaar Spa offers the treatment, as do various other salons around the city.

Coffee at Cava Jazz and Coffee Lounge.

has rooms for singles or couples and a large tiled room for a full-on body scrub followed by a reclining shower fed by eight shower heads. Sit at the *jamu* bar and drink some traditional herbal elixirs, or spend time relaxing by the pond (smoking and mobile phones are wonderfully banned here).

CHECK OUT www.marthatilaarspa.com/salondayspa

11 JUNIOR HIGH SCHOOL
Post spa, walk down the road and, to the left, will be the **Sekolah Menengah Pertama** (Junior High School), Built in 1885, it's where all of President Sukarno's children were educated. The school became famous on November 30th, 1957, when Sukarno was attending a function there and two grenades were lobbed on to the premises. It was the first of six failed assassination attempts against the leader and, while he survived, unfortunately 11 others died, including six children.

12 JL. RADEN SALEH TO CIKINI STATION
Continue on and turn left on Jl. Raden Saleh. Walk up the street, past the Aljazeera Restaurant on the left, and later, on the right, the grand **Oasis Restaurant**, which was built in 1928. Even today, the staff here ring a gong as patrons enter along a red carpet, a *gamelan* group plays and a long line of lovely, well-dressed ladies welcome guests to a luxurious dinner.

From the restaurant, continue up the street keeping an eye out for the **Rumah Sakit PGI Cikini** (PGI Cikini Hospital). The building became a hospital in 1898, but before that it was the residence of Raden Saleh Syarif Bustaman, Indonesia's most

prominent 19th century painter. Known for his portraits, dramatic landscapes (think exploding volcanoes) and romantic depictions of animals (lion wrestling with buffalo), Raden Saleh had a hand in Cikini's slow development during the late 1800s and early 1900s since he reserved his land here for the preservation and exhibition of plants and animals.

Most folks can stop here, but for those who still want more, backtrack a bit to Jl. Cimandiri, which is on the same side of the street as the Oasis Restaurant, and go up the road until it T-junctions with Jl. Cilosari. Turn right on to Jl. Cilosari and then left once it runs into Jl. Cikini/Jl. Pegangsaan. Across the street is the Cikini Train Station which, until recently, was home to Pasar Cikini, a well-kept market specializing in rattan and woven crafts. Don't forget to grab a bouquet of flowers for your loved one on the way out at the flower market, **Pasar Bunga Cikini** (Cikini Flower Market) aka **Pasar Kembang** (Flower Market), just next door.

HEADS UP
Watch out for the women dressed in long, distinctive *batik* print skirts and blouses hauling a half dozen long-necked bottles filled with colorful liquids in baskets slung over their backs. These are *jamu gendong*, or traditional herbal medicine sellers. Within their arsenal are cures for the chills, loss of appetite, fertility problems, menstrual pain, low sex drive, obesity, oily skin and more. Even if you are not sick, the *jamu* lady can whip up a drink to bolster general health.

GETTING SIDETRACKED For those looking to blaze their own trail and to get off the busy streets and explore *kampung* life, a good place to start is a walk along the historic Ciliwung Canal (which was once a river). Jl. Raden Saleh crosses over the Ciliwung and there is a small, paved road on the eastern side called Jl. Inspeksi, heading south, and Jl. Cikini 10, heading north. Both of these roads are safe and easy to walk along, while allowing at the same time a peek into the lives of those who live along the waterway here. Head along Jl. Inspeksi and then dip into Kampung Kenari via Jl. Kenari 1 or Kenari 2 and the small maze of narrow, friendly lanes.

Walking Tour 10

TANAH ABANG
A Walk through Jakarta's Arab Quarter and a Lesson in Batik Making

1. **Goat Market and Traditional Market**
2. **Zinc Market**
3. **Tanah Abang Market**
4. **Tanah Rendah Market**
5. **Textile Museum**

Tanah Abang (Red Earth) is home to one of the city's most famous textile markets, and this is shown by the amount of traffic leading into the neighborhood at midday. Things were quite different four centuries ago, when the canals that helped cultivate the area were just being built. As implied by its name, the earth in this area is red clay, which worked well for growing crops. This helps explain the names of neighborhoods, such as Melati (Jasmine Garden) and Kebon Kacang (Peanut Garden), although few remnants of the former agricultural heyday remain.

The arrival of the Arabs brought the establishment of a goat market and the beginnings of Zinc Market. Then, in 1735 a rich Dutch landowner opened a full-on market, **Pasar Tanah Abang** (Tanah Abang Market), at roughly the same time he set up Pasar Senen and built a road connect-

The green and beige Pasar Tanah Abang in Jl. Jati Baru.

ing the two. Since that time, Pasar Tanah Abang, in its various forms, has been nearly destroyed by fire or rioting at least three times, the first coming on the heels of the 1750 riots in which the Chinese residents were brutally killed during a period of unrest.

Present-day Tanah Abang is marked by a towering green and cream colored shopping complex with an exotic-looking Arabic façade. Reputed to be the largest textile market in Southeast Asia, it packs a wild array of goods that are often bought in bulk and can be a shopper's dream–or nightmare. Half a dozen less formal markets and new shopping centers have sprung up alongside it.

Compared to most of the walks in this book, this one is fairly short. It begins at the live **Pasar Kambing** (Goat Market), meanders through the **Kebon Kacang** (Peanut Garden), cuts over to **Pasar Seng** (Zinc Market) for rugs, dates and oil lamps, and then heads into the mammoth **Pasar Tanah Abang**. Next, the tour buzzes by a quirky little market specializing in appliance parts and workshop doo-dads before finishing up at the **Museum Textil** (Textile Museum), where you can try your hand at the art of *batik* making.

WHO? Anyone can do this walk, but it's definitely more adult oriented–except for the *batik* making at the Textile Museum.

HOW LONG? It should take around 1.5 hours, but should be started no later than 9am, as the later it gets, the hotter it gets, and the traditional market will start to wind down. Traffic eventually comes to a standstill in front of Pasar Tanah Abang, which adds to the havoc.

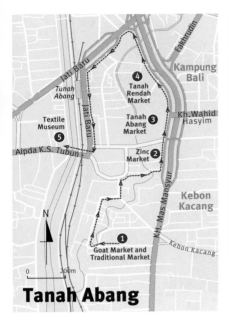

Tanah Abang

HOW FAR? 3km, including driving; 2km for the walking section.

GETTING THERE To avoid the legendary traffic, park at Plaza Indonesia or Grand Indonesia and take a taxi or *ojek* to the starting point. Ask the taxi to drop you at Pasar Kambing, which is located just off Jl. Mas Mansyur and a little over half a kilometer from Pasar Tanah Abang, on Jl. Kebon Pala. Look out for the small white sign announcing its presence just past the Caravan Hotel and across the street from the Thamrin City JCC mega mall.

1 GOAT MARKET AND TRADITIONAL MARKET

Pasar Kambing (Goat Market) is exactly that. Open 24/7 all year round, this is the prime spot for those with a hankering for live goat. Come prepared to bargain, and be careful where you step. Some goats are left to wander freely, often just resting in the middle of the road. On a good day, you might see a family load one on its motorbike and drive off with the poor soul bleating for mercy.

Next, walk past the goats on Jl. Kebon Pala, away from Jl. Mas Mansyur, which runs parallel to the **Pasar Tradisional** (Traditional Market) in Kebon Kacang (Peanut Garden). Early risers can watch the *kaki lima* fruit

sellers slice, dice, trim and skin their fruit selections before loading up their carts and rolling out. Surrounded by chickens getting quartered, tofu sellers peddling their soy-based wares by the block, the rumbling of machines shredding coconut meat and piles of leafy vegetables, guests can be forgiven for thinking they are in a village rather than the middle of Jakarta.

> ## *FAST FACT*
> While in the market, look out for the large chunks of *tempeh* which appear to be covered with orange mold. That's because they are. This type of *tempeh* is called *oncol* and it comes in both red and black varieties. Traditionally, it's an important part of West Javanese cooking and is made through fermentation.

Follow Jl. Kebon Pala as it naturally curves to the right, crosses over a small canal, goes straight and then curves right again. It will soon T-junction at Jl. Lontar. Take a left there. Turn right at the major road, Jl. Jati Bunder, and very soon on the right will be Jl. H. Said. Follow this road back to Jl. Mas Mansyur and you'll end up in the middle of Pasar Seng.

2 ZINC MARKET

Pasar Seng (Zinc Market), rumored to take its name from a market in Mecca where similar goods are sold and the roofs of the shops there are made from zinc, is an interesting collection of pseudo-Arab tents and shops selling raisins, rugs, shisha, henna, teapots, beads and veils. Best yet, it carries dates year round; don't be shy to sample first. Explore the market in both directions, then walk with the traffic to Pasar Tanah Abang. It's connected to Metro Tanah Abang by a green indoor pedestrian corridor.

3 TANAH ABANG MARKET

Pasar Tanah Abang (Tanah Abang Market) is a towering textile market that offers clothes, home furnishings and bargain prices on cloth and its various end products. With roughly a million stalls and what feels like a billion people rummaging through them, the place buzzes like a beehive. Head on in, wander around (keeping a close eye on your purse, backpack and wallet), and when hunger strikes, don't miss the food court on the

Local children during the street festivities for Idul Adha at Tanah Abang.

top floor, which has great selections from across the archipelago.

Some people might want to end the walk here and hop over to the Textile Museum. For those who want more, go back out to Jl. Mas Mansyur and take a left, following the flow of the traffic and keeping to the sidewalk when there is one. Note the roadside vendors, particularly the natural stone polishers who turn volcanic rocks into ring-ready pieces.

4 TANAH RENDAH MARKET

For people in search of a quirky, outdoor market, or those in need of new blender parts, the informal **Pasar Tanah Rendah** (Lowland Market), named for its proximity to the canal, has an eclectic array of stalls that specialize in new, used and dismembered irons, fans and car stereos as well as power tools, cart wheels, keys, knives and machetes. Walk past the **bird shop** on the left and keep an eye out for the **leech specialists** who can help with erectile dysfunction. The roadside market fun finally peters out as the road hooks to the left and becomes Jl. Jati Baru. Now it's time for the Textile Museum. Wave down a taxi or grab an *ojek* and he'll help you cover the short distance there.

5 TEXTILE MUSEUM

The building in which the **Museum Textil** (Textile Museum) is located is a wonderful example of French architecture, and was originally a private residence. Indeed, the building rivals the display of goods found inside. It was constructed in the 1800s and opened as a museum in 1976. Here, visitors can get some peace and quiet from the hectic road out front. It's kept cool inside to preserve the fabrics and there are some fine looking displays of *batik* cloth from the various islands in Indonesia. Outside, you can visit the garden where vegetable dyes are grown for coloring new *batik* pieces. *Batik* making courses are available in a small house at the back.

FAST FACT

The collection of 1,000 or more pieces of *batik* are rotated in and out of display regularly so repeated visits may result in new discoveries.

Batik, along with *wayang* puppetry and the magical *keris*, is part of UNESCO's intangible cultural heritage list.

A tourist trying her hand at making batik using the canting at the Textile Museum.

MASTERING THE ART OF BATIK MAKING

Anyone can make *batik*, but few can master the craft. The word *batik* actually refers to the technique of using wax to create a design on fabric that is later dyed, revealing simple designs or intricate motifs. While the process may seem relatively simple, the slightest twitch can throw the whole project into disarray (though there are certain tricks that can help salvage a few slips of the hand). In the **Batik Workshop** next door to the Textile Museum, the staff guide newcomers through the basic steps of designing, drawing, waxing and finally dyeing their piece of cloth.

Hot wax 'pens' or canting for batik making.

Begin by either selecting a pre-drawn design from the hundreds available or whipping out your own. Next, trace or copy the design on to a square piece of cloth. Then don an apron and plunk down on a tiny wooden stool set before a hot pot of wax.

Use a small bamboo and brass tool called a *canting* to scoop up a teaspoon's worth of hot, smoking wax, rid it of excess, tip it at just the right angle and draw out thin, delicate lines with the wax. One little jerk, hiccup or wobble of the hand, though, and the craftsperson and his or her cloth will be gobbed in blobs of unsightly wax.

When the design is finally traced out, the staff will dye your undoubtedly fine piece of cloth the color of your choosing by dunking it in a series of tubs filled with water, dyes and other additives. Then hang it out to dry and revel in the glory of a job well done.

GETTING THERE Jalan K. S. Tubun #4. If driving, there is plenty of parking within the compound.

GETTING IN Open 9am to 3pm, Tuesday to Thursday; 9am to 2pm, Friday and Sunday; 9am to 2.30pm, Saturday.

Walking Tour 11

JATINEGARA TO SENEN

A Market Tour Featuring Gems, Songbirds and Vintage Clothes with an Added French Twist

1. **Gemstone Market**
2. **Bird Market**
3. **National Library of Indonesia**
4. **French Cultural Center**
5. **Senen Market**

Some of the most fascinating places in Jakarta are the *pasars* (markets), which are often considered the pulsing heart of a neighborhood and the lifeblood of a community. Here, you find old women sitting among piles of vegetables, teenage girls hawking pirated DVDs, middle-aged mothers peddling fake leather belts and mustachioed men with assorted kitchenware. *Ojek* and *bajaj* drivers generally wait out front to whisk plastic bag-laden housewives home to their mortars and pestles, stray cats scurry about in darkened corners looking for food, and scavengers gather up anything that is possibly recyclable.

This tour strays from the norm, though, in that it provides access to three very unique markets, each with its own peculiar scents, sights and shopping scene. It kicks off with the **Pasar Rawabening** (Gemstone Market) in east Jakarta, which only recently moved to a newly constructed building. Even with the loss of the tarp-topped shops outside and ramshackle construction of the original market, the upgraded version is still an exciting place to find not just precious stones and shiny knock-offs, but unusual bits and pieces associated with magic and mystery, such as talismans and charms.

From here, the tour heads north to the **Pasar Burung** (Bird Market), where far more than just cocks and crows are traded. The overwhelming collection of fauna makes for

a market that must be experienced, though animal lovers may find themselves squirming. Next, the tour travels past one of Jakarta's largest libraries as well as the **Pusat Kebudayaan Perancis** (French Cultural Center) before ending up at the **Pasar Senen** (Monday Market), a behemoth secondhand goods market that offers wares ranging from frozen sharks to police uniforms.

It should be noted that trying to get to all these markets on foot is highly unadvisable as they are a fair distance apart and the roads are not suitable for a pleasurable stroll. This is ultimately a driving tour that will require taking a private car, taxi or *ojek* between each location.

WHO? This tour can be done by anyone. However, the markets can be crowded and the bird market unnerving. You may not consider it kid-friendly.

HOW LONG? A full day if all three markets are explored thoroughly, although ultimately the day depends on the amount of dilly dallying, traffic and buying.

HOW FAR? 9km driving.

GETTING THERE Take Busway #5 to the Pasar Jatinegara stop, then head up Jl. Bekasi Barat Raya, staying on the right side.

Drivers coming from the south should take the Ir. Wiyoto Wiyono toll road and exit at Kampung Melayu/Jatinegara, then turn left on to Jl. Bekasi Barat Raya.

From the west, take Jl. Casablanca as it turns into Jl. Kampung Melayu Besar, then turn left at the toll road, follow the toll road on Jl. D. I. Panjaitan, then turn left on to Jl. Bekasi Barat Raya. The Gemstone Market is directly across from the Jatinegara train station. There is parking out front.

GETTING IN All the markets are open from around 9am to 5pm daily, but many of the individual stalls have their own operating hours. Sunday is a good time to visit, starting around 9.30am.

1 GEMSTONE MARKET

Pasar Rawabening (Shiny Swamp Market) is better known as the Gemstone Market. It sits In a nice, multistory complex built in 2009. The Jakarta government decided to raze the scrappy, indoor/outdoor market to modernize things. Most of the former tenants have relocated to their new home and have retained some of their former traditional market ambience. Of course, the present

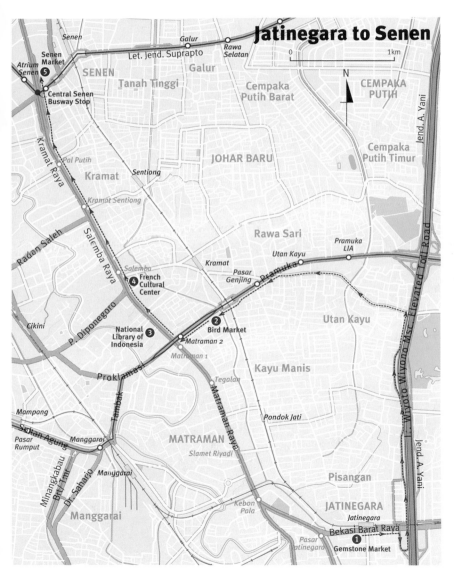

Examining goods at the Gemstone Market.

of rock that exhibit the inner stones in their natural state.

HELPFUL HINT

Some sellers are unscrupulous. If a vendor claims a ruby from Africa costs only Rp150,000, use logic to decide whether you are getting the real deal.

---

hides the past well as the area was originally called Rawa Bangkai (Corpse Swamp) due to the large number of dead bodies dumped here during Dutch colonial times. Later on, the name changed to Rawa Bunga (Flower Swamp) in light of the prevalent sex trade going on in the neighborhood, before finally becoming Rawa Bening, referring to the shiny stones being traded.

Small, square kiosks with glass display cabinets greet shoppers as they walk through the front doors. Circle around the mall's inner perimeter, picking up, testing out and weighing up all the interesting tidbits and collectibles, souvenirs and oddities. Many shops display *keris*, the legendary wavy blade daggers whose name comes from the old Javanese word for 'to stab.' They were traditionally used for executions, protection and to wear into battle, striking down enemies by piercing the dagger through the clavicle and into the heart. A true *keris*, however, possesses magical powers granted by a shaman, grants good luck and provides protection to its owner. Allegedly, a magical *keris* can act of its own will and kill those it views with displeasure.

Western, Indonesian, Chinese and Arab expert buyers stroll among the stalls holding small lights and magnifying glasses to examine the gemstones' quality and authenticity. Vendors here sell both natural stones and synthetic imitations, including rubies, emeralds, topaz, jade, sapphire and amethyst, with a host of precious metals as well.

Many of the gemstones come from Africa (Tanzania and Madagascar), but there are also Asian varieties from Burma, Sri Lanka, Thailand and China. In Indonesia, Central and East Java are big producers. Stones are priced by the gram, but the sellers are ready to bargain. Several shops sell cleaved chunks

Jewelers can cut stones, set them and add some artful frills to handmade pieces. Ready-made jewelry can also be purchased. The artisans craft their trade right in their little booths in the marketplace, and it can be interesting to watch them get out the blowtorch and blast away at a precious metal, melt it down, pour it into a mold and shape it for sale. Feel free to pull up a stool and chat with a craftsman about his work. Jewelry making hobbyists can also buy supplies here.

Moving away from gemstones, watch for the odd assortment of incense and the peculiar aromatherapy oil varieties. Old coins are for sale, as are other collectors' trinkets, including brass Buddha and Hindu statues, pig tusk jewelry, antique-looking Korans with animal skin covers, petrified wood, horseshoes, crystal balls and magic jewels found in snake and worm heads. Watch out for large bottles of a white glue-like substance. It's reportedly elephant sperm. Leech oil is another curiosity that can be purchased for those who are challenged by impotency.

With wonderful variety and some real characters running the place, it's a fun market to walk around for an hour or two. Stop and listen to the sifting and sorting of stones as they clink against each other and container walls, the tink-tink-tinking of the small hammers, polishing machines whirring away and the ubiquitous *dangdut* music playing on a distant radio.

From Pasar Rawabening, go east on Jl. Bekasi Barat Raya, turning right as the road loops around and heads north, following the toll road. Turn left on Jl. Utan Kayu, which runs into Jl. Pramuka heading west. Just past the train tracks, on the left, is Pasar Burung. You'll know you have reached the market when you start seeing small shops selling bird, hamster, rabbit and cock-fighting cages on the street. Across the street from the entrance to the market, you can see two green and white apartment towers.

The Bird Market sells not only birds and hand-made cages but also a host of other exotic wildlife.

GETTING IN The market is open seven days a week from roughly 8am to 5pm, though shops have staggered opening and closing times as they seem to run on their own schedules.

⊐ BIRD MARKET

Pasar Burung (Bird Market) is located just behind a pharmaceuticals shopping plaza called Pasar Pramuka, a mildly interesting site itself as it's packed with every medical device, aid and pill you could need. For those already feeling top notch, go around to the rear of the building to enter the bird market.

Established in 1967, the market initially only sold birds. Throughout the 1980s the type of animal sold here diversified rapidly, and today it is crammed with seemingly more animal life than the whole of Kalimantan. The market's incredible, if not overwhelming, collection includes bats, slow lorises, snakes, mongooses, owls and monitor lizards as well as scores of exotic birds found throughout Indonesia. Most reside in cages made onsite.

Animal lovers be warned, this market is not for the faint of heart. Many sellers see their birds and animals strictly as a commodity and not as living creatures to be handled

with care. Most cages are overcrowded and dirty, the air is thick and pungent and can be somewhat overpowering at times, while the wildlife is tossed about like a tennis ball. It's not rare to see dead or dying creatures lying at the bottom of cages and new shipments of animals are often transported here in burlap bags. That said, some sellers obviously take more care than others, although this might have more to do with the fact that many of these animals sell for millions of rupiah and are better off healthy and alive.

Note that if you show interest in a creature, a guy with a dangling cigarette may well yank it from its cage and thrust it into your arms. This sales trick may not always work, but be careful when it comes to the cute little slow loris with its large, adorable eyes. This animal has sharp teeth, which the traders remove so the little one can't deliver a nasty bite, tinged with poison from its elbow patch.

If the market seems a bit overwhelming, try going to the small road around the back to watch the action from a distance. It's a good vantage point for viewing the haggling and trading, and also offers good photo ops of the motorbikes as they go zipping off with cages strapped to their seats. Houses in the surrounding neighborhood are also getting

Birds add color and noise at the Bird Market.

in on the animal trade. One home directly behind the green-roofed buildings specializes in albino animals, including small albino monkeys and squirrels.

Pet food is also available. Check out the wooden crates massed with crickets, plastic tubs writhing with grubs, and rattan trays that look to contain drying bits of rice. These are actually the guts of an ant nest, complete with dead and live ants and larvae mashed into one creepy, crawly mess. They serve as bait for fishermen or special treats for birds.

> ### HEADS UP
> If you suspect the critter you want to buy is endangered or has been mistreated, please don't buy it. Remember, purchasing an animal here means another will be captured or bred to replace it.

GETTING THERE DIRECTLY Take Busway #4, getting off at either the Matraman 2 or Pasar Genjing stops. Drivers can come via Jl. Matraman Raya or Jl. Sultan Agung. There is parking at Pasar Pramuka.

After Pasar Burung, it's time for a snack, a large cold drink and a dose of culture, all under the cool caress of air-conditioning at the French Cultural Center. Head southwest on Jl. Pramuka to Salemba Raya via the flyover. The National Library of Indonesia is to the left as you come down the flyover.

③ NATIONAL LIBRARY OF INDONESIA

The newish, nine-story-high **Perpustakaan Nasional RI** (National Library of Indonesia) is what's known as a 'closed' library, meaning that browsing is not generally allowed. Instead, search through their catalogs and ask the librarian for a specific title and they will retrieve it for you.

The second floor holds maps and old picture collections, while the fifth floor offers access to more than 10,000 manuscripts and displays of ancient Indonesian writing on bamboo sticks. The top-notch reading room has stained-glass windows, large chairs and tables and a nice view of the city. Most floors have electronic filing systems and catalogs, wi-fi and study spaces. On the ground floor is the magazine and newspaper section, along with a snack mart, internet cubicles and an information center, where visitors can obtain a library card.

> ### HELPFUL HINT
> If you ever need extra assistance, ask for a *kelompak layanan informasi* (librarian specialist) who will be ready to help. Not everyone speaks English, but if you ask for help in English, they may be able to dig someone up.

WHERE TO GO #28A Jl. Salemba Raya.

GETTING THERE DIRECTLY Take Busway #4 and exit at Matraman 2, or Busway #5 and exit at Matraman 1. Drivers can come via Jl. Sultan Agung or Jl. Matraman Raya.

CHECK OUT www.pnri.go.id

GETTING IN 9am to 5.30pm, Monday to Friday; 9am to 1pm, Saturday.

4 FRENCH CULTURAL CENTER

Leaving the library, continue up Jl. Salemba Raya until reaching the Salemba Busway pedestrian bridge. Walk over the bridge, follow the direction of traffic and the **Pusat Kebudayaan Perancis** (French Cultural Center) is on the left.

The center offers French lessons from beginner to advanced. It also boasts a pleasant little courtyard in the back with a café (no French food or wine, unfortunately) and two TVs playing French channels. Next to the café is an art gallery, a cinema for the occasional film screening and a hall for dance performances and music concerts. There is a pleasant two-story library with a multimedia room and comfortable listening stations up top. It's a good place to chill out before continuing the day's adventure.

CHECK OUT www.ccfjakarta.or.id

GETTING IN 8am to 7pm Monday, Tuesday, Thursday and Friday; 8am to 4.30pm Wednesday and 9.30am to 4.30pm Saturday

Once break time is over and your French hello and goodbye is passable, pack up and head northwest again on Jl. Salemba Raya. The road turns into Jl. Kramat Raya, and goes over the Senen flyover, leading to Pasar Senen on the right. Busway users can take Busway #5, getting off at the Senen stop.

5 SENEN MARKET

Pasar Senen (Monday Market), which was first opened in 1733 by Dutchman Justinus Vinck, is the mother of all markets and nirvana if you're into used or vintage clothing. Pasar Senen was once connected directly to Pasar Tanah Abang, also built by Vinck, via the still existing Jl. Prapatan and Jl. Wahid Hasyim Originally called Pasar Vinck, Pasar Senen was later referred to as Gang Weng Seng (Gate of Business) before finally becoming Pasar Senen, as Mondays seemed to be the busiest days. The modern-day version of the market appeared from the 1960s to the 1990s, with five main buildings making up the complex.

The market boasts more than 500 stalls covering multiple floors. Concentrated on the west side of the market are the secondhand clothes, including belts, shoes, jackets, suits, dresses and even lingerie, most of which is offered at bargain basement prices. Listen for the sellers shouting out bargains, and if haggling is your thing, this is an excellent spot to practice it. For those looking for a unique hat, their Halloween costume or some fancy duds for the next Bollywood dance party, there is no better place to start.

Aside from clothes, the south end of this massive bazaar has everything from police uniforms to eyeglasses and electronics to trophy makers, with the array of choices often overwhelming. On the east side are the consumables, with a meat market, groceries section, seafood stalls and even live animals. Don't be surprised to see a pick-up truck filled with massive, headless, frozen shark bodies being unloaded and hauled inside. The majority of the booksellers have settled along the Pasar Senen Bus Station at the northern end of the market, creating the largest used book market in the city. Most literature is in Indonesian but there may be a few English language treasures as well. Don't be surprised to find a large number of photocopied books, often done in very high quality.

Note that this market is not considered to be a tourist site, so security can be lax and the interior stuffy. The perimeter is a magnet for debilitated beggars, so consider bringing some coins to satiate them.

In the painfully early hours of the morning (1am–4am), Pasar Senen hosts **Pasar Kue Subuh** (Dawn Cake Market). Myriad stalls sell every kind of cake and pastry imaginable, from sponge rolls to tarts, layer cakes to pudding cakes, pies to the infamous must-have *mochi* from Sukabumi. It's not all cakes and cookies, though, as a large variety of traditional foods are bought and sold here as well. Many of the products are made at home and then transported to the market, a process some sellers have repeated for more than 20 years.

GETTING IN Contrary to its name, Pasar Senen is open every day from early until late. Pasar Kue Bubuh is open Monday to Saturday mornings. The action at the Dawn Cake Market wraps up around 7am.

Walking Tour 12

BENDUNGAN HILIR
A Meander down Narrow Lanes in a Neighborhood at the Heart of the City

1. **Benhil Traditional Market**
2. **Darussalam Mosque**
3. **Blind massage parlors**
4. **Community composting area**
5. **Man-made fishing pond**
6. **Canal Ferry**

Bendungan Hilir (Benhil) is an up and coming residential neighborhood located along a canal just off Jl. Sudirman, the city's primary thoroughfare. With its dynamic mix of city center commerce and cheap and cheerful food stalls, Bendungan Hilir is one of the most eclectic, laid-back neighborhoods in town.

Jl. Bendungan Hilir scores the neighborhood in half and is jam-packed with delicious

A beggar in disguise.

street food, salons, cafés and restaurants. It's also brimming with *bemos, bajajs, mikrolets,* cyclists and vendors on wheels. However, the *gangs* (narrow lanes) to either side of Jl. Bendungan Hilir are pleasant and well-kept, little local parks get good use and residents take pride in their neighborhood. The Benhil area is very diverse, with lower-income homes, middle-class houses and large new residences all cozied up together and connected by the threaded filaments of lanes which are weaved together like a web. Visit in the cool hours of a Sunday morning to stroll along the canal, through the *gangs* and into two adjacent graveyards offering spacious grounds for an hour of peace and greenery.

The walk begins at a nice park behind the **BRI Building** before passing through the **Pasar Benhil** (Benhil Traditional Market). A ride on a kooky little *bemo* gets into the meat of the walk, which wends through the neighborhood's tiny back streets, well-kept and prettied with potted plants. Watch for the snack vendors, kids on bicycles and the occasional motorcycle helmet planter box. The tour passes a number of **blind massage parlors** and a **local composting area** before crossing the main road and winding alongside the canal.

The low-income neighborhoods parallel to the canal are both fascinating and friendly, as long as you greet the inhabitants with a smile. Half a dozen little bridges cross the waterway, and the backs of the ramshackle buildings built on a tottering edge over the water are something to wonder at. Watch for the **monkey in a cage** and the **local recycling business**. Stroll past the **Batavia Apartments**, favored accommodation amongst expats, then cross over the canal using a super cool **hand-powered ferry**.

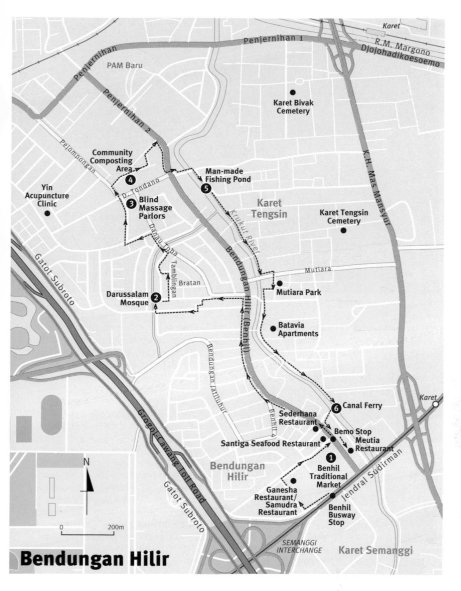

Karet

Penjernihan 1

Karet
R.M. Margono
Djojohadikoesoemo

Penjernihan

PAM Baru

Penjernihan 2

Karet Bivak
Cemetery

Perampongan

Community
Composting
Area **4**

D. Tondano

3 Blind
Massage
Parlors

Man-made
Fishing Pond

5

Karet
Tengsin

Karet Tengsin
Cemetery

Yin
Acupuncture
Clinic

Datau Toba

Tamblingan

Bratan

Krukut River

Bendungan Hilir (Benhil)

Mutiara

Gatot Subroto

Darussalam
Mosque **2**

Mutiara Park

Batavia
Apartments

K. H. Mas Mansyur

Bendungan Jatiluhur

Benhil

Sederhana
Restaurant

6 Canal Ferry

Karet

Bemo Stop

Meutia
Restaurant

Santiga Seafood Restaurant

Grogol-Cawang Toll Road

Bendungan
Hilir

Gatot Subroto

N

Ganesha
Restaurant/
Samudra
Restaurant

1

Benhil
Traditional
Market

Benhil
Busway
Stop

Jendral Sudirman

0   200m

SEMANGGI
INTERCHANGE

Karet Semanggi

Bendungan Hilir

WHO? Anyone can do this walk, although the canal portion may challenge some people's comfort zones.

HOW LONG? This walk should take around two hours, depending on the amount of stopping and chatting. Make sure to eat lunch in Benhil when you finish, as the neighborhood is famous for its food.

HOW FAR? 4.2km, including the *bemo* ride; 3.5km not including the ride.

GETTING STARTED Take Busway #1 to the Benhil stop, and walk against the traffic as you come off the Busway bridge by the BRI building. Enter the complex at the *pejalan kaki* (pedestrian) guard shack. Turn left, cross in front of the BRI I building and turn

Narrow residential lanes form a complex web in the Bendungan Hilir district.

right to walk up the pedestrian path adjacent to BRI II. If driving, park at the BRI building on Jl. Sudirman, just across from Semanggi Mall.

The walk starts at the brick path that fronts Starbucks in the Sentra BRI building, also home to the tasty **Ganesha** and **Samudra** restaurants. Walk along the path to the small guard post where pedestrians and motorcycles enter and exit. Leave through here and turn right. Follow this narrow road, which is lined with small *warungs*.

The road soon curves left, but instead of following it, continue straight and head into the dark, makeshift-looking entranceway to the Benhil Traditional Market. Look for the ANZ building looming over the entrance in the distance. Walk along the market corridor and pass the highly recommended Santiga seafood restaurant. This is the indoor branch of the very popular streetside **Santiga** restaurant located on Jl. Benhil near the BCA ATM. The outdoor restaurant is open in the evenings only and often features a live band.

1 BENHIL TRADITIONAL MARKET
Pasar Benhil (Benhil Traditional Market) is officially recognized as one of the cleanest traditional markets in the city. In the early mornings, when the marketplace is at its liveliest, the grocery stalls spill across the pavement. Most of the bottom floor is dedicated to caféteria-style eating and a wet market laden with fruit, vegetables, eggs, fresh meat and fish. At around 11pm, the fruit and vegetable sellers take over the inner parking lot, spreading out their recently delivered wares, ready to sell to both the public as well as the cooks of restaurants and cafés. The second floor of the market houses clothes retailers, tailors and tiny salons.

Back on the walk, exit the market at Jl. Benhil and hop in a waiting *bemo*. (A *bemo* is an ancient blue and yellow three-wheeled puttering and sputtering little dinosaur of a vehicle, which you enter through the back. The interior benches hold six passengers, with room in front for one.) Tell the driver you are going to Jl. Danau Toba. It should cost Rp2,000 per person, which is paid upon arrival.

In the *bemo*, pass Pizza Hut and then a large white building on the left, which is a hospital. Get out just a few meters past the hospital. Turn left into Jl. Danau Toba. Don't follow the road as it bends to the right. Instead, continue straight by taking the narrow lane of Jl. Buyan passing a black and white striped gate post. A few houses up on the left is a lamppost, and the entrance to the very tiny Jl. Bahari II. Follow this lane until reaching the bridge over the canal.

> ### FAST FACT
> Some house fronts have signs that say *kost*, which means you can rent a room there. Some *kosts* are large and elaborate places with dozens of rooms, while others are small homes offering just a room or two.

② DARUSSALAM MOSQUE

When you reach the bridge, don't cross it. Instead, turn right. It looks like this is a personal driveway but it is not. This narrow lane intersects with **Masjid Darussalam** (Darussalam Mosque) and turns right. Take a moment to peek inside the mosque and then continue straight on to the faux log fence. Turn left here, going up a beautiful *gang* called Jl. Tamblingan. Walk along this lane and turn down the second *gang* on the left, which will be just before Jl. Tamblingan widens and hooks to the right. This little lane soon ends at a T-junction and across the street is some playground equipment. Turn right here and follow the narrow park, which borders the canal to the left.

At the four-way intersection with Jl. Danau Toba, turn left, cross the canal and turn left again on Jl. Limboto. Continue up the road until you see a green and white street sign noting Pejempongan and Slipi overhead. Just before a school on the right is a narrow lane called Jl. Sekolah. Turn up this lane, which has a tiny drainage channel skirting it on the right. Follow the lane, and just a few houses before it ends you'll see a sign on the right that reads **Panti Pijat Tuna Netra Karya Hasta** (Blind Massage Parlor).

③ BLIND MASSAGE PARLORS

Panti Pijat Tuna Netra (Blind massage parlors) are generally located in converted houses with sectioned-off curtained rooms. Like any massage experience, guests lay face down on a raised bed with clothing reduced to a minimum. The masseurs' movements are slow and deliberate. They *feel* their way across the skin, seeking out the sore spots. With a heightened sense of awareness, they seem apt at locating troubled areas deep below the surface. This is a unique local neighborhood adventure on the cheap and an hour well spent. Note that if your masseuse is massaging you to the point that it hurts, try saying *Kurangi keras*, which is asking for them to be more gentle.

Continuing on the walk, Jl. Sekolah ends at the busy Jl. Tondano. Cross this road and go up Jl. Pejompongan. Pass a small hotel on the right and turn up the wonderful Jl. Pengairan, passing under a rectangular metal archway.

④ COMMUNITY COMPOSTING AREA

Immediately on the left is a small basketball court, followed by a community building and a community garden. Look for the little steps farther up on the right, which lead up to a small embankment and **Pengolahan Kompos Warga** (community composting area). It feels a bit like someone's backyard, but don't feel shy about poking around. Return the way you came and continue along the road as it winds its way along. On the right, at #16B, is another blind massage parlor.

Jl. Pengairan eventually ends in a T-junction with the busy Jl. Benhil. Turn right and walk along the road to the four-way intersection with the broken stoplights and a host of *ojek* drivers. Turn left here, crossing the street and then the canal. To the left is a tall public housing building. Turn right after crossing the bridge and follow the path that skirts the canal. This is where things really get interesting.

Say *Permisi* as you pass residents chatting and going about their daily chores. They will answer with *Mari* (come along). Stop and chat often, always asking permission to take photos. A short way after the first little bridge, you will come to a small, recently closed, man-made fishing pond behind a bamboo fence on the right.

⑤ MAN-MADE FISHING POND

Hanging out at a **Kolam Pancing Buatan** (man-made fishing pond) and bagging the night's dinner is a cheap and fun way for low-income Indonesian men to spend their day—while tapping into the outdoorsman within them. Impromptu fishing holes are found throughout the city; some are rectangular holes dug into the ground, others are small ponds located along a canal, yet others comprise fenced-off areas within a reservoir or lake. Regularly restocked with farmed fish, you are always guaranteed that somewhere below the murky waters lurks a fillet ready to be turned into a fine curry.

Fish ponds are open to the public and generally have fishing poles, bait and all the other needed gear for rent or sale from the pond manager. After you have everything you need, you should find an open spot, make a cast, light a cigarette, order a coffee from the passing lady with the thermos of hot water and instant coffee packets and then wait until the big one is landed.

To find a fishing pond in your local neighborhood, ask around for a *pemancingan*. A few big name places are Setu Babakan and Taman Mini in south Jakarta or Sunter Lake in north Jakarta.

6 CANAL FERRY

Back on the walk and after passing a total of four bridges, the path merges with a road, with **Masjid Nur At-Taqua** at the confluence. Continue along a short way until this road ends at Jl. Karet Pasar Baru Barat 4. Cross the street, turn left and go straight until the first little lane on the right. Go up this small road, passing the rundown **Taman Mutiara** (Mutiara Park). The lane turns to the right and wiggles along, eventually leading back to the path along the canal. Watch for the neighborhood **recycling collection business**.

The path passes in front of **Batavia Apartments**, where a wide bridge spans the canal to the right. Just past the apartments is a cute little pond and beyond this is one of two canal ferries. Skip the first ferry (*getek*), but take the second one, another 300m along. Pay Rp1,000 per person and alight on the far side. Go up the steps, turn right and follow the road as it turns left, leading back to Jl. Benhil and a number of lunch options.

One choice is to cross the street and pop into **Sederhana** for some tasty Padang food (try *rendang*, buffalo stewed in rich coconut sauce). Conversely, turn left and, near the BCA ATMs, is excellent Acehnese food at **Meutia** (try the fried noodle dish *mie goreng* or flat bread with curry *roti canai*) and wash it down with a *teh tarik* (pulled tea), a frothy black tea and condensed milk drink which is fun to watch being made. For some excellent North Indian food, return to the start of the walk and go to the 9th floor of the Sentra BRI building to eat at **Ganesha**. Dim sum lovers should try **Samudra** on the 8th floor of the same building.

ADDITIONAL DIVERSIONS While the Benhil walk is an excellent way to see the neighborhood, there are a number of other interesting places to visit.

GET STUFFED People come to Benhil to eat, since the options are more numerous than the islands in Indonesia. Most are food hawkers, food stalls and small restaurants and cafés. The majority are all located along Jl. Benhil, starting at the market. Popular choices are *martabak* (a thick sponge pancake) that comes either sweet or savory; *ayam bakar*, grilled chicken; *bubur ayam*, shredded chicken porridge, and *mie Aceh*, an Acehnese noodle dish which can be ordered with a *ganja sambal*, marijuana hot sauce. The latter can be found in RM Aceh Seulawah, just up from the Batavia apartments.

THE DAIRY DUNK An invitation to a **cream bath** may evoke images of being submerged neck deep in a large, ivory white tub full of frothy, fresh milk. Actually, it is a scalp, shoulder, arm and hand massage offered at many local salons, of which Bendungan Hilir has no shortage.

A cream bath starts with a hair wash followed by a dollop of a hair conditioning cream—choose from avocado, strawberry, ginseng or aloe vera. The salon attendant massages the cream into your scalp, then wraps your head in a towel before massaging your upper body. You'll feel as fresh as a daisy once the cream has been rinsed out.

HEADS UP

Take full advantage of the spa facilities in Indonesia as they are one of the best reasons to be here. Pedicures, manicures, cream baths, reflexology and facials are relaxing and inexpensive. Even men should experiment!

A SHOCKING THOUGHT For a truly extraordinary Asian experience, try fire therapy, which is designed to aid in weight loss, or electroshock therapy, used to cure chronic pain, spasms and paralysis. For **fire therapy**, a clinician smears a concoction of Chinese herbs on your exposed stomach, over which a damp towel is laid. Next the towel is moistened using a syringe filled with a 96 percent alcohol solution, a lighter is struck and the towel is set ablaze. Once the fire has burned down, the process is repeated twice more. With each new blaze, the room gets noticeably hotter and you can feel the heat penetrating to your inner core.

Once the flame is permanently out, an assistant smears more herbs on the stomach

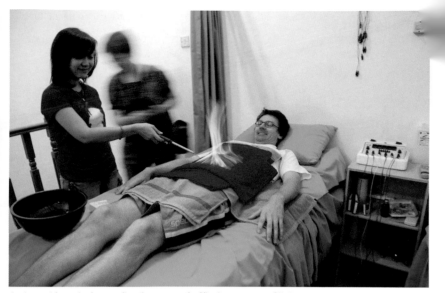

An intrepid tourist braves fire therapy at the Yin Acupuncture Clinic.

and then tightly wraps a thin cling film around your body, leaving you to feel a bit like a hot ham and cheese sandwich to go. When you remove the plastic wrap an hour later at home, supposedly the pounds will have melted away. Note that while this all seems a bit extreme, the situation is quite safe and manageable.

Electroshock therapy involves a series of needles, which an acupuncturist sticks into your head, neck and back. The therapist takes six colored wires, each with an alligator clip attached at the end, and connects them to the needles embedded in the skin. The acupuncturist flips a power switch and cranks some dials, causing the skin to leap about. The power pulses every half second, quickly immobilizing you. Deep within your back you will feel the throb of electric magic.

WHERE TO GO Klinik Akupuntur Yin—Jl. Danau Limboto C1 #2.

WHO TO CALL 021 787 5465

BETTER OFF DEAD When it comes to prime land in the city, those that have died actually have it much better than the living. With winding walking paths, radiant flowers, nubby shrubs, frangipani trees, general quiet, kids with kites, a handful of drink sellers, goats as lawnmowers and curious gravestones, who wouldn't want to be anywhere other than the graveyard?

Just east of Benhil are two wonderful cemeteries. **TPU Karet Bivak** (Karet Bivak Cemetery) is smaller and a short ways behind the Batavia Apartments, while adjacent is **TPU Karet Tengsin** (Karet Tengsin Cemetery), much larger at twice the size. Both of these cemeteries allow for peaceful strolls among the hundreds of graves and they merge with the *kampung* west of Jl. Benhil.

> ### *FAST FACT*
> These two cemeteries have the word *karet* in them, meaning rubber, as this area was originally a giant rubber plantation.

Not on the tour but interesting to note, the neighborhood also includes a mini menagerie of pythons and monkeys on Jl. Mesjid 1, a discretely disguised wine shop on Jl. Taman Bendungan Asahan 1, two lending libraries of Indonesian books, one just off Jl. Danau Bekuan and one on Jl. Taman Bendungan Jatiluhur 2, a magic shop on Jl. Danau Toba, an occasional street fair on Jl. Tondano and a tattoo/piercing parlor on Jl. Jatiluhur.

alking Tour 13

SENAYAN

A Long Stroll through Jakarta's Main Sports Area and Shopping District

1. Jakarta Convention Center
2. Aries Shooting Club
3. Plant Market
4. Madya Stadium
5. Gelora Bung Karno Stadium
6. Indonesian Heritage Society
7. Plaza Senayan
8. Senayan Golf Course
9. Senayan City
10. Youth Statue
11. National Library of Education
12. FX Mall
13. Senayan Golf Driving Range
14. Senayan Sports Palace
15. Krida Loka Park
16. Swimming Stadium
17. Pacific Place Mall
18. Bengkel Night Park
19. Manggala Wanabakti Museum of Forestry
20. Plaza Semanggi

Senayan is a centrally located hot spot that includes upscale shopping and sports venues populated by both people in tailored suits and those in track suits. Dominated by ever-multiplying high rises, the neighbor-hood proffers a shopper's orgy of delights, with four of the city's hottest malls, includ-ing **Senayan City** and its escalator with a stiletto heel facade. It also contains **two driving ranges** plus the 18-hole **Padang Golf Senayan** (Senayan Golf Course), which should satisfy any Tiger Woods wannabes. The **Klub Meembak Aries** (Aries Shooting Club) targets those who like to pack heat, while the **Museum Manggala Wanabakti** (Museum of Forestry) is sure to interest arborists.

Malls aside, the central feature of the area has to be the Senayan Sports Complex. More formally known as **Stadion Gelora Bung Karno** (Gelora Bung Karno Stadium), it encompasses a large swath of land in the heart of the city and is the go-to place to stretch your legs, break a sweat and join like-minded people who want to get fit. Visitors will also find an array of non-sport activities here, such as concerts, exhibitions, rallies and festivals.

President Sukarno started construction of the sports complex in the 1950s with the goal of hosting the Asia Games, a regional version of the Olympics. It required a large-scale relocation of the area's residents, and unfortunately, developers continue to gobble up more of the area each year. At the time of writing, five new office towers and a parking garage have recently been built just outside the Sports Complex, near Plaza Senayan, all on land that was supposed to have been set aside as a green area and for sports-related activities.

This walk starts in the sports complex to break a sweat, strays off to some malls to get gifts, swings past the firing range to fire off a few rounds and finishes up at a nice little park and swimming pool for a cooling-off dip. Not everyone goes shopping in the same get-up they wear to exercise, so dress sporty in case the desire to sprint a few laps on the track arises.

WHO? This walk is suitable for anyone and everyone.

HOW LONG? The whole walk should take around two hours, longer if you join an impromptu game of football.

HOW FAR? 7.75km.

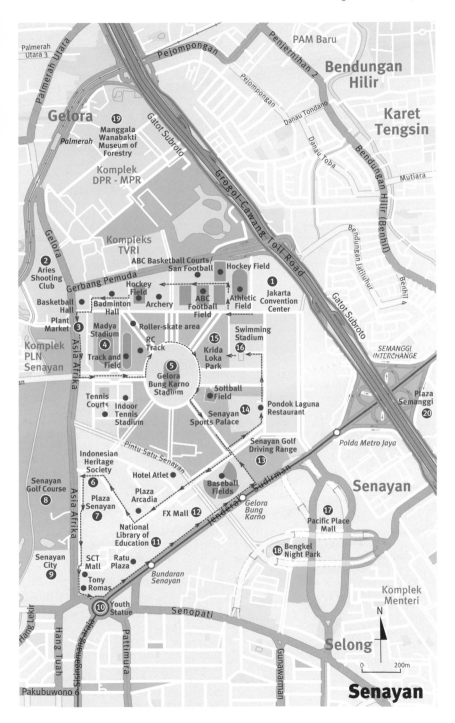

GETTING STARTED There is ample parking inside the sports complex, but when the Jakarta Convention Center is hosting a large event, which it often does, traffic getting into the complex can border on nightmarish. Police may close certain gates to manage the flow, so drivers should plan far in advance or take a motorbike, if possible. Busway passengers should disembark at the Gelora Bung Karno stop on corridor #1. Ultimately, your best bet is to come by bicycle.

An archery competition in progress.

① JAKARTA CONVENTION CENTER

The tour begins at the front gates of the **Jakarta Convention Center** (JCC). Every week, the JCC hosts exhibitions, ranging from arts and crafts to homebuilding supplies to diving and extreme sports to new technology. Keep an eye on their schedule through their website. The whole east side parking lot that fronts JCC and stretches to the driving range is often used for temporary exhibitions and concerts, and is also the staging area for rallies; you never know what will pop up next.

CHECK OUT www.jcc.co.id

Standing facing the JCC, turn left and follow the road, noting the **athletic field** to the right. At the road to the left of this field, turn right and continue straight. Runners use the **dirt track** circling the field to the right, and football games take place in the middle. Some of the city's **largest music festivals and concerts** are thrown here as well. To the left, a better maintained football field gets used by special teams, such as the national football team. As the road nears its end, turn left. To the right is an **artificial turf field**, which hosts field hockey, rugby and Ultimate Frisbee games.

Further down the lane sit four recently renovated outdoor **basketball courts**, **volleyball courts** and two **sand football fields**, all to the right. Two more **football fields** are on the left. When the lane meets one of the main roads into the complex, cross over and enter the gate on the other side. Turn left on to the large football field, which doubles as an **archery field**. Turn right and walk in front of the small stadium seats, crossing through a gate into a grassy area with an **artificial turf field** to the left. This field is also used for field hockey, Ultimate Frisbee, touch football, archery and rugby.

Hook to the left, following the contour of the field. Once you're past the locker rooms in front of the field, turn right and walk straight. Building C is a **basketball hall** and building B has two indoor **badminton courts**. Building A, also a **basketball hall**, is sometimes used for rock concerts. Exit out of this area through the black gates on the left, cross the street, turn right and exit Gelora Bung Karno on to Jl. Asia Afrika. Gun enthusiasts can take a short detour here by crossing the street and turning right. Up the road a few hundred meters on the left is Jakarta's preeminent shooting range.

② ARIES SHOOTING CLUB

Frequented by military personnel, police officers and members of the public–some nicknamed Guided Missile, Grizzly and Magnum–the **Klub Meembak Aries** (Aries Shooting Club) is for those looking to fire off a barrage of bullets and enjoy the feeling that only unleashing a loaded gun can bring. The club has an indoor two-story area for rifle practice, with metal targets shaped like goats, rabbits, squirrels and other fuzzy creatures at distances of 10, 25 and 50 meters. There is also a pleasant outdoor arena with chirping birds (not for shooting), shade trees and benches. Visitors can rent one of Aries' guns or bring their own.

WHO TO CALL 0813 1000 5991

GETTING IN Open 9am to 5pm daily.

③ PLANT MARKET

To continue the walk from the sports complex gates, turn left and stroll along the sidewalk flanking Jl. Asia Afrika. This is **Pasar Tanaman** (Plant Market), one of the best nurseries in Jakarta. Walk along the stretch of plants and gardening accessories, found

Guidebook photographer Melanie Wood receiving a lesson at the Aries Shooting Club.

on both sides of the road, and peek behind the wall of pottery to see the guys make the planters. An array of colorful flowers occupy the stalls across from Taman Ria, on Jl. Gerbang Pemuda. If the urge to buy plants strikes, delivery trucks are available.

4 MADYA STADIUM

To the left of Pasar Senayan is the entrance gate to **Stadion Madya** (Madya Stadium), but hands off the track, it's for national athletes only. The west gate into the sports complex is just past Madya. In the evening, youths like to gather here, hang out and eat at the *warungs* that pop up in the early evening. Late at night, car and motorcycle street racers often gear up here for rallies, which can be quite exciting to watch. Unfortunately, they usually take place in the wee hours of the night. The area is also popular for concerts and commercial events.

Pass through the gates with two archer statues up top, and on the left is the **track and field area**, followed by a track for **radio-controlled cars**. At the RC track, anyone can plunk down a small chunk of change to rent a zippy little car and send it flying around the serpentine track a few hundred times. To the right of the entrance street are nearly 20

outdoor **tennis courts** and just past them is the **indoor tennis stadium**, which doubles as a **concert venue** that hosts some of the biggest concerts that come to the city.

CHECK OUT www.deathrockstar.info to stay on top of what's coming to both Jakarta and the region.

If it's hot out and you need to slake your thirst, watch for a guy carrying a long thin stick with four bamboo tubes lashed to it. Inside each tube is a cool, refreshing palm *aren* sugar drink called *nira*, made from the *pohon aren* (sugar palm tree), and is guaranteed to add spring to your step.

5 GELORA BUNG KARNO STADIUM

The next set of gates leads smack into the center of the Senayan sports universe, **Stadion Gelora Bung Karno** (Gelora Bung Karno Stadium). This is where all the **big football games** are held, although it's used mostly by hometown favorite Persija, identified by their bright orange jerseys. The stadium's outer perimeter holds smaller sports halls used for **martial arts**, **capoeira** (a Brazilian martial art/dance), **weightlifting**, **gymnastics**, **fencing** and more.

Baseball at Gelora Bung Karno, where major sports competitions are held.

Joggers, **walkers**, **cyclists** and **skaters** use the asphalt space around the stadium, which also hosts **parkour** (an urban gymnastics type sport), **football**, **badminton**, **martial arts**, **line dancing** and **marching band rehearsal**. The weekend brings out groups such as the Y GO English Club; the Sweet Iron Low Riders, with their tricked-out bicycles sporting leopard skin seats and fuzzy dice; and the University of Indonesia's Nursing Program, which occasionally offers blood tests for low blood sugar. Keep an eye out for the suction cup healers.

FAST FACT

Metode bekam is a form of healing in which various-sized suction cups are placed on a person's body. As air is sucked out of the cup, the skin beneath rises to fill up the space. The method is used to extract toxins from the body, regardless of whether you are sick or healthy. Next, the healer removes the cups and doles out a well-oiled massage and superb head rub.

To the left, past the RC racetrack, is a recently repaved **roller skate area**, which stretches out like an asphalt tentacle. These asphalt arms extend out from points all around the stadium, and play host to countless football games, especially on the weekends. Between the tentacles, past the roller skate area, is a large plant nursery.

Most of the spaces sandwiched by the tentacles could be classified as parks. Generally used as hang-out spots by street sweepers or bored teenagers, they are shaded by large trees and have dirt or paved paths. Squeezed behind the **Masjid Al Bina Senayan**, one of the most attractive of its kind in the city, in the southwest part of the complex are dirt paths that encircle and cross over a small hill, good for exploring by bike.

Continue around the stadium until you pass Pintu VIII (Gate 8) and exit out the black gates to the left. The **Cemara Softball Field** is off to the left near the large statue of an archer, the symbol of the sports complex. There are numerous dirt paths amongst the trees both to the left and right here which could be explored by the more adventurous types.

Exit through the next set of black gates, where a defunct fountain sits. Turn right and cross the road, walking past the softball and baseball fields on the left. Complete with batting cages and pitching machines, these fields are popular among the small community of softball and baseball fans. They also offer a great place to just sit in the bleachers and be a spectator.

Like most things in Jakarta, sporting events seem to happen spontaneously. Games and practices can relocate at the

Outdoor suction cup therapy near the central sports stadium.

last minute and it can be tough to find an upcoming schedule. The best bet is to go to the area where the sport you're interested in is played and hope someone is around to provide more information. If not, try again on a different day, query a drink or food vendor, or ask Google. The process can be frustrating, but in a city where it's hard to meet new people and make friends, Senayan holds the potential for both.

Back on the walk, exit out of Gelora Bung Karno through the big gates, cross the main road, Jl. Pintu Satu Senayan, and continue straight. When passing **Hotel Atlet** on the right, try to spot the three big tanks labeled *sambal*, pizza dough and ketchup–a remnant of the days when there was an Italian eatery inside. At the T-junction at the top of the road, turn right. On the corner is **Plaza Arcadia**, and while it won't be too happening in the morning, come back at night to check out the highly recommended **Black Cat Jazz Café** and their live music, **Hacienda's** Mexican grub with the absolute best frozen margaritas in the city, and **Din Tai Fung's** *dim sum* (different small servings of food on plates or in steamed baskets).

CHECK OUT www.plaza-senayan.com/arcadia

6 INDONESIAN HERITAGE SOCIETY

Cross the street, turn right and continue on to **Sentral Senayan I and II**. In the first tower, on the 17th floor, is where the Indonesian Heritage Society is located.

The **Indonesian Heritage Society** is a gathering point for anyone eager to know more about the country. Not only does it have a fabulous library with more than 5,000 books in five languages, but there are also loads of magazines, pamphlets, movies and CDs. The library, which has wi-fi, also serves

Kids line up for their martial arts practice at the central sports stadium.

as a meeting place and discussion spot. The Heritage Society hosts museum tours, language classes, study groups, lectures and an Explorers Group. Note that there is a yearly membership charge.

CHECK OUT www.heritagejkt.org

7 PLAZA SENAYAN

From the towers, turn left and pass through a plaza. It used to have founts which squirted water up from the ground, but now it's used as a resting spot by office workers. Make a beeline for Starbucks in **Plaza Senayan**.

This upscale mall, once the premier place to be seen in Jakarta, still manages a crowd despite the growing competition. Much like Plaza Indonesia, Plaza Senayan is filled with designer handbag and watch stores that no one ever seems to go into. Yet it is also home to two great bookstores, **Kinokuniya** (5th floor) and **Periplus** (3rd floor); an excellent eatery, **Rustique** (4th floor), which does gourmet burgers; and **Taichan Ramen** (3rd floor), which offers giant bowls of tasty noodles.

CK OUT www.plaza-senayan.com

SENAYAN GOLF COURSE

continue the walk, skirt the front of Plaza Senayan and turn right, heading out to the sidewalk along Jl. Asia Afrika. From here you can either cross the street and head to the 18-hole **Padang Golf Senayan** (Senayan Golf Course), to the right, or you can pop into another mall, Senayan City.

9 SENAYAN CITY

The massive **Senayan City** complex is a hopping place to shop, with several indoor/outdoor restaurants on the lower levels, including alcohol-offering Domain on the bottom floor near the billiards hall. For one of the mall's highlights, which is actually on top of the roof of the building, visit **Fitness First's** infinity pool. For a more unusual activity, try the fish spa.

CHECK OUT www.senayancity.com

FISH SPA This curious process begins with a quick scrub of the feet and calves. Next, customers are sat before an elongated tank full of hungry little fish. A customer drops their twinkle toes into the cool blue waters and watches the melee unfold as the fish nibble bits of dead skin off the feet and legs. It sounds disgusting, but it works wonders. The peck of a few hundred tiny fish lips feels a bit like being buzzed by a vibrator and it usually tickles. The fish, Garra Rufa, are originally from Turkey, and they produce an enzyme that makes the skin smooth as they chomp away. After 30 minutes, a person's feet should be as soft as a peeled *rambutan*.

WHERE TO GO Kenko Reflexology and Fish Spa at Senayan City, lower ground level.

CHECK OUT www.kenkoindonesia.com

10 YOUTH STATUE

If you're in the market for electronics, arts and crafts, a new bicycle or dance lessons, check out the partially deserted **Mal STC** (STC Mall) across from Senayan City and to the left of Plaza Senayan. Otherwise, follow the road as it wraps around to the left. The **Patung Pemuda** (Youth Statue) will come into sight straight ahead. Probably the most recognizable statue in the city, it depicts an incredibly muscled young man hoisting a

flame above his head. He was supposed to be unveiled at Youth Pledge Day in 1971, but unfortunately he came a little late. Today, he is commonly referred to as the Flaming Pizza Man.

11 NATIONAL LIBRARY OF EDUCATION

Follow the road around, noting **Tony Roma's** to the left, a US-based restaurant known for its ribs. Then, on the left, is **Ratu Plaza**, a good spot for electronics and pirated DVDs. One building past Ratu Plaza is the **Perpustakaan Pendidikan Nasional** (National Library of Education). Once belonging to the British Council, the library was later turned over to the Ministry of Education, and they have done a good job of keeping it going. While they have an extensive catalog of English-language guides, they also have fiction, non-fiction and reference books (18,000 English titles in total), not to mention movies, music, magazines, wi-fi, internet and a café.

12 FX MALL

Continue past the library to find the **Mal FX** (FX Mall) on the left. This is the sister mall to EX, next to Plaza Indonesia, and for once the mall's builders got the size right. Rather than being the size of Sumatra, FX is a funky mid-sized mall where you are unlikely to get lost. Some floors are translucent and it's got a snappy color scheme. For fun, the mall sports a multistory transparent slide that plunges down the center of the building, and there's even a store that sells clothes for dogs. For a good meal and live music, head straight to **Tartine** in the basement and then stop by **Bloeming** for specials on beer.

13 SENAYAN GOLF DRIVING RANGE

After passing FX, cross the street and walk along Jl. Sudirman, admiring the skyline of modern towers. Walk through the fairly grand entrance gates to the sports complex and up the large pedestrian path. Off to the right is the multilevel **Driving Range Golf Senayan** (Senayan Golf Driving Range).

14 SENAYAN SPORTS PALACE

Once at the main road (where the dry fountain you saw earlier sits), turn right. To the left is **Istora Senayan** (Senayan Sports Palace), which hosts various sports competitions, concerts and exhibitions. Note: A lot of buildings in Jakarta get the label 'palace,' when they are anything but. Continue walking past the **Pondok Laguna Restaurant** (or step in for a seafood feast), pass by two asphalt strips leading to the stadium and enter left into the Swimming Stadium.

15 KRIDA LOKA PARK
Head around to the back of the stadium where **Taman Krida Loka** (Krida Loka Park) is located. Inside this pleasant park is a decent kilometer-long jogging path that has distances marked for those who want to tally their laps. The park is stuffed with large, leafy trees, mildly dilapidated exercise stations and has restrooms with lockers to change and store your bags. It's a solid, little area but bring anti-mosquito cream.

16 SWIMMING STADIUM
Leave the park and check out the giant **Stadion Renang** (Swimming Stadium) with its Olympic-style diving boards and grandstand seating. It's generally open to the public from 7.30am to 4pm, so have a swimsuit handy to take a dip.

With that, you have come full circle and the walk is complete.

17 PACIFIC PLACE MALL
THE SENAYAN SUPPLEMENT One of the latest gifts to those who love all things shopping is **Mal Pacific Place** (Pacific Place Mall). It's much like every other massive, upscale mall, but it certainly has elements of surprise. Check out the creative and fairly extensive dining area options. A highlight is **Le Seminyak** on the 5th floor, which offers excellent Balinese food. **Blitz Megaplex** on the top level has **Velvet Class seating**, where you can lie in bed and get served dinner while watching the big screen. Kids get to play at being adults at **Kidzania**, while parents can indulge at the **Ritz Carlton Hotel's** rooftop bar, **Eight**, where patrons imbibe high above the traffic and can run their toes through real grass. Movie classics are shown some Friday nights on an outdoor screen here. Note that this bar cannot be accessed via the mall, but must be entered through the hotel's outside entrance.

WHERE TO GO Just off Jl. Sudirman near the Semanggi interchange.

CHECK OUT www.pacificplace.co.id, www.kidzania.co.id, www.blitzmegaplex.com

18 BENGKEL NIGHT PARK
The **Bengkel Night Park Concert Hall** is a little-known concert venue often referred to as the Bengkel Café. This venue hosts some rocking concerts, with both local and big name acts passing through, and even has a bar right smack in the middle of the auditorium floor. The place is large enough to hold a thousand people but small enough to where rabid fans can edge right up to the stage and nearly touch their favorite rock stars.

19 MANGGALA WANABAKTI MUSEUM OF FORESTRY
The **Museum Manggala Wanabakti** (Manggala Wanabakti Museum of Forestry) is definitely slanted toward the commercial use of forests. It sports over 700 artifacts, including fossilized wood and examples of different wood types. A number of dioramas add visual effects and a small section focuses on reforestation and rehabilitation. The second floor has picture displays of different types of forests, as well as a wonderful resource library with books in both Indonesian and English. Outside is the **Forest Park** with a number of displays, a pond, a monument and labeled trees.

WHERE TO GO Jl. Slipi and Jl. Gelora 1.

HOW TO GET THERE The nearest Busway stop is Polda Metro Jaya on Busway #1. It can also be reached by car, exiting off Jl. Subroto. There is plenty of parking inside.

WHO TO CALL 021 570 3265/ 021 570 3246 ext. 5557/8

OTHER 9am to 4pm, Monday to Friday.

20 PLAZA SEMANGGI
In some countries, karaoke is something done only by lonely drunks in back alley bars, but here in Jakarta it's *the* thing to do. The infamous *dangdut* sex bomb Inul Daratista started up her own chain of karaoke clubs, **Inul Vizta**, which have proven very popular and are generally family friendly. There are venues all over the city, but try the one on the 6th floor of **Plaza Semanggi** on the corner of Jl. Sudirman/Subroto, just north of Senayan.

CHECK OUT www.vizta.co.id

Chapter 4

South Jakarta

The leafy neighborhoods of south Jakarta are home to much of the expatriate community and offer world cuisine, homely pubs, cultural centers, fruit orchards, recreation parks and trails for running and cycling.

South Jakarta encompasses a huge area stretching from the central business district of Kuningan to Depok 15km away. It's more practical to divide the area into south Jakarta, far south Jakarta and super far south Jakarta, as those living in Kebayoran Baru, a five-minute walk from Pasaraya Grande mall, aren't at all close to the residents around the University of Indonesia, a drive of over an hour away.

South Jakarta used to be rice fields, plantations and forests, with roaming animals and a scarce population. These days, it's the suburbs with golf courses, residential estates, luxury housing, international schools and offices. For parents with children at one of the international schools, the outdoorsy types, and those wanting space for a yard or a pool, south Jakarta, far south Jakarta and far-flung south Jakarta offer many possibilities.

What south Jakarta lacks in historical interest, it makes up for in outdoor adventure opportunities, greenery and activities other than mall hopping.

The physically fit can head for the **JPG Mountain Bike Course**, where riders meet en masse to blast down hillsides and along sweeping country trails, cross rickety bridges and spray mud. Runners can head to **Ragunan Zoo** early on Sunday mornings to join the **Jakarta Free Spirit** running club, while trekkers, trail runners and cyclists can strike for the hills of Sentul to explore the labyrinth of village paths, roads and goat trails. The **rock climbing walls** in Kuningan are the best place to work on the upper body and make new friends. The Kuningan area also boasts the largest and most diverse range of cemeteries in the city; cemeteries are among the rare green

Neat white crosses amid green grass at the Ereveld Menteng Pulo War Cemetery.

The Snow Bay Water Park from the sky gondola at Taman Mini Indonesia Indah.

spaces in the city and make peaceful venues for morning walks.

For some family fun, **Mekasari** is a sprawling fruit orchard with water activities and children's rides. You can escape undisturbed for hours amid the acres of fruit trees. **Taman Mini Indonesia Indah** is worth several visits. The park's attractions include an insectarium, museums, aviaries, an IMAX theater, the Snow Bay Water Park and gondola lifts. The grounds are extensive and suitable for exploring on one of the rented tandem bicycles. **Ragunan Zoo** is set in leafy, spacious grounds and is a good place to walk or cycle freely amongst the old trees, spotting the animals along the way.

The **Pondok Indah** walking tour passes through or near 18 of the more than 50 local parks and green areas. Rise at the crack of dawn to do some bird watching, catch the dog trainers at work in Terrasering Park or join in with a group using a local park to practice Tai Chi.

For culture, the smartly housed **Gedung Dua8** (Indigenous People's Museum) in Kemang presents multiple floors of ethnic artifacts, while cultural center **Salihara** hosts performances, poetry slams, lectures and art shows, often with a slant to the modern and experimental. Enroll at the **University of Indonesia** for an Indonesian

language course, or simply stroll around the campus grounds enjoying the greenery and sense of academia.

Kemang has a lively concentration of bars, restaurants, nightclubs and party spots, and is well-known as an expatriate neighborhood. Kemang caters for a range of budgets: the Kemang Food Fest dishes up good meals for good prices, and the Bremer bar serves a well-priced pint. Further up the scale, visit Anatolia for Turkish cuisine and Kinara for Indian. Shy at the Papilion is a magnet for rich, fashion-conscious teenagers, while Eastern Promise is a down-to-earth pub for the more casually dressed.

Blok M is an edgier neighborhood with a more rock and roll attitude. The streets are lively at night, and the plentiful dining options include Indonesian, Japanese, Korean and European fare. Blok M is also an underground fashion area rich with tiny one-off clothing stores, hair salons and massage parlors.

Blok M has another claim to fame—Bar Street. Jl. Palatehan holds enough bars within stumbling distance of each other that a beer at each would be enough to put most to bed.

For shopaholics, there is the bustling indoor market at the **Mal Ambassador** and the simple **Pasar Festival**, while Pasaraya Grande and the Pondok Indah malls offer more complete ranges of retail goods.

Walking Tour 14

KUNINGAN
A Walk through Verdant Cemeteries to Some of Jakarta's Newest Malls

1. **Pasar Festival**
2. **Bakrie Tower**
3. **Menteng Cemeteries**
4. **Yasda Islamic School**
5. **Mega Kuningan**
6. **Ambassador Mall**
7. **Erasmus Huis Dutch Cultural Center**
8. **Grass Market**
9. **Armed Forces Museum**

It may mean 'brass', but Kuningan is more about the gold of money. Located in an area known as the Golden Triangle, it is part of the city's central business district. In addition to the embassies, five-star hotels and luxury apartments, there are middle-income neighborhoods, slums and some of the city's best cemeteries.

Kuningan's main artery is **Jl. Rasuna Said**, named after Indonesia's first female minister, a national heroine who made a name for herself by fighting for gender equality. This smooth stretch of road is a breeze to travel down when traffic is light, on Sundays for example, but during rush hour the gridlock brings cars to a halt and drivers to their knees. Served by one of the city's Busway corridors, though, commuters can make a fairly quick trip from one end to the other, going all the way down to the zoo, in fact. As well as office towers, the street has plenty of great places to eat, such as **Setiabudi 21**, and places to drink, as seen at the ever-popular **Aphrodite Sports Bar**.

Some of the skyscrapers are quite captivating, particularly the snakeskin-looking façade of the **Bakrie Tower**, just outside the Taman Rasuna Apartment block. Also near here, the down to earth **Pasar Festival** mini-mall offers shopping and sports facilities, while the **Menteng Pulo cemeteries** make for a rewarding outdoor walk. For museum lovers, there is the worthwhile **Museum Satria Mandala** (Armed Forces Museum), where you can thoroughly explore the historical armed conflicts of the country. For culture hounds, the Dutch Embassy's **Erasmus Huis** has year-round activities and events. The **Four Seasons Spa** rounds out a good day by offering saunas, steam rooms and great massages.

The highlights of the Kuningan walk include three interesting cemeteries complete with fragrant flowers and goats bumping heads between burial plots. The walk goes via the best rock-climbing walls in town; allows you to see wheeled vegetable vendors winding down narrow lanes of a cool little *kampung*; follows wide, tree-lined streets; shows off sky rises with fine dining and takes you to spacious, motorbike-free sidewalks that you can actually walk on.

It's best enjoyed if you stray from the beaten path often, linger when the mood strikes and chat with the locals along the way.

WHO? Just about anyone can do this walk, although the stretches in the *kampung* may require an adventurous spirit.

HOW LONG? Around three to four hours. A 7am or 8am start on a weekend is the best way to enjoy this walk to the fullest as it should be at its quietest.

HOW FAR? 5.8km.

GETTING STARTED Start the walk by either parking at Pasar Festival on Jl. Rasuna Said, or taking Busway #6 and get off at the GOR Sumantri stop.

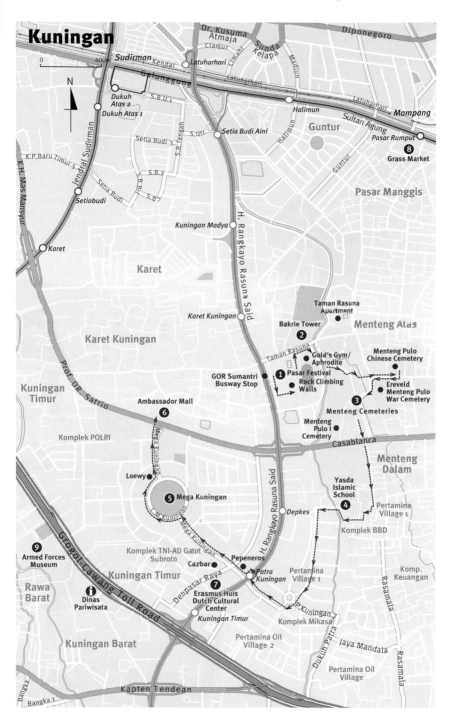

Rock climbing at Pasar Festival.

1 PASAR FESTIVAL

Just a few buildings down from the Australian Embassy is **Pasar Festival**. As Jakarta malls go, it's a mere mite in a field of elephants. It does, however, have a wide variety of sports facilities, including an indoor basketball court that is often used for exhibition tournaments, such as boxing.

To the right of the mall are two **Dinding Panjat Tebing** (artificial rock climbing walls). Groups often use the surrounding space here to practice martial arts or parkour, an urban, gymnastics-type sport. Next door is the Universitas Bakrie.

Rock climbing in Indonesia is still in its infancy, but hardcore climbers come to Pasar Festival nearly every Saturday and occasionally during the week. One of the walls is flat, meaning that climbers of any level can manage. The other wall is geared toward intermediate and advanced climbers. There is also a bouldering wall downstairs, under the stadium, which is great for those that want to work on strength training and improve technical skills. It's also good for use during the rainy season when the outdoor walls are too slick to climb on. Gear is usually available for use, though it helps to have climbing shoes.

For more information, call Panji Susanto (0813 11209767, panjiclimb@gmail.com), a real-life Spiderman with muscles etched out with a samurai sword. This former X-games competitor and professional athlete for the Indonesian government runs the climbing wall when he's not training.

2 BAKRIE TOWER

After scaling or scoping out the wall, walk left along the front of the sports stadium, popping out on to Jl. Taman Rasuna. Note that on the left is a public swimming pool. Turn right and walk past **Gold's Gym** on the right, which is next door to **Aphrodite**, a popular bar among guys looking for beer, ball games on the big screen and babes. It's also got a popular billiards scene where teams come to practice and compete (check out: www.jakartapoolleague.com). On the left is the magnificent **Bakrie Tower** with its accompanying **Rasuna Epicentrum**, which boasts the largest Cinema XXI in Jakarta, seating over 500 people. The canal in front of Epicentrum is an excellent example of a successful waterway reclamation project. Along the canal, which has been cleaned of garbage, is now a winding jogging/cycling path lined with flowers, shrubs and trees. Benches and garbage cans have been installed. The area has become very popular with the locals and there is talk of the project extending to include longer sections of the canal.

Straight ahead is a roundabout, and beyond it stand the **Taman Rasuna Apartments**, a city unto itself, with its 18 residential towers and more than 4,000

Tourists walking along the canal at Epicentrum.

Ereveld Menteng Pulo War Cemetery, a lush oasis in a city of skyscapers.

apartments in a 50-hectare area. The site is popular with expats thanks to its central location, adequate facilities and reasonably priced apartments.

3 MENTENG CEMETERIES

At the roundabout, turn right. Just up on the left is a bridge over a canal. Cross the canal and enter **TPU Menteng Pulo I** (Menteng Pulo I Cemetery). Follow the broken brick and dirt path, keeping to the left. The path soon heads out of the cemetery and up a path with a canal on the left and a brick wall on the right. Pass the SMP Negeri 145 school on the right. At the first intersection, the white crosses of a cemetery should be visible through the gate just ahead. To the right is the Kantor Lurah Menteng Atas (Menteng Village Office). To the left is a road off into the *kampung*.

FAST FACT

The term Golden Triangle refers to the area of expensive real estate contained within Jl. Rasuna Said, Jl. Subroto and Jl. Sudirman.

Walk straight, going up Jl. Menteng Pulo, keeping the white crosses on the right and passing a traditional market on the left (it's tucked among the buildings so you need to walk in to explore it). The **Pemakaman Cina Menteng Pulo** (Menteng Pulo Chinese Cemetery) will appear on the left. A green and white sign saying Masjid Al-Falah indicates the spot to turn in.

Stroll around the cemetery, noting that most gravesites are marked by crosses with Mandarin writing. There are enough goats and chickens here to fill a petting zoo, but their nibbling has not kept the vegetation from consuming many of the burial sites. In some places nothing more than a headstone's top peeks out from the green, offering an interesting lesson on nature's habit of reclaiming anything left unattended. Although many plots have been vandalized or left in a sad state of affair, it's still a nice place to spend a few minutes, away from the hustle and bustle.

Cross to the far side of the cemetery to find a dumping ground and the homes of those who make their livings off the rubbish. The people here are generally friendly, but be polite with the picture taking. After mingling for a bit, exit back on to Jl. Menteng Pulo, and return to the intersection where the white crosses were visible. Turn left, walk up the road a bit and enter the **Pemakaman Belanda Ereveld** (Ereveld Menteng Pulo War Cemetery).

The gates to this cemetery are always locked, but generally a caretaker there will open them when asked. The grounds here are stunning, the landscaping pleasing, and the simple church seems almost brand new. This is by far one of the most surprising locations in the city and definitely the best cemetery.

The view from the top of the church over the immaculate grounds, surrounded by skyscrapers, is impressive. Take an extended walk through the graves and into the graveyard next door, where commonwealth men and soldiers are buried. Grave markers are shaped according to sex and ethnicity. The serenity of the surroundings may seduce some into wishing they had a sun lounger, a good book and all morning to just lay back and relax, cemetery or no cemetery.

Ereveld Menteng Pulo War Cemetery.

ue until reconnecting with a cement path. Walk on with a wall to the right separating you from the cemetery. Pass a concrete football field on the left that may have wooden, hand-built circus rides for kids and continue until reaching the canal. Turn right, walk up a ways and cross the canal using the bridge up on the left. Use the **Sekolah Islamic Yasda** (Yasda Islamic School) next to the bridge as a sign that you are on the right track.

HEADS UP

The existence of ghosts is accepted in Indonesia so don't be surprised if you come across a lost soul stuck somewhere between our world and the next. If you do run into one, it's likely to be a *pocong*, a hopping, mummy-looking ghost, which is meant to be a person buried in the Islamic style of being wrapped in clean white sheets with the feet bound.

HEADS UP

If you get lost going through the village, just say *Mau ke Jl. Patra Kuningan* and people will point you in the right direction.

Exit the cemetery and turn left. Pass the SMA 79 school on the right and note the apartments on the left, which one of the caretakers of the Menteng cemeteries claims were built on cemetery land and are therefore haunted, thus leading to a high rate of vacancy. Cut through the small parking lot with all the *warungs* and exit diagonal from the left, following the main road and through the cemetery. Exit on to Jl. Casablanca and you should see a big, ugly, unidentifiable statute just past the archway that reads PU Menteng Pulo on the outside.

Cross over the road using the pedestrian bridge. On the other side, enter the PU Menteng cemetery once again, stopping to chat with the flower sellers and to buy a few roses or some rose water to sprinkle on the graves. Inside, check out all the beautiful flowering trees and unique gravesites. The place seems wild, yet tended to. Again, venture off the main track as needed.

④ YASDA ISLAMIC SCHOOL

At the end of this road, there is a wall separating the cemetery from the village. Don't enter the village here. Turn right and walk a short distance, then turn left and take the next right on to a broken brick and dirt path. Pass a fishing hole on the right and contin-

On the far side of the bridge is a very well-off community evidenced by an immediate and obvious change in house size and road width. Walk up Jl. Patra Kuningan 15 to the junction and turn left. Head straight up Jl. Patra Kuningan (a red and white striped gate may block the road), passing the football fields and tennis courts in the median between the roads. Go through the next roundabout and take the next right on to Jl. Patra Kuningan Raya. Look for an overhead green and white sign pointing toward Jl. Rasuna Said.

Cross over Jl. Rasuna Said using the Busway bridge. On the other side, walk against the traffic to Jl. Gilimanuk and turn right. Pass (or go into) the highly recommended **Pepenero Restaurant** in Menara Karya tower, cross the main intersection and pass the RNI building, also on the right.

⑤ MEGA KUNINGAN

At this point, you have reached **Mega Kuningan**, which can be viewed as the heart of the golden triangle, with the Ritz Carlton and JW Marriott Hotels being two of the main attractions. People come here for upscale shopping, fine dining or to work at any one of the many embassies in the area. What's special about this neighborhood is that there are smooth, wide sidewalks. The roads are also clean and spacious and you can bicycle and walk in relative peace.

Cross the road any time and note **Cazbar** on the left in Menara Anugrah (Anugrah Tower). If you are thirsty and need some alcohol to wet your lips, pop in to find a great selection of drinks, sports on the TV and often live music. The bar is at Taman Kantor Unit A.

At the next intersection, head left, following the circular road of Jl. Lingkar Mega Kuningan. Pass Menara Prima, The East and Oakwood, which are all on the left-hand side. If a meal is a must and you want to go somewhere where you'll be seen, head to the trendy **Loewy** (www.loewyjakarta.com), a French-inspired bistro/bar at the Oakwood Condominiums. It has pleasant outdoor seating and the bar is often packed. It is advisable to call ahead for reservations.

6 AMBASSADOR MALL

At the Oakwood, hook left and follow Jl. Mega Kuningan as it runs straight into the **Mal Ambassador** (Ambassador Mall).

Just across from Mega Kuningan, separated by Jl. Prof. Dr. Satrio (often referred to as Jl. Casablanca), is Mal Ambassador. The mall has two sides. One is more of a giant bargain basement, while the other sports standard clothes shops and electronic goods stores. The place is known for its deals, and draws shoppers like moths to a reduced-priced candle. As with most malls, Sundays can be a real mosh pit when trying to get from shop to shop, but most other days it is a bit more relaxed.

THE KUNINGAN SUPPLEMENT

7 ERASMUS HUIS DUTCH CULTURAL CENTER

Located next to the Dutch embassy is the **Pusat Kebudayaan Belanda Erasmus Huis** (Erasmus Huis Dutch Cultural Center). The center offers seminars, exhibitions, workshops, concerts, lectures and film screenings. Members of the public can catch one of the popular presentations from the National Heritage Society's lecture series (see p. 141) and bookworms can take advantage of the well-stocked library which has more than 22,000 titles including newspapers and magazines that focus on the Netherlands and Indonesia. There is also a good music collection that can be tapped into for a small fee.

WHERE TO GO Jl. Rasuna Said Kav. S-3.

CHECK OUT www.mfa.nl/erasmushuis

8 GRASS MARKET

Pasar Rumput (Grass Market) is a bit of an oddity. Despite its name, it's the go-to place for refurbished toilets, crutches, old treadmills, boots, racquets and wheelchairs. The real reason to come here, however, is for bicycles. There are models for everyone, from tiny tots on training wheels to the hardcore mountain biker. Many are cheap, both in price and in quality, and most are new. Secondhand foreign brands, such as Trek, Giant and Specialized, are also on hand. The stock changes daily, and bargaining hard is a must.

WHERE TO GO Take Busway #4 to the Pasar Rumput stop. It's on Jl. Sultan Agung.

9 ARMED FORCES MUSEUM

The **Museum Satria Mandala** (Armed Forces Museum) is run by the Indonesian Armed Forces (Tentara Nasional Indonesia or TNI). The museum provides the public with an opportunity to glimpse the country's long, often bloody history as well as the weaponry and hardware used to fight the epic battles. The complex of buildings is filled with the usual sword and gun collections, military outfits, furniture used by generals of bygone eras and a lot of old black and white photos.

History buffs should not miss the extensive range of dioramas, which depict significant battles from all across the archipelago. Most of them center on the years of 1945 and 1946, when Indonesia fought for freedom from Japanese control during World War II and the TNI was formed to protect the fledgling republic and its new constitution. Beyond the buildings, there is a lovely grassy area with a pond and benches that is free of noise and congestion, where you can just chill out and enjoy the surroundings. Also outside are loads of military vehicles and weaponry, including a fleet of airplanes that visitors can pose with and play on.

WHERE TO GO Jl. Gatot Subroto #14.

HOW TO GET THERE Head northwest on Jl. Gatot Subroto toward Semanggi. The museum is just off the road on the left-hand side, opposite Hana Bank. There is plenty of parking inside.

OTHER Open 9am to 2.30pm, Tuesday to Sunday.

Walking Tour 15

BLOK M
A Fun Walk through One of Jakarta's Coolest Neighborhoods, Complete with Parks, Barbecued Ribs and Pubs

1. Police Museum
2. Pasaraya Grande Mall
3. Blok M Bus Station
4. Little Japan
5. Blok M Square
6. Martha Tiahahu Park
7. Blok M Plaza
8. Ayodia Park
9. Langsat Park
10. Barito Animal Market
11. Mayestik Market
12. Taman Puring Market
13. Puring Park

Blok M is ground zero for Jakarta's alternative street crowd. Forget the glamour and hype of the mega malls. Funky shops, great cafés and the latest fashions at breakneck prices pack the streets around Blok M. Competing with the rock music are also a plethora of spas, dozens of small parks and more teens sporting tattoos and pierced body parts than anywhere else in the 'Big Durian,' Jakarta's rather apt nickname.

Starting with the **Museum Polri** (Police Museum), the tour then goes underground to the **Blok M Bus Station,** a secret shopping hot spot. Grab some super tasty and affordable barbecued ribs at the infamous **Warung Ayam Bakar Ganthari** before wending through a couple of cool parks and the **Pasar Barito** (Animal Market), where you can either buy a squirrel or protest that squirrels are for sale. Finish up at the cute little **Pasar Taman Puring** (Taman Puring Market) and its accompanying park, **Taman Puring** (Puring Park). If refreshments are in order, a quick zip back to the start of the

tour goes past **Bar Street**, which has the highest concentration of bars in the city (along with some friendly local ladies who like to keep Western men company).

Of course, the places mentioned in this walk are just the tip of the iceberg. To really discover Blok M's endless surprises, indulge in some detours and aimless wandering.

WHO? Anyone.

HOW LONG? The tour takes at least two hours and could extend to a full day. It's best done in the morning, around 9am, to avoid the accumulated bus exhaust and midday heat. It is designed to show off the best spots in Blok M, but many won't be open in the morning and may need to be revisited later.

HOW FAR? 4.3km.

GETTING STARTED Those coming by Busway (Route #1, getting off at the Blok M stop), will need to backtrack to the Police Museum. If coming by car or taxi, start in the parking lot of the museum.

1 POLICE MUSEUM

Museum Polri (Police Museum) on the corner of Jl. Trunojoyo and Jl. Sultan Hasanuddin, is a much-welcome addition to the cadre of museums in Jakarta and is easy to identify by the police helicopter perched out front. Housed on three floors, the museum showcases undercover gear, such as lighters with built-in cameras, calculators embedded with radio trans-

mitters and lock picking equipment. Guns, riot gear, swords, shields and uniforms also are not in short supply, and there are old police motorcycles, bicycles and a car inside.

Check out the timeline of police history, wall of fame and Kids Corner, complete with tiny police outfits, a forensics lab, narcotics and bomb sections and videos looped on flat-screen TVs. Not to be missed are the splendid murals that cover different aspects of police activity and are combined with large photos and cartoon renditions of reality.

GETTING IN Open 9am to 4pm, Tuesday to Sunday.

2 PASARAYA GRANDE MALL

Leaving the Police Museum, cross the intersection in the direction the statue of the policeman is looking. The sign for the giant **Mal Pasaraya Grande** (Pasaraya Grande Mall) will be visible ahead. Cross the pedestrian bridge over Jl. Sultan Hasanuddin and find the entrance to Pasaraya to the left. The mall was better before its recent makeover, but it still offers a sea of goods, including the

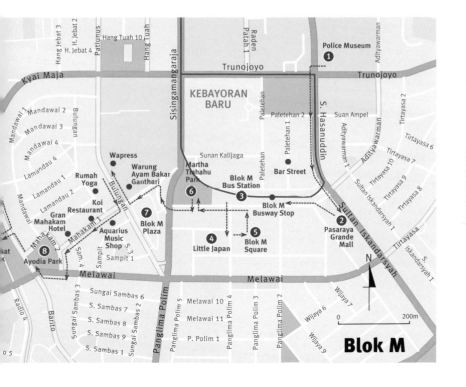

largest supply of camping gear in the city. The lower floors contain a warehouse's worth of crafts and souvenirs as well as a decent selection of art supplies.

③ BLOK M BUS STATION

The road from the pedestrian bridge also branches off to the right, toward **Terminal Bis Blok M** (Blok M Bus Station). It is marked by a sign that reads 'Mal Blok M.'

The Blok M Bus Station is a major daily transit point for hundreds of buses, including the Busway. The main terminal leads down to a market that spans out into one long underground shopping center. The myriad stores here sell everything from rock star fashions to the usual mishmash of hand-phones, belts, hats, perfume, sunglasses, T-shirts, magazines and bras. Get caught up in the mass of 20 somethings as they do what they do best—wander aimlessly. Many of the shops are *distros*, small clothing shops stocked with locally designed and produced goods. They are the place to find original, retro-funk threads.

After descending the stairs, head straight into a sales corridor with the Ramayana department store to the right. This is the point where the **Busway** people join the tour. As they exit the Busway, they will go down a flight of stairs, turn right and pass Ramayana before turning right to walk along the sales corridor. Two-thirds of the way down is an escalator that goes one floor down to karaoke, cheap reflexology, pirated DVDs, $1 haircuts at the Johnny Andrean Training Center and old rock cassettes.

FAST FACT

The Blok M area is filled with young *pengamen* (musical buskers), generally identifiable by their punk clothing, tattoos, piercings and, of course, the ubiquitous musical instrument. Many of them are living on the streets or supporting family members, so be sure to give them a bit of money.

---

④ LITTLE JAPAN

Continue straight until you reach the Robinsons department store with its army of young, bored salesgirls, each armed with a megaphone or handset to a PA system. Turn left here, go up the stairs, turn right and up the stairs again, emerging on to Jl. Melawai I.

Blok M Bus Station is clearly marked.

This street is laden with tattoo artists who draw real and fake tattoos. It also borders **Little Japan**.

Little Japan consists of a variety of Japanese restaurants, karaoke bars, executive clubs, massage parlors and hotels.

⑤ BLOK M SQUARE

Off to the left is the Dr Seuss-style **Blok M Square**, with its red and white checkered spiraling tower. The mall sells gold and silver jewelry and has a good selection of camera gear and reject clothing from upscale shops like Zara.

⑥ MARTHA TIAHAHU PARK

Walk straight up Jl. Melawai I and cross it at **Taman Martha Tiahahu** (Martha Tiahahu Park) on the right. This park sports concrete deer, elephants and dinosaurs along with chickens in a giant cage and small groups of punk kids playing guitars, cuddling up to each other, smoking or just chilling out. The occasionally functioning fountain in the center is probably the ugliest ever constructed, but no one seems to care. There is a resident monkey that roams the well cared for, fenced-off grounds which visitors can enter if they ask the caretakers nicely. Note the banana trees, paths, composting and biopore holes which have been dug to alleviate flooding.

⑦ BLOK M PLAZA

Leave the park the same way you entered and take the pedestrian bridge over Jl. Panglima Polim. Here, in the afternoon, guys sell body piercing jewelry, drumsticks, stylish and industrial anti-pollution masks and fashionable belts and hats. At the bottom of the bridge, go straight to the taxi/*bajaj*/*ojek* stand and swing left. On the left is **Blok M**

The Dr Seuss-like Blok M Square.

A concrete deer at Martha Tiahahu Park.

Plaza, which sells a million tweeny things for the million hip youngsters parading the halls. Jl. Mahakam starts at the tiny roundabout marked by a clenched fist holding a Simpati card. Across the street, visit the **Warung Ayam Bakar Ganthari** for its famous barbeque chicken and ribs. Turning right at the roundabout leads to **Wapress**, on the right, a great venue for quality live Indonesian music.

Straight off the roundabout is the **Toko Aquarius Music** (Aquarius music shop) on the left. The shop, worth popping into, has a wide selection of cassette tapes and CDs.

Across the street is Jl. Lamandau, and up one block and on the right is an incredible massage at **Rumah Yoga**. Here, you can lay in a darkened room filled with lovely scents and light music as a masseur places warm rocks between your toes, up your legs and across your back and shoulders. For some, the hot stone massage is as close to heaven as they'll get.

CHECK OUT www.rumahyoga.com.

Past Rumah Yoga on the right is the **Koi Restaurant**, one of the best eats in the city. Koi specializes in Indonesian, French,

At Blok M Plaza there is something for everyone, especially its mostly teenage patrons.

Cosying up to a rabbit at the Animal Market.

European and North African delights. It sells a rhubarb crumble that could bring an elephant to its knees. The beautiful building on the right, just past Koi, is the Hotel Gran Mahakam, which is good stop for a cup of tea.

8 AYODIA PARK
Further on is **Taman Ayodia** (Ayodia Park), a lovely little place for families to gather around the small fountain pond in the center. Paths circling the pond lead up to gazebos and benches, and nice patches of grass make ideal spots for lounging. As the park is still new, most of the trees are quite young, but

one day one of them could be the grand-daddy of all trees in Jakarta.

Cross the street to Taman Langsat and enter the park just before the fruit vendors on the right. Turn left inside the first nursery and then look for the path ahead that leads to the right and over a bridge. Follow the path to the small parking lot, cross it and then continue up the path. Take a moment to shed your shoes and try out the reflexology stone paths here. In fact, many parks in Jakarta now have walkways with small embedded stones poking upwards to walk barefoot on, thereby giving a stimulating foot massage.

FAST FACT
The general idea of reflexology is that areas of the feet are connected to other parts of the body and by applying pressure to the right spot on the foot, you can aid an afflicted body part. For example, the toes are aligned with the head and the heel is linked to the lower back.

9 LANGSAT PARK
Taman Langsat/Langsia (Langsat Park) is a cute little forest park with a 750-meter path which undulates in a serpentine roller-

Hitching a ride on the winding serpentine-like path in the forested Langsat Park.

A myriad of baskets for sale along Jl. Barito.

Bajajs at the entrance to Mayestik Market.

coaster fashion, crossing bridges and wrapping back upon itself. The park is perfect for walkers and joggers. Although it was designed and designated for senior citizens, kids come to swing, teens come to play basketball and all others come to zone out and listen to the frogs croak and the birds chirp. Watch for trees whose leaves occasionally turn a bonfire red and orange, scorching the surrounding vegetation with their color. Come early Sunday morning to join a Tai Chi session.

10 BARITO ANIMAL MARKET

Exit the park where you entered and turn left. Pass the fruit vendors and continue on to **Pasar Barito** (Animal Market). Buses ply the road here, but the variety of strange creatures provides plenty of distraction. The market sells everything from flying foxes and loris to squirrels, monkeys and owls. There are also a host of amphibians and rodents, such as iguanas and guinea pigs, as well as animal supplies.

At the end of Jl. Barito turn left and continue on to Jl. Kyai Maja. Pass through the small intersection and find Pasar Mayestik.

11 MAYESTIK MARKET

Until recently **Pasar Mayestik** (Mayestik Market) was a clean and bustling traditional market filled with fresh fruit, vegetables, chicken and fish. The city demolished the original building in mid-2010 and is now rebuilding it, but the site still has a number of good quality fabric shops and tailors. The market also has a wide range of kitchen hardware and hard to find cooking ingredients. It's a diverse place with many vendors

of Pakistani, Indian and Chinese descent. Explore the streets of Jl. Tebah I–V to see all the options.

12 TAMAN PURING MARKET

Leave the market via the same road in and cross over. When the road splits, continue straight and on the right will be a police station. Next to it is **Pasar Taman Puring** (Taman Puring Market).

Pasar Taman Puring is a friendly two-story, pint-sized market selling a hodgepodge of sports equipment, musical instruments, shoes, chainsaws, motorcycle parts, watches, wallets, cassettes, used blenders and stereo speakers. It's jam-packed and a bit claustrophobic but fun for a quick stroll around.

13 PURING PARK

Next door is **Taman Puring** (Puring Park), which used to be overrun by small carts and two-bit businesses. After officials evicted them, a nice little park emerged with playground equipment, loads of shade trees and paths to stroll around on.

If all this walking has worked up a thirst, hail a taxi or *bajaj* and head back to the Blok M Bus Terminal. Ask to go to Jl. Pelatehan, aka The Street of Shame, aka The Street of Broken Dreams aka The Street of Fun–home to pubs with names such as **Oscar**, **The One Tree**, **G String**, **Top Gun**, **My Bar**, **M Club**, **D's Place**, **Highway to Elle**, **Everest Café** and **Sportsman's**. Although grizzled male expats and the ladies of the night mostly frequent these places, they are also good for a beer, a game of billiards or sports watching. They really get going from 1am to 4am, with Top Gun and D's Place being the bars of choice.

Walking Tour 16

KEMANG
A Walk in the Quiet Upscale Residential Lanes around Jalan Raya Kemang

Many expatriates consider Kemang an escape. It's the closest thing to a Western suburb that Jakarta offers. With large homes, tree-lined streets, cool cafés, a bustling bar scene and a wide range of dining options, most a walkable distance from each other, it's a great source of comfort and familiarity for many. The majority of shops cater to the wealthy residents. Everything that many expats expect to have are there, from pet stores to galleries to gourmet kitchen supply outlets, to numerous small businesses offering specialty services like party planning. Being in close proximity to a number of international schools and with a notable absence of malls and sky rises certainly doesn't hurt either. The area also offers craft classes, salons and unique fashion outlets for children and adults.

Kemang is probably best known for its nightlife. Home to some of the best bars and lounges in the city—many just a stumble away from one another—this is where late-night revelers go to chat, dance and drink shoulder to shoulder with the city's hardcore party people. Gangs of youths gather at the **Kemang Food Festival** on Saturdays for cheap eats, while older, more refined groups dine at one of the dozens of places along Jl. Kemang Raya.

Most clubs have live music on the weekends, with the clubbing scene starting late and finishing much later. Large groups of rabble-rousers head home just as the rest of the city is rising. **Eastern Promise**, a local icon, has a large stage area, a bar and plenty of seating, while **365 Ecobar** prides itself on its DJs. **Elbow Room**, a self-proclaimed gastro pub, has a bar upstairs where live bands play until late.

For parents, Kemang has more kid-friendly shops and entertainment stops per square kilometer than any other Jakarta neighborhood, with **Playparq** and **The Playground** being two of the best play spots.

The Kemang walk is not about getting somewhere; it's about going nowhere but enjoying every minute of it. There are no museums, no waterslides and no statues of muscular men in loincloths carrying burning pizzas. There are, instead, pleasant shaded lanes used by families for early morning strolls. As many of the opulent abodes are up for rent, have a look around one and make Kemang your home. To get plugged into the expat social scene, pop into the **Jakarta International Community Center**.

During the walk, keep a look out for **joggers**, or better still, families of cyclists (a rarity in Jakarta); **a horse and cart** filled with children and **pet fish for sale** in plastic bags hanging from bicycles and pushcarts. Also watch for **frangipani flowers** drying on racks, **mussel vendors** offering up fishy snacks and the *kaki limas* selling ever-tasty *toge goreng*, a bowl of bean sprouts, orange tofu, green onions and peanut sauce. Check the trees from time to time for birds, squirrels and little lizards.

Despite the residents' wealth, little money has been put into making the main streets pedestrian-friendly. In other words, though Kemang is an oasis in Jakarta, it is still Jakarta.

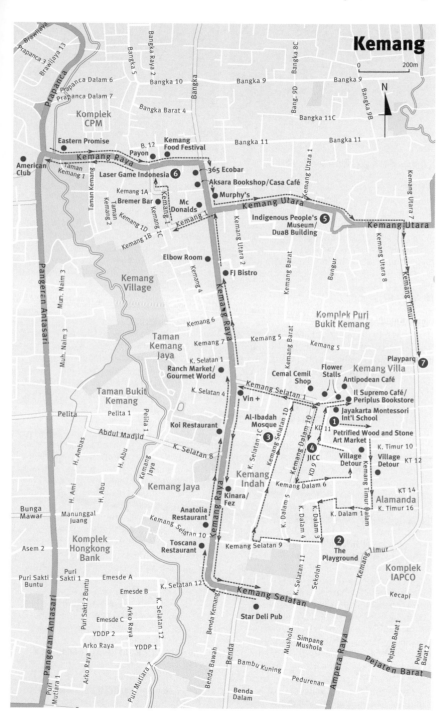

A frangipani collector showing off his flowers.

Traveling vendor with locally grown fruit.

WHO? Anyone can do this walk, and it's one of the more children-friendly.

HOW LONG? The walk should take 1.5 hours at most if you stroll straight through. But what's the hurry? Take your time, talk to as many people along the way as you can and occasionally daydream on an empty bench.

HOW FAR? 3.5km.

GETTING STARTED Enter Kemang via Jl. Kemang Raya. Turn right at the T-junction, pass McDonalds on the right and continue on to Jl. Kemang Selatan I on the left. There should be a sign for Hero Supermarket and Amigos Restaurant indicating a left turn. Drive down to Hero and park there.

1 PETRIFIED WOOD AND STONE ART MARKET

If you are read for a coffee, drop into the **Antipodean Café** in the Hero Supermarket arcade for a strong brew and breakfast or try **Il Supremo Café** next door in the **Periplus Bookshop**, which also has excellent coffee (try the mint mocha) and pastries straight from a German bakery. With the caffeine buzzing, head back up Jl. Kemang Selatan I to the flower stalls on the left. Turn left here, passing the **Sekolah Internasional Jayakarta Montessori** (Jayakarta Montessori School), and take the first left at the crossroads. On this corner there is an informal market selling **petrified wood and stone art products**.

Continue up this road (Jl. Kemang Dalam XI) to the T-junction and turn right on to Jl. Kemang Timur Dalam. Just up the road on the right is a small **Muslim cemetery**. There is not much to see inside, but it's interesting that this plot of land has survived the onslaught of construction around it. Continue past the cemetery. Passing

Jl. Kemang Timur XII, watch for a mosque on the left beside a small graveyard.

As a tiny side detour, you can go up to the end of this lane to see **squirrels**, **chickens** and **birds in cages**. Back on the main road, continue on to Jl. Kemang Dalam I and turn right. Follow Jl. Kemang Dalam I until it reaches a T-junction, turn right, go up a short way and take the first left on to Jl. Kemang Dalam IV.

2 THE PLAYGROUND

Watch for the **small vegetable market** that is generally bustling early in the morning. Then continue on to Jl. Kemang Dalam III and turn left. Follow this road to Jl. Kemang Dalam IIIB. Parents and children can check out **The Playground**, which sits up this road on the right.

3 AL-IBADAH MOSQUE

Continue along Jl. Kemang Dalam III to the Puskesmas Health Clinic on the left. Take the narrow lane on the right to the four-way intersection. Cross the intersection and take the second right at the Putra Tehnik shop. This is Jl. Kemang Selatan ID. Look at the first house to the left here, since it's where frangipani collectors often dry their flowers, which they later sell by the kilogram to factories in East Java. As the road continues, it does a small zigzag and then shoots straight until it ends in a T-junction at Jl. Kemang Selatan I. Along the way it will pass the lovely green-tiled **Masjid Al-Ibadah** (Al-Ibadah Mosque) with its stained-glass windows.

4 JAKARTA INTERNATIONAL COMMUNITY CENTER

Turn right at Jl. Kemang Selatan I, watching for the cozy **Cemal Cemil** on the left selling old-fashioned toys, sweets and crockery. Then

Exterior of Dua 8, the Indigenous People's Museum.

turn right at the next corner, Jl. Kemang Dalam X, where the **flower stalls** are located. Along the way, check out the **Jakarta International Community Center** (#E6A), which is an excellent resource for those just settling into the city and looking for language courses, help with the kids, domestic staff assistance or ways to make friends (www. jicconline.com). Follow this road to a four-way intersection, with the Posyandu Nusa Indah on the right.

Turn left up Jl. Kemang Dalam VI and follow the road bending left into Jl. Kemang Dalam VIII. Follow it until it ends in a T-junction. The **ambassador's residence for Papua New Guinea** is right ahead. Turn right here and follow the road back to the flower market from which you started.

At the flower market, buy some gerbera flowers to freshen up your kitchen, then grab a *bajaj* or walk back up Jl. Kemang Selatan I until it reaches the main road, Jl. Kemang Raya. Cross the street to the **Ranch Market** supermarket with the **Gourmet World** restaurant upstairs. Go inside to soak up some air-conditioning, pound a beer and indulge in a fine meal. Or turn to the left to Vin+ for a reviving bowl of tomato soup and a four-cheese pizza.

> ### HEADS UP
> Passing cars will honk at you. If it's a taxi, the driver is trying to get your attention. If it's a private car, the driver is sending a message that he is coming up on you. Generally, drivers are not telling you to get out of the way, as long as you aren't in the middle of the road.

ADDITIONAL DIVERSIONS

5 INDIGENOUS PEOPLE'S MUSEUM

Gedung Dua8 (The Indigenous People's Museum) is definitely one of the best museums in the city, probably because it's not government owned. Located in a modern glass building, the museum spreads over five floors that are connected by stairways and ramps. Representing around 20 indigenous peoples, this museum has excellent displays of art and everyday tools that come from far-flung locales, such as Timor, Sumba and Papua.

Tour through a maze of wood carvings, baskets, jewelry, spectacular weaponry, pottery, textiles, masks, drums and frightening body-length costumes. As all the displays are written in Indonesian, guided tours are recommended. The museum also has a library with more than 1,500 books in five languages on Indonesian arts and culture.

WHERE TO GO Gedung Dua8 on Jl. Kemang Utara. Look for the 'Dua8' sign.

CHECK OUT www.gedungdua8.com

Jl. Kemang Timur is a long road lined with furniture and antique shops. Many of the places are also workshops, with the carpenters working out front. Shops stock everything from busted-up secondhand pieces to gorgeous, artistic, one-of-a-kinds and many are willing to take custom orders. Plan to bring something home since it's hard to pass up on a rocking chair, secondhand trunk or tiny stool, though prepare to bargain. Keep in mind that this stretch is not particularly enjoyable to walk along with all the automobiles and cruddy sidewalk.

HOW TO GET THERE Enter the street from either Jl. Kemang Selatan or Jl. Kemang Utara.

Although not technically in Kemang, the **American Club** is a great place for sports and social gatherings. It also hosts the **Jakarta Players**, an amateur acting troupe that puts on performances throughout the year. For those who starred in a high school production of *Romeo and Juliet* but haven't been back to the stage since then, try the club's informal drama circles on the last Friday of each month. They are open to anyone, regardless of experience.

WHERE TO GO Jl. Brawijaya IV #20.

CHECK OUT www.amclubjakarta.org

GETTING FED AND DRUNK The following is a snapshot of the many places to eat and drink in Kemang. Be warned, however, that most bars and restaurants still cater to smokers.

Payon (Jl. Kemang Raya 17) is one of the best spots in the city for affordable Javanese cuisine. It has an excellent indoor/outdoor atmosphere (which comes with biting mosquitoes), and offers traditional Indonesian music in the evenings. Try the house specialty, *iga bakar* (barbequed ribs).

The **Koi Restaurant** (Jl. Kemang Raya 72; www.koiindonesia.com) is one of two branches in town and is renowned for its great food and drinks, pleasant staff and buzzing atmosphere. The space also hosts a furniture gallery, which sells many pieces made from reclaimed wood.

For excellent Indian food, don't miss **Kinara** (Jl. Kemang Raya 78B, www.kinara.co.id). With candlelit tables, arched doorways and a central pool, the décor and ambience make it a special place to dine. After dinner, move downstairs to sports bar **Fez by Aphrodite** to shoot some pool.

To sink your teeth into some upscale Turkish food, try **Anatolia** (Jl. Kemang Raya 110A), which makes a succulent *kasarli kofte* meatball and a delightful *baklava* as a finale. Plunk down in the *shisha* lounge after and kick back for an hour or two. Vegetarians are well catered to here.

One of the best kept secrets, until now, is **FJ Bistro**, hidden away behind the Fj'L boutique (Jl. Kemang Raya 25, www.fjljakarta.com). This bistro offers a posh dining experience with excellent fare, such as pulled pork with spinach, and fine drinks. The smoking area toward the back is also divinely decked out, enough so that even a non-smoker may be enticed to be seated there.

When someone suggests Italian, someone else should suggest **Toscana** (Jl. Kemang Raya 120; www.toscana-italianrestaurant.com), which has been catering to a mixed crowd of Indonesians and expats for nearly 15 years. In a city where a glass of wine can now break the bank, Toscana tries to ensure that bottles are reasonably priced.

Eastern Promise (Jl. Kemang Raya 5) is the top spot to load up on curries followed by mass quantities of beer. With a friendly atmosphere where everybody seems to know each other, it's the perfect place for an after-work drink. The main bar caters to men over 50 wearing polo shirts, but you can also escape to the bar out back which has a stage and hosts bands on the weekends. Check out 'Free-beer Fridays' from 5pm to 6pm when everyone drinks for free until someone leaves to pee. There is also a dining section where they serve excellent Indian grub, so tuck into a curry and smile.

Murphy's Irish Pub and Restaurant (Jl. Kemang Raya 11; www.murphysjakarta.com) is a new addition to the Kemang Raya strip. The clientele is more of a mix than Eastern Promise and the band sets up in the corner. Quiz nights happen weekly and happy hour keeps the prices reasonable. It's not the hippest spot in town yet, but it has

Walking and cycling through relatively quiet residential streets is one of Kemang's attractions.

potential. It has a well polished all-wood interior which gives it a classier feel.

Bremer Beer House (Jl. Kemang I, next to Little Baghdad) boasts a great off-street, outdoor seating area with big beers at small prices. A bit off the beaten track, a young, laid-back crowd frequents this joint.

GETTING A GOOD READ AND COFFEE

Aksara Bookstore (Jl. Kemang Raya 8B; www.aksara.com) has a good selection of graphic novels, great local music, cool gifts and unique home accoutrements. Head upstairs to the all-smoking **Casa Café** to enjoy a drink in what feels like an Indonesian living room from the 1960s. People come here to see and be seen while having something light to eat (try the carrot cake).

Antipodean Café (Kemang Selatan I, Hero Kemang Complex; www.antipodean coffee.com) is a convenient and comfy café with great coffee, delightful pastries and a smoke-free environment. It's a small place with a well-stocked menu scrawled on a giant blackboard. It's a good place to run into friends and neighbors if you live in the area.

Il Supremo Café, inside the **Periplus Bookshop** (Kemang Selatan I, Hero Kemang Complex), is a good place to burrow into a newly purchased read. The coffee is excellent and loads of treats are available. Although the wi-fi connected coffee shop is tiny, it is a suitable place to wile away an entire day.

WHERE TO SEND THE KIDS

6 LASER GAME INDONESIA

(Kemang Raya 16A; www.laser gameindonesia.com) is a family-friendly version of paintball that doesn't leave kids with welts the size of baseballs and covered in mosquito bites. This competitive game requires players to strap on vests with built-in sensors, arm themselves with laser shooting shotguns and race around a maze of walls and obstacles, trying to shoot their enemies.

7 PLAYPARQ

Playparq (Kemang Timur 72; www.playparq. com) is a favorite spot for moms and their little ones. An outdoor water world with fountains, slides and various playground equipment complements the trampoline and mini ferris wheel inside. Moms are well taken care of in the café, which comes complete with wi-fi.

Playparq's main competitor is **The Playground** (Kemang Dalam IIIB B6), which also offers good quality play equipment in a pleasant and safe environment. The highlight is the site's outdoor space, which includes a track that kids can bicycle and rollerblade on, a playground, a flying fox and basketball hoops. Tennis lessons are available, as are areas that can be rented out for barbecues or birthday parties. An attached café has a decent menu for when hunger strikes.

Walking Tour 17

PONDOK INDAH

A Wonderful Stroll through Parks in Jakarta's Most Elite Neighborhood

1. **Alam Segar Park I**
2. **Alam Elok Park V**
3. **Alam Elok Park VII**
4. **Kartika Alam Park II**
5. **Gedung Pinang Park**
6. **Pinang Merah Park**
7. **Posko Gedung Hijau Park**
8. **Hijau Baru Park**
9. **Bukit Hijau Park**
10. **Pondok Indah Plaza II**
11. **Puspita Park**
12. **Kencana Permai Park and Terrasering Park**
13. **Patung Kuda Park and Duta Niaga Park**
14. **Jakarta International School**
15. **Golf Hill Park**
16. **Water Park**
17. **International Sports Club of Indonesia**
18. **Kite Museum**

Pondok Indah (Beautiful Cottage) was originally home to a fig plantation, but in the 1970s it began its transformation into the suburban spread it is today. Long dominated by well-off expats (estimated at roughly 70 percent), this neighborhood is divided into east and west halves and comprises more than 50 small parks, wide leafy lanes populated with children on bicycles, at least 26 different chirping bird species and a plethora of ostentatious mansions with Romanesque columns and showy domes. Most of the streets are locked down at night by guard posts, but by day you are free to roam.

One thing that sets Pondok Indah apart is that its roughly 12,000 residents seem to care for the community as a whole, rather than just their personal plot of land. This sense of both camaraderie and civic duty has kept the area clean, well tended and safe. The back streets are generally quiet and light on traffic, and a 'no burn' rule that prohibits residents from burning leaves and garbage is adhered to better than in most neighborhoods. The parks are meeting places rather than dumping grounds, and the recently formed Pondok Indah Green Map Community has produced a map outlining the best green go-to spots.

This walking tour kicks off just outside one of the city's premier malls, **Mal Pondok Indah II** (Pondok Indah Mall II). From here it wends its way through a lovely leafy neighborhood, stringing 18 postage stamp-sized parks together. Stop off at **De Hooi** for a great bite to eat and a cocktail before strolling up the road to **Flower Park**, one of the most popular parks in Pondok Indah with early morning Tai Chi and playground equipment for the kids. Once the tour hits the **Jakarta International School**, those with an adventurous spirit can walk among the banana trees while skirting the **Kali Grogol** (Grogol Canal).

Near the end of the walk is **Bukit Golf**, a lavish neighborhood lined with fruit trees and ensconced within a golf course. Here, statues of galloping horses adorn front lawns and Porsches and Hummers line the driveways. For those with endurance, the walk comes full circle after twisting through more down to earth neighborhoods peppered with little parks.

WHO? Anyone can do this walk, but note its length (12km), so perhaps only the fittest will be able to complete the entire stretch.

HOW LONG? The full walk should take five to six hours. Breaking it up into two or three more manageable sections is also recommended. It's also very bicycle-friendly, so oil

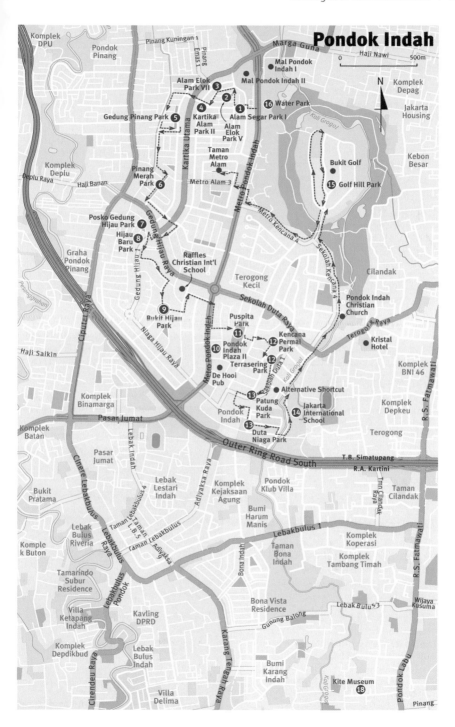

your chain, grab your helmet and get back
on the banana seat.

HOW FAR? 12km.

Pondok Indah is connected to central and
west Jakarta by Busway Corridor #8, as well
as by the Outer Ring Road and Jl. Sultan
Iskandar Muda. Drivers can park at Mal
Pondok Indah II. Those coming by bicycle
or walking, can begin the walk just to the
left of the PIM II parking entrance on
Jl. Metro Pondok Indah II, which is almost
directly across from the Busway stop.

1 ALAM SEGAR PARK I
Walk under the black and white gate pole,
which should be raised, and continue
straight until reaching the first park, **Taman
Alam Segar I** (Fresh Nature Park I). To enter,
turn right and immediately left, going up
Jl. Alam Elok I. Turn left again and you'll see
the entrance. This park has a lily and fish
pond, basketball and badminton courts,
swings, lots of trees, dark red dragonflies
and is great for bird watching. Watch out
for the horse and cart, which offers rides.

> ## FAST FACT
> For those who want to do some birding, be
> on the lookout for the Olive-backed Sunbird,
> Red-breasted Parakeet, Plaintive Cockatoo,
> Yellow-bellied Sunbird, Straw-headed Robin,
> Scaly-breasted Munia and Pacific Swallow.

2 ALAM ELOK PARK V
Exit the park the same way you entered and
turn right, going up Jl. Alam Elok III. On the
left is **Taman Alam Elok V** (Pleasant Nature
Park V), which can be circled before moving
on. Continue along Jl. Alam Elok III, turning
left at the next street, Jl. Alam Elok VI. As you
turn the corner, note the wicked shards of
glass lining the exterior wall of house UXI
to the right.

3 ALAM ELOK PARK VII
Walk up the street and on the right will be
Taman Alam Elok VII (Pleasant Nature
Park VII). It has a tiny grove of old-growth
trees with newer trees planted around
them. Take a close look to find that many
may be bearing fruit, depending on the
season.

A quick note at this point. It's easy to just
cruise through these parks, but take the time
to sit down once in a while and chill out. It's
only then that you'll notice all the lizards,
butterflies, birds and small critters stirring
about.

4 KARTIKA ALAM PARK II
Continue following Jl. Alam Elok VI as it
hooks to the left and moves toward the triangular **Taman Kartika Alam II** (Star Nature
Park II). Turn right and follow the road, crossing a mildly busier one, as it turns into Jl.
Pinang Perak IV. Go straight until reaching a
wall flanking a waterway. Turn left and follow
the little path, which parallels a nice canal
and comes loaded with plants, trees, birds
and butterflies. As you walk along, note the
little bridge to the right that leads into the
adjacent *kampung*. Feel free to cross over and
explore the vibrancy of the neighborhood.

5 GEDUNG PINANG PARK
Continue along the path until it ends at the
Pos Keamanan (Security Post) and turn left,
going one block to **Taman Gedung Pinang**
(Betel Nut House Park). Circle around or cut
through this park and return back to the path
at the Pos Keamanan.

Canal-side footpath in Pondok Indah.

6 PINANG MERAH PARK

Continue walking along the canal on Jl. Pinang Perak I, catching glimpses of *kampung* life to the right. Follow the road as it veers to the left. Turn right at **Taman Pinang Merah** (Red Betel Nut Park), which runs along Jl. Taman Pinang Merah Barat. Follow this road to its terminus and turn left, going up Jl. Kartika Pinang. At the intersection of Jl. Metro Alam I and Jl. Kartika Utama, turn right and follow this busy road, going under an archway that reads 'Selamat Jalan–Terima Kasih' (Thank you–Bon Voyage).

7 POSKO GEDUNG HIJAU PARK; 8 HIJAU BARU PARK; 9 BUKIT HIJAU PARK

Keep going straight, around the roundabout, then pass the ordinary **Posko Taman Gedung Hijau** (Green House Post Park) on the right. Cross the street (Jl. Gedung Hijau I) to check out the row of *kaki limas* for some street food. Then continue along Jl. Gedung Hijau I, noting the tiny **Taman Hijau Baru** (New Green Park) on the left, before turning left on Jl. Bukit Hijau II. Turn right when the road hooks to the right and follow it to **Taman Bukit Hijau** (Green Hill Park). The park is circular and crammed with trees, which makes for good bird watching. A peripatetic vendor often sells organic vegetables here and Tai Chi groups gather early in the morning.

> ### HEADS UP
> Bird watchers need to get here early as the birds are much more active in the early hours and can be difficult to spot as the day progresses.

Next, take Jl. Taman Bukit Hijau III to where it meets Jl. Taman Bukit Hijau VIII. Turn left and walk up the road. **Sekolah Kristen Internasional Raffles** (Raffles Christian International School) will be on the left. Turn right on Jl. Metro Hijau II, which is one road before the main road. Go straight until hitting the very busy Jl. Metro Pondok Indah. Turn left, go up to the intersection, cross to the other side of the street and turn right, going along Jl. Metro Pondok Indah until reaching Jl. Metro Duta on the left.

10 PONDOK INDAH PLAZA II

Now it's time for another break. Stop in at **Pondok Indah Plaza II**, which offers both Asian and Western cuisine. Depending on the time, pop into **De Hooi Pub**, which is arguably the best bar in south Jakarta. With live music, open mic nights, good drink specials and solid grub, it's good for an early breakfast or late night double shot. Find it set back in Pondok Indah Plaza 2, right next door to Pondok Indah Plaza 1.

11 PUSPITA PARK

Continue up Jl. Metro Duta, past the hospital on the right, until reaching a gaggle of *kaki limas*, which are parked in front of **Taman Puspita** (Puspita Park), the best park on the tour. It boasts a community building, benches, trellises, jogging paths and playground equipment that make it a great spot for kids, readers, nappers and walkers. To catch the park at its busiest, be here between 5am and 7am. Anyone that rocks up mid-morning will pretty much have the place to themselves.

> ### HEADS UP
> For those who have never eaten a fried snack from a street vendor, now is the chance. A good bet is *pisang goreng* (fried bananas). They are cheap and tasty energy boosters. Keep on the lookout for one of these guys rolling his cart around or parked under a nice, leafy tree, just waiting for you.

12 KENCANA PERMAI PARK AND TERRASERING PARK

Exit the park opposite the side from which you entered. Turn left and then an immediate right, going up Jl. Duta Permai I. At the tiny triangular **Taman Kencana Permai** (Kencana Permai Park), give the big old beautiful tree a hug and then hook right, walking along Jl. Sekolah Duta II. Turn left on Jl. Duta Permai VII and follow this road until reaching the oblong-shaped **Taman Terrasering** (Terrasering Park). Play King of the Mountain on the short little walls in the park, and keep an eye out for the dog trainers and bird watchers if you are here early enough.

13 PATUNG KUDA PARK AND DUTA NIAGA PARK

Take Jl. Sekolah Duta I and head right on it to **Taman Patung Kuda** (Horse Statue Park), where there is a chunky, rough-looking statue of a man on a stallion. Continue along Jl. Sekolah Duta I until Jl. Duta Indah III and turn left. Follow this road to Jl. Duta Niaga and turn right. Follow this road past **Taman Duta Niaga** (Trade Ambassador Park), then turn left on Jl. Duta Niaga III. Take it until it terminates at the canal.

From here there are two choices. The first is to turn left on Jl. Duta Indah, then left again on Jl. Duta Niaga I, a road lined by a retaining wall and wall of bamboo trees. Then backtrack past Taman Patung Kuda, this time turning right on Jl. Duta Indah III. This will lead to Kali Grogol (Grogol Canal) which you should follow to the left using a dirt path.

14 JAKARTA INTERNATIONAL SCHOOL

The second choice, for the more intrepid, is to turn right and watch for the break in the fence, just before the bridge that crosses over to the **Jakarta International School**. Take a few steps down to a cement retaining wall that forms a path you can follow along the canal. When the wall ends, walk/scramble along the dirt path and through the tall grass and banana trees until emerging about five minutes later where Jl. Duta Indah meets the grassy strip along the canal.

Either way, continue on the makeshift path along the canal, enjoying a slice of nature. Eventually, the path will end at the Pos Keamanan on Jl. Duta Indah I. Go up Jl. Duta Indah I, which is parallel to the canal, and in a few moments you'll reach the busy Jl. Sekolah Duta I. Cross the road, turn left and take an immediate right. Follow this road, Jl. Sekolah Kencana IV, past the SMU Tirta Marta Christian School and the **Gereja Kristen Pondok Indah** (Pondok Indah Christian Church). A sidewalk will appear on the left for a short ways, just after the church. Continue until the road comes to a T-junction, then turn right on to Jl. Bukit Golf.

15 GOLF HILL PARK

Follow the signs to enter the **Bukit Golf** complex, which is surrounded by a golf course, and enjoy the peace and quiet that only money can buy. Take Jl. Bukit Golf Utama on the left, and at the end of the road watch for a number of frolicking horse statues and some rocks sporting biblical quotes. At the top of the road, follow it to

the right and head back down Jl. Bukit Golf II. There are five main roads here, each lined with a variety of fruit trees, including rambutan, star fruit, mango and mangosteen. At the confluence of Jl. Bukit Golf I and II is **Taman Bukit Golf** (Golf Hill Park). This micro-neighborhood is a good place for jogging, tooling around on a bicycle or bird watching.

Exit the complex along Jl. Bukit Golf and go straight until the road turns into Jl. Metro Kencana IV. Follow this road until it terminates at the incredibly busy Jl. Metro Pondok Indah. You can either take a taxi down to the roundabout and then back up to Pondok Indah Mall I (PIM I), or you can walk there along Jl. Metro Pondok Indah. Once you reach PIM I, cross the road via the mall's skybridge to PIM II. For those who want to walk more, go with the traffic from PIM I to Jl. Metro Alam III and turn left. From here, you can wend and weave your way back up through the neighborhood, popping back out at **Taman Alam Segar I**.

Note: An excellent walking guide to Pondok Indah, which highlights all the green spaces, bird watching sites, flower gardens and more, can be found on their very own Peta Hijau (Green Map). For a copy, contact Ricky Lestari at rickylestari@gmail.com or Roosie Setiawan at roosie.setiawan@yahoo.com or call 021 684 65892 for the Green Map Jakarta office.

THE PONDOK INDAH SUPPLEMENT

Mal Pondok Indah I and II, which are connected by two double-decker skybridges, are some of the best malls in the city, as they are approachable, fun and friendly places to shop. PIM II is considered to be the more upscale version of the siblings while PIM I has more down-to-earth shopping opportunities. PIM I was built in 1991, making it one of the first big malls in Jakarta. PIM II was added in 2004.

WHERE TO GO Jl. Metro Pondok Indah.

CHECK OUT www.pondokindahmall.co.id

16 WATER PARK

Water Park is a low-key water park that is easy to get to and offers a solid afternoon of splish-splash fun, although it is not as developed as some of the city's other big water attractions.

WHERE TO GO Jl. Metro Pondok Indah Blok 3B, next to PIM I Mall.

WHO TO CALL 021 7506750 ext. 128/144

17 INTERNATIONAL SPORTS CLUB OF INDONESIA

For those with cash to flash and a love of sports, the **International Sports Club of Indonesia** is one of the best spots in the city for indoor and outdoor workouts. Located a short distance south of Pondok Indah, ISCI is a private club set on five hectares of land and boasting more than 12 sports facilities. Try taekwondo, badminton, football, squash, rugby or netball. There are also eight tennis courts and five squash courts for those who want to raise a racquet. On the weekend, the KidzKlub offers loads of tyke-friendly activities for families.

At one point, there was a full lake behind ISCI where you could do a bit of sailing, though due to an accidental draining of the lake this hasn't been possible for some time. Repairs are ongoing, though, and hopefully it will be full once again.

WHERE TO GO Jl. Ciputat Raya #2 (some maps may say Jl. Ir. H. Juanda).

HOW TO GET THERE From PIM I and II head south on Jl. Metro Pondok Indah, crossing under the toll road. It will be on the left, just off Jl. Kertamukti.

CHECK OUT www.isci-jakarta.com

Just a step out of Pondok Indah is the Kristal Hotel, which often holds lectures supported by **Go Wild! Indonesia**. Three British men formed the non-profit group in 2009 to host discussions and lead adventure trips around Jakarta, as well as further flung locales. In the past, they have ventured up rivers, trudged through mangrove forests and trekked into national parks during trips to Komodo Island, Gunung Halimun National Park, the Thousand Islands and Kalimantan among others.

The lectures at the Kristal Hotel are given by experts in their fields, and can be on anything from Sumatran elephants to diving in West Papua. For more on Go Wild! events, check out its website (www.gowildindo.multiply.com). After the talk, grab a cold one at the **Satu Lagi** bar.

The Kite Museum exhibit across the country.

WHERE TO GO The Kristal Hotel, Jl. Terogong Raya, Cilandak Barat.

18 KITE MUSEUM

The **Museum Layang-Layang** (Kite Museum) makes for a fun afternoon, as it's set in lovely surroundings with a nice courtyard, lots of greenery and a swimming pool. Visitors can watch a kite video, take a tour (available in English), make their own kite or paint an umbrella, ceramic creation or a shirt to take home.

The indoor/outdoor museum boasts an extensive collection of kites from around Indonesia, as well as other Asian countries and beyond. Giant ones hang outside in wonderful designs, such as a horse-pulled cart, a dragonfly and a cyclist. There are fighting kites from Kalimantan, batik kites from Solo, a Peacock Queen Dancer kite from West Java, stunt kites, kites used to kill bats, fishing kites and what might be the world's smallest kite at the size of a Rp500 coin. Many kites are made from leaves, banana tree bark, pineapple fibers and Swedish duck feathers.

In an adjacent building, the owner showcases a private collection of cloth from around the archipelago, as well as some statues, furniture and a carriage.

WHERE TO GO Jl H. Kamang #38, Pondok Labu, a short way south of Pondok Indah.

HOW TO GET THERE Come by taxi or grab a bus at the top of Jl. R. S. Fatmawati and ride it southward, getting off at Jl. H. Kamang. For drivers, head south on Jl. Fatmawati, cross under the Outer Ring Road, and the museum will be on the right, just past Swadarma University and the BNI Building.

Walking Tour 18

RAGUNAN ZOO

A Family-friendly Walk on the Wild Side through the Spacious Wooded Grounds of the Zoo

1. **North Entrance**
2. **Schmutzer Primate Center**
3. **Children's Zoo**
4. **Ragunan Orchid Garden**
5. **Ministry of Agriculture Park**

Ragunan Zoo is undoubtedly one of the best excursions in Jakarta. With 140 hectares of green space, the zoo offers plenty of activities as well as the opportunity to take a breather from the city for those who don't have the time or the means to take a trip further afield.

Visitors to Ragunan can get much closer to the animals than a Western zoo might allow and those who come early enough may even see some uncaged animals, such as an elephant or giraffe, grazing the facility's lawns. The zoo has the usual array of wildlife, but some of the more famous residents are the **Malayan sun bear**, **Sumatran tiger**, **Komodo dragon**, **Sumatran elephant**, **western lowland gorilla**, **orangutan** and **hippo**. It shouldn't be hard to find your personal favorite from the more than 3,500 creatures here. Get into the **Tourist Forest** for a nice solitary stroll amongst the trees.

For additional entertainment, try paddling around in a **swan boat**, attending an **animal show**, taking a **camel**, **horse** or **elephant ride** or heading to the **Children's Zoo**. Once your legs have worn out, rent a **pony cart** or hop on the **zoo train**. Cycling is another option. In the early mornings, you can ride free and fast, enjoying the kilometers of paths, fresh air and the animals at their liveliest.

An accordion busker entertains zoo visitors.

> ### *FAST FACT*
> The zoo is one of the best places in the city to run. The Jakarta Free Spirit running group gathers here on Saturdays at 6.30am (www.jakartafreespirit.org).

NOTE The afternoon is when it's hottest, the animals sleepiest and the crowds thickest, so come early to see the animals in action.

WHO? This is the No. 1 family-friendly walk, though it's also appropriate for lovers, single nomads and groups of friends. It's excellent also for cyclists, joggers and runners.

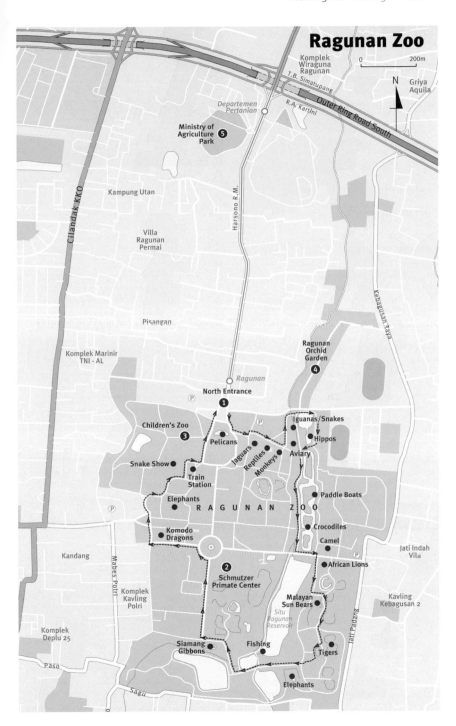

Ragunan Zoo

Komplek
Wiraguna
Ragunan

T.B. Simatupang

Griya
Aquila

0   200m

N

Departemen
Pertanian

R.A. Kartini

Outer Ring Road South

Ministry of
Agriculture 5
Park

Kampung Utan

Harsono R.M.

Villa
Ragunan
Permai

Pisangan

Kebagusan Raya

Komplek Marinir
TNI - AL

Ragunan
Orchid
Garden 4

Cilandak KKO

Ragunan

North Entrance
1

Children's Zoo
3

Pelicans

Iguanas / Snakes

Hippos

Jaguars

Reptiles

Aviary

Snake Show

Monkeys

Train
Station

Paddle Boats

Elephants

R A G U N A N   Z O O

Komodo
Dragons

Crocodiles

Camel

Jati Indah
Vila

Kandang

Mabes Polri

African Lions

Schmutzer
Primate Center
2

Kavling
Kebagusan 2

Komplek
Kavling
Polri

Malayan
Sun Bears

Komplek
Deplu 25

Situ
Ragunan
Reservoir

Jati Padang

Paso

Siamang
Gibbons

Fishing

Tigers

Sagu

Elephants

HOW LONG? This walk should take around four hours, although it all depends on the amount of meandering and stamina you have. Bring a bicycle or rent one there to speed things up.

HOW FAR? 4km at a minimum.

GETTING THERE The zoo is located at Jl. Harsono R. M. 1 in Pasar Minggu. Take Busway #6 to the Kebon Binatang Ragunan stop. Drivers should take Jl. Harsono to its terminus at the zoo. Parking depends on the crowds, though a large lot is available.

GETTING IN Opening hours are 7am to 5pm daily.

GETTING STARTED To get in, buy the cheap entrance ticket and be sure to request one of their poorly printed maps if you have somewhere specific you want to go.

1 NORTH ENTRANCE

Enter at **Pintu Masuk Utara** (North Entrance Gate) and watch for the big map straight ahead to get oriented. Turn left at the sign, passing a cute garden to the left and Pintu Keluar Utara I. Just to the right is the well-done **pelicans** enclosure and some massive trees that hint at what the jungle must have looked like here before the bulldozers came through.

Follow the path as it curves and watch for the brick road to the left (it's marked with a 'do not enter' sign prohibiting vehicles only). Head up this lane, viewing the **raccoons** off to the left. Just behind them are the largest of the rare **civet cats**, the **binturong**. Off to the right are **jaguars**, followed by some green buildings that house the terrariums for **turtles**, **lizards**, **snakes** and other **reptiles**. Past the reptiles are four circular **monkey** cages. Far off to the left is a row of *warungs*, useful for feeding any hungry humans.

After the monkeys, look for a road with a directional signpost listing various big name animals such as lions and hippos. Follow the road to the left until you reach the **aviary** on the right. Just across from here is an interesting enclosure packed with a writhing mass of **iguana/snakes**. It can be tricky to see them at first, though, so take the time to let your eyes see them all. The keepers toss guinea pigs in as prey which can be interesting to watch.

Jaguars are among the big cats at the zoo.

Take the path past this enclosure (keeping the enclosure on the right), and it will curve to the right, leading to the **hippos**. Continue to the far side of the hippo lake and walk until reaching some blocks that look like Tetris game pieces and serve as a bridge over the water. Cross both sets of blocks to the main path and turn left.

Follow this path until the **sepeda air** (paddleboats) can be seen off to the left. Now you're in **crocodile** territory, where some particularly large individuals are laying in wait. Continue straight to the big T-junction. If a long version of the walk seems a bit daunting at this point, turn right and head toward the roundabout where the **primate center** is located. To stick to the long route, turn left toward the sun bears and tigers. Just past the lake, on the left and up the stairs, are the **camels**, across from which are the **African lions**. Running parallel to the outer wall is a path that goes past various **white tiger** enclosures. Up and on the right are the **Malayan sun bears**, which seem to suffer deplorable conditions in punishment for bearing the name of Indonesia's number one rival country—Malaysia.

> ### FAST FACT
> The Ragunan Zoo was founded in 1864 and originally located in central Jakarta, where Taman Ismail Marzuki now is. Later, in 1964, it was moved to its current position which gave it much more space.

Continue down the path but make sure not to miss the incredible **Sumatran tigers** on the left. Go down the stairs to the right and cross the road to where a large electricity tower is located. Check out the additional

A visitor to the zoo holding a snake.

Affectionate orang-utans at the primate center.

tigers on the other side and, at the white tiger enclosures, cross the path to see more African lions. At the front of the African lion cage descend the steps to a larger road. Turn left and go up the road, following it as it curves to the right. On the left will be some **elephants**. Go straight, past the **memancing** (fishing area), and follow the main road as it curves to the right. Listen for the yipping and yapping monkey calls as reassurance you are on the right track. The road will go uphill a bit, curve to the left and on the left are **siamang gibbons**, a type of ape (different from a monkey because they don't have a tail).

2 SCHMUTZER PRIMATE CENTER

Turn right here and walk straight along the road. At the roundabout, which sports a nice park and monkey statue, is the **Pusat Primata Schmutzer** (Schmutzer Primate Center). This center, which opened in 2002 to great fanfare, has 13 hectares all to itself. It was created in a unique way that allows visitors to feel like they're viewing the collection of great apes in their actual habitat (or as close to it as is manageable). Walk along the **canopy bridge** for views down into the ape enclosure, and then wander about the maze of walkways, which bring visitors face to face with an incredible array of primates. Afterward, check out the theater and museum for an extra dose of knowledge.

Food is not available in the primate center, so if you're feeling peckish, head to the other side of the roundabout and get some grub from the row of small *warungs* to keep energy levels high. From the *warungs*, head west to see the giant **Komodo dragons** and the **elephants** just behind them. Continue north, past the elephants, until reaching the zoo's **Stasiun Kerata** (mini-train station). Take

a ride on the wheeled train or check out the **Pertunjukan Ular** (snake exhibit) next door.

With a collection of impressively large snakes, this venue lets visitors hold, pet or take their picture with one of the creatures. The photos on the walls seem to assure parents of the safety in plunking their infants amid the massive coils of a python for a photo op. You can assume either the snakes here are so well fed they are not hungry enough to munch on visitors, or they have been drugged into a sluggish state.

3 CHILDREN'S ZOO

After the snake show, pass in front of the train station and turn left, going north past the **emus** and **kijang**, not only a type of deer, but also one of the most common brands of cars in Jakarta. Finally, on the left, is the **Children's Zoo**, just before the main gate where you first entered.

4 RAGUNAN ORCHID GARDEN

After departing, stop off at the plant sellers that line the street leading away from the zoo. Another option is to take the road to the right, which follows the zoo's outer wall. This leads to the mightily impressive **Taman Anggrek Ragunan** (Ragunan Orchid Garden), which contains an ocean of beautiful flowers, all for sale.

5 MINISTRY OF AGRICULTURE PARK

Note: If you don't want to enter the zoo but still want to stroll around the area, check out **Taman Departemen Pertanian** (Ministry of Agriculture Park). It's directly across from the Department of Agriculture, just a few minutes up Jl. Harsono R.M. from the zoo. It's free to enter, quiet and relatively unknown, so visitors should have plenty of elbow room. Bring the dog along for a run around.

Walking Tour 19

TAMAN MINI INDONESIA INDAH

A Family-friendly Day at Jakarta's Best Tourist Attraction: A Showcase of Indonesia's Incredible Diversity

1. **Golden Snail Flower Gardens**
2. **Asmat Museum**
3. **Freshwater Aquarium**
4. **Insect Museum**
5. **Heirloom Museum**
6. **Army Museum**
7. **Transportation Museum**
8. **Komodo Museum**
9. **Stamp Museum**
10. **Fishing Pond**
11. **Museum of Energy and Electricity**
12. **Oil and Gas Museum**
13. **Bird Park**
14. **Center for Science and Technology**
15. **Sky Gondola Station**
16. **Rare Books Market**
17. **Children's Palace**

Indonesia is the world's largest archipelago, stretching across an area as wide as the United States, and that's something to be proud of. Its 17,000 islands are home to an incredible array of ethnic groups, with their own distinctive cultures, as well as flora and fauna, but its vast size makes it difficult to see everything the country has to offer. Taman Mini Indah Indonesia (TMII) provides a taste, by highlighting the different indigenous cultures, dress and architecture. Opened in 1975 by Ibu Tien, the wife of President Suharto, the park aims to create a sense of pride and unity among Indonesians when they see the complex diversity of the country's 33 provinces.

Within the 165-hectare park is a plethora of activities, including cultural performances (such as *dangdut*), letting the kids go wild in

a **children's amusement park**, **taking a boat** around a miniature Indonesia, doing some tricks at the **Green Skate Park** and **BMX dirt track**, and checking out the park's most identifiable feature and singular piece of architecture, the giant **Golden Snail** that houses an **IMAX theater**.

Animal and plant life are exhibited here, and there is an **insect museum**, **reptile gardens**, **aviaries** and an **aquarium**, all quite well done and rewarding to stroll through. There are also some nicely landscaped green spaces boasting ten different gardens, including one solely for orchids. As a nod to Indonesia's religious pluralism, the park also has **places of worship** for Catholics, Protestants, Buddhists, Muslims and Hindus, which are all open to the public.

The buffet of cultural delights includes an excellent array of **traditional houses** packed with art, crafts, furniture and other accouterments. Most display mannequins in local dress, and often a guide will be on hand to provide additional information. While many of Indonesia's museums are fairly decrepit, understocked and underwhelming, some of the best ones are here in Taman Mini. Be sure to spend some time browsing any or all of the 14 on offer, which cover topics from stamps to science.

The options for getting around the park are also varied. Rent a tandem bicycle near the Imax Theater, ride the mini-train or monorail or take a leisurely ride up on the gondola. Conversely, if the sun is baking hot and you don't want to move another inch, take a break and cool off at **Snow Bay Water Park**.

Definitely try to get an early start as it can get quite hot and the crowds thick as the day progresses. Drink plenty of water and stop

regularly for fresh coconut juice, straight from the nut. There are also quite a few *warungs* spread out across the complex, so be sure to stop from time to time, take your shoes off, settle yourself down on one of the ground mats provided and bulk up on some fried rice or noodles.

Taman Mini can be overwhelming so don't try to do everything in one visit. In fact, it's best not to rush as it's a massive complex with an incredible array of activities and is worth many return visits. The following itinerary includes more than a dozen sites, which will require great stamina and energy to finish. Thus, the walk is only a suggested route and you should feel free to meander off at any time, skip certain locales, visit those not listed or even just spend the day reading a book in the flower gardens.

WHO? This is an excellent place for everyone, especially families.

HOW LONG? It should take from a half to a full day, though consider breaking the walk up over several visits.

HOW FAR? 4.5km if you stick to the path. Wandering around aimlessly could easily add a few more kilometers.

GETTING THERE Take Busway #7 to the Kampung Rambutan stop and then hop on a T15 Metro Mini to the front gates. Drivers can come via the Jagorawi toll road.

GETTING STARTED The walk starts at the path between the **Keong Emas** and the **Handicraft Center**. Don't do it now, but at some point check out one of the films at the **IMAX theater**. One of the regularly screened films takes viewers on a wonderfully scenic tour across the country, Discovery Channel style. Generally, films are in Indonesian with subtitles.

1 GOLDEN SNAIL FLOWER GARDENS

Head up the sidewalk on the right, watching for the **Kebun Bunga Keong Emas** (Golden Snail Flower Gardens). They are wonderfully landscaped with fountains and statues that tell the story of the Golden Snail, a tale that centers around a princess subject to an evil spell. Behind the flower gardens, visitors can rent a bicycle buggy to tool around on while kids can zip around in a mini *becak* on the nicely shaded path.

2 ASMAT MUSEUM

Just past the gardens is the **Museum Asmat** (Asmat Museum), a small, dimly lit but very cool museum about the Asmat people, an ethnic group from Papua famous for their wood carvings. It's one of the more peaceful places to pop into.

3 FRESHWATER AQUARIUM; 4 INSECT MUSEUM

Immediately next door is the **Akuarium Air Tawar** (Freshwater Aquarium), but be sure to check out the **Museum Serangga** (Insect

View the park from the sky gondola or monorail.

Museum) nearby. It includes a butterfly house, which can be a bit short on butterflies, as well as an artistic presentation of the country's mind-blowing array of insect life. Some of the critters on display are the size of a small bird, certainly not something you want crawling up your trouser leg.

5 HEIRLOOM MUSEUM
The **Museum Pusaka** (Heirloom Museum) is up next and contains Indonesia's widest array of *keris*, the magically infused, wavy-blade daggers famous across Southeast Asia for their connection to spirits and mysticism. On show are a diverse range of blades, sheaths, hilts and decorations. This type of thing isn't for everyone, so if time is running short, feel free to skip it.

6 ARMY MUSEUM
Following is the **Museum Keprajuritan** (Army Museum), which is housed in a castle-like fortress surrounded by a swampy moat. It's definitely worth a peek at the manne-quins inside, both male and female, cloaked in a wide variety of armor and warrior outfits and armed to the teeth. Each one represents a different tribe or region, and their dress is specific to the role they served in battle. Get up close and look one in the eye, study the eerily realistic facial hair and small wrinkles in the skin and think about whether you'd want to be trapped in here overnight.

7 TRANSPORTATION MUSEUM
Further on, the **Museum Transportasi** (Transportation Museum) displays the trains, planes and automobiles that move

the country's people and goods. It is more interesting for kids than adults, however, so skip it if you don't have little rug rats.

8 KOMODO MUSEUM
Pushing on, head to the **Museum Komodo** (Komodo Museum), wonderfully built in the shape of—what else—but a komodo. This cool attraction gets people up close and personal with the archipelago's fine range of reptiles and amphibians, including the Komodo drag-on, the world's largest lizard. Ever seen a snapping turtle eat a live baby chick? If you are lucky enough to be there at feeding time, this may be your chance.

9 STAMP MUSEUM
After seeing the ancient lizards, it's a bit hard to get excited about the next attraction, the **Museum Perangko** (Stamp Museum). But it's a dream for any philatelist. It's also a good opportunity to stroll through postal history and watch how the process of sending a letter has changed over time. Check out the display with the old mail-delivery bikes, which were used back when it actually meant something to be a postman.

10 FISHING POND; 11 MUSEUM OF ENERGY AND ELECTRICITY; 12 OIL AND GAS MUSEUM
At the very back of Taman Mini is the **Pemancingan Telaga Mina** (Fishing Pond), the largest of its kind in Jakarta. It is catch

A traditional house with a soaring roof.

A section of the gardens at the 165-hectare Taman Mini Indonesia Indah.

and release, with the point being fun and relaxation. Next door is the **Museum Listrik dan Energi Baru** (Museum of Energy and Electricity) and also the **Museum Minyak dan Gas Bumi** (Oil and Gas Museum). These museums may be of more interest to those who work in these sectors rather than the general public. But since they are not big visitor attractions, they can provide a good respite from the crowds.

13 BIRD PARK

Around on the northern side of the park is **Taman Burung** (Bird Park). There are several pleasant walk-in aviaries as well as caged birds. The grounds are quite pleasant and the birds look healthy. This is definitely a recommended stop-off, and a good place for kids to explore.

14 CENTER FOR SCIENCE AND TECHNOLOGY

From here, head into the central part of the park, just south of Taman Burung, to see the kid-focused **Pusat Peragaan Ilmu Pengetahuan dan Teknologi** (Center for Science and Technology). Some of the activities and displays are fairly tumble-down, or simply don't work anymore, but a number of them are quite entertaining. The center has a higher entrance fee than most places but it may be worth letting the kids run around inside for an hour trying out the different interactive offerings. Ride the bicycle mounted along a suspension wire.

15 SKY GONDOLA STATION

Now it's time for a break, so head to the **Stasiun Kereta Gantung** (Sky Gondola Station), which is where the sky gondolas are located. The trip along a suspension cable provides a wonderful view of the action below. The best part is sailing over an artificial lake modeled to look like a map of Indonesia in miniature. Note: The lines for the gondola can be long, so try riding it either early or late in the day.

16 RARE BOOKS MARKET

Back on the ground, just up from the gondola station near the Papua Pavilion, is the **Pasar Buku Langka** (Rare Books Market). In addition to some rather curious and remarkable old books (in a range of languages), magazines, comics, dictionaries and encyclopedias fill book stalls and outdoor tables. This is a great place to browse for those interested in old Indonesian documents.

17 CHILDREN'S PALACE

Complete the day by stopping at the traditional houses from Maluku, Sulawesi, Kalimantan and Aceh while walking back toward the parking lot. Although the kids will probably be tired, be sure to note the castle-shaped **Istana Anak-Anak** (Children's Palace) off to the left, which boasts an impressive display of fairy tale paintings from around the world.

CHECK OUT www.tamanmini.com

ADDITIONAL INFORMATION Buying the entrance ticket to get in is only the first step. Keep your wallet handy as you will need to pay a minimal fee for just about every single garden, museum, park or attraction you enter.

Walking Tour 20

MEKARSARI TOURISM PARK
A Leafy Day of Family Fun in a Giant Fruit Orchard

1. **Garden Center**
2. **Paradiso Park**
3. **Amusement Park**
4. **Central Park**
5. **Waterfall Building**
6. **Labyrinth Park**
7. **Durian Orchard**
8. **Water Zone**
9. **Water Park**
10. **Zona Family Walk**

Mekarsari is officially dubbed an 'Amazing Tourism Park'. This family-oriented attraction *is* rather 'amazing' in that it is a massive **264-hectare orchard** full of nature's own goodness. Not only is it green and buffeted by a nice cool breeze, dangling from most trees and vines is an extensive array of fruit. In fact, it is the cultivation of this very fruit that lies at the core of the park's existence. Mekarsari's spatial plan, best appreciated by looking at a map, is laid out like five giant, leaf-covered branches. Each branch, plus Central Park at the core, is an area with its own distinctive activities and feel: Family Walk Zone, Mediterranean Zone, Water Zone and Green Land Zone.

Visitors can either stroll or cycle the maze of roads and trails, passing through mangosteen, rose apple and starfruit **orchards**. Macadamia nuts, Brazil cherries, coffee and chocolate also grow on the grounds, as well as bigger fruit varieties such as durian and coconut. Some food stands have information about local produce and offer samples, including freshly made durian ice cream, chocolaty coffee and dried mango.

Of all the designated areas, the **Wisata Air** (Water Zone) is by far one of the most popular. You can ride a **banana boat** for

a bit of a laugh, take a short, laid-back cruise on a **dragon boat** or rent a **water bicycle** for some exercise. For those feeling rather goofy, there is the incredible **Giant Bubble**, an inflatable plastic hamster ball you flounder about in while floating on the lake. If that's not enough of a thrill, grab your friends and try spinning around in the **Floating Donut**. There is an **outbound course** for kids who like to climb, as well as a water park for the little guppies. Don't forget to bring your Speedos.

The **Zona Family Walk** (Family Walk Zone) is also very popular for fishing and pony riding. It includes a miniature zoo, picnic garden and paddy village. For something more organized, take a tour into the rice paddies, learn the art of cultivation or explore some of the more exotic fruit offerings via the **Paddy Legend**, **Smart Cultivation or Tropical Exotic tours**. Or stroll through the sandy, cactus-strewn **Taman Mediterranean dan Oasis** (Mediterranean Park and Oasis) and get a load of the waterfall building in **Central Park**. If one day isn't enough, stay overnight in a **tree house** at **Rumah Pohon Leo** (Leo's Tree House).

A day at Mekarsari will be long, hot and tiring. Be sure to bring snack food and drink loads of water to keep energy levels up. Don't forget a hat, sunscreen, comfortable shoes and an umbrella, which will be useful in both rain and shine.

WHO? This attraction is geared toward families.

HOW LONG? A full day.

HOW FAR? 6.4 km, not including cycling or train rides.

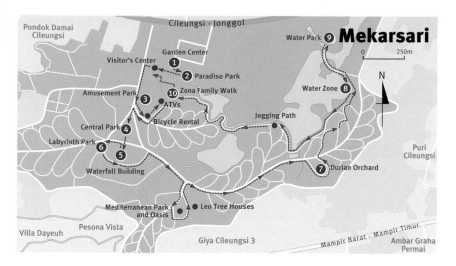

GETTING THERE

Mekarsari is located on Jl. Raya Cileungsi-Jonggol km 3 in Cileungsi. The only way to get there besides taxi is by private car, with a private car definitely the recommended option. Go via the Jagorawi toll road, exit at Cibubur and take Jl. Trans Yogie. Later cross Jl. Narogong and the road will turn into Jl. Cileungsi-Jonggol. Look out for Mekarsari on the right. There is plenty of parking inside.

GETTING IN

Open 9am to 4.30pm, Tuesday to Sunday.

CHECK OUT

www.mekarsari.com

GETTING STARTED

Mekarsari's mission is written clearly over the entrance gates: Conservation, Reforestation, Education, Recreation (Konservasi, Reboisasi, Edukasi, Rekreasi). Opened in 1995, the park is one of the largest public areas near Jakarta devoted to showcasing the natural and agricultural apects of the country. Set as it is closer to the mountains, be sure to notice the Gede and Pangrango volcanoes due south, as well as their cousin, Mount Salak, which sits a bit more squat on its own just off to the west.

After entering the park, head straight to the Information/Visitor Center, which holds all the brochures, information and maps of the grounds. Here, there are a number of package deals families can sign up for, including field planting with a buffalo, guided tours of Melon Park, Deer Park or Snake Fruit forest, and bicycle tours of Passion Fruit Park or the Rare Plants Orchard.

① GARDEN CENTER

To jump right into the walk, turn left and start with the **Garden Center**. This is mainly a commercial area for those who want to buy fruit plants, but it's also a nice place to observe what the plants look like that produce the goodies on your morning fruit platter. The selection is excellent: durian, dragon fruit, pineapples, figs, tamarind, pomegranate, cherries, starfruit, mangoes, avocados, grapes and oranges. You'll also find cloves, cinnamon and a small red berry called the miracle fruit (*Synsepalum dulcificum*), a sneaky little fruit which tricks the taste buds into thinking that sour food actually tastes sweet. There's a selection of bonsai trees as well.

② PARADISO PARK

Pass through the Garden Center to **Taman Paradiso** (Paradiso Park), which includes a house plants section. One of the more interesting plants here is the mother-in-law's tongue, which has long, tough, green and yellow streaked leaves. These plants are a Jakarta resident's best friend because they are famous for scrubbing benzene from the air. Also found here are elephant ear plants, philodendrons, flower-bearing antheriums and succulent agave, a notable mention as it has of late become a sugar substitute. Stroll

A tram bus traversing Mekarsari Tourism Park.

along the paths, check out the water feature, cross under the vine-covered trellises and sit on a bench to enjoy the flitting butterflies and the peace and quiet. Then head back to the main entrance area.

For those who want an overview of the park but aren't up for a long trek, tram buses depart from near the **Pusat Informasi** (Visitor's Center) for a 20-minute tour of the park. The drivers point out all the interesting aspects and share facts about the park's main areas. Note that the tour is only in Indonesian. For those who are not into motorized tours, the train is a useful way to get to the other side of the park, with drop-off and pick-up points at the Water Zone.

③ AMUSEMENT PARK
Those who would rather strike out and get some exercise can head up the road to the right of the Visitor's Center. Pass the kid's **Taman Hiburan** (Amusement Park) and its antiquated-looking roller coaster and on the left is a spot for **renting tandem bicycles** and *sepeda tuktuk* (bicycle cars). The bikes are cheap and fairly junky, but since people are only allowed to ride them around this part of the park, it doesn't much matter that they aren't suitable for long rides. Mount your trusty, rusty, two-wheeled steed and have fun rolling around amongst the avocado trees and adjacent camping area. Heading off to the left leads to the water's edge where you can sneak away and pedal along the path for a good bit of fun. Technically, bikes aren't supposed to go this far, but a little joy ride outside the rules won't hurt.

Near here are kite rentals, where kids can send a string strung eagle soaring on the breeze which buffets the park. For the mud boggers, mini ATVs are available for a rip-roar around a little dirt track.

④ CENTRAL PARK; ⑤ WATERFALL BUILDING
Back out on the main road, continue straight to **Central Park** and **Plaza Air Mancur** (Waterfall Plaza), a pleasant area with trees, bushes, flowers and benches. Central Park offers a good view of the unique **Bangunan Air Terjun** (Waterfall Building), an unusual seven-story, plant-covered building with a waterfall cascading from the roof. It was designed to look like a hillside and, while it looks like it would make for a great hotel, the building is meant for administrative purposes only. The philosophy behind the building is that the mountains and hills provide water and therefore life for both humans and nature.

⑥ LABYRINTH PARK
Just to the right of the Water Building is **Taman Labirin** (Labyrinth Park), a shrub maze swarming with butterflies, featuring a small statue of a person deep in thought in the center. It won't be tough for an adult to navigate through, but for anyone who is less than three feet tall, it should be a fun puzzle to solve. The maze is located in a grove of *belimbing* (starfruit) trees, and is a bit neglected, but that adds a certain magic and mystery to it.

Next, head west toward the **Mediterranean Zone**, which features the **Rumah Pohon Leo** and **Taman Mediterranean dan Oasis**. Take a few minutes to stroll around the park and its accompanying 'oasis,' a small pool of water. Paths meander through the sandy grounds dotted with cactuses and benches, while a small footbridge crosses over the oasis. It's lightly shaded with palm trees. Off to the side of the park is the treehouse hotel. The rooms are fun in a kitsch, Swiss Family Robinson sort of way, with cute little wooden beds and furnishings. They are located on the second floor of the tree, which provides a good vantage point to fend off the forest bandits.

Rumah Pohon Leo (Leo's Treehouse) has bicycles for guests only, but if you ask nicely they may let you have a ride. The bicycles have one pedal in the salvage yard, but that's OK because they can only be ridden around in the Mediterranean Zone. Take advantage of this, though, and head out on the small, breezy, orchard-lined paths, until reaching the outer walls of the park, then wheely-skip back again.

7 DURIAN ORCHARD

Now head west again, just past the waterlily-covered pond on the right. There is a path to the right that leads to **Kebun Durian** (Durian Orchard). Tours are led here from time to time and a fresh durian ice cream vendor may be stationed in among the trees. If durian ice cream sounds like the last thing on earth you'd want to try, think again. What they serve here is soft and lovely, not too strong and very fresh. If no one is selling, it can definitely be found back at the main building near the souvenir stands.

> ## *HEADS UP*
> Durian fruit are large, heavy and covered with spikes. Hanging from the trees, they are like medieval weapons waiting to fall. If you are walking in a durian orchard, note that a plummeting durian can literally kill, so be aware at all times of what is overhead.

Leo's Treehouse for overnight accommodation.

8 WATER ZONE

Continuing on the path will lead you to the **Wisata Air** (Water Zone). There are plenty of things for kids to do here, and a few adult-friendly activities as well. Rent a **canoe** or **kayak** (the family-friendly, touristy type), ride a **banana boat**, pedal a **floating three-wheel bicycle** or try spinning around inside the **Floating Donut**, a large, colorful, spool-shaped inflatable that a number of people can stand inside and try to spin. Another fun water toy is the **Giant Bubble**, which is basically a hamster ball for humans. Get inside and the attendant will inflate it, seal it and roll it on to the lake while you try to stay upright. Five minutes of flipping and flopping about inside makes it a steaming, sweat sauna of fun. For those looking for something a bit more laid back, take a **dragon boat** ride around the man-made lake. This is also a good way to get back to the other side of the park.

9 WATER PARK

This end of the park with the Water Zone is not nearly as peaceful and quiet as other parts. Many companies come here for staff gatherings and large groups of children participate in activities that require high-pitched MCs to shout into microphones and thump '80s techno music. There is also a **water park** with slides, pools and all the

rest that can be reached via a footbridge, but it's hardly the highlight of Mekarsari.

10 ZONA FAMILY WALK

People who don't take the dragon boat or train back to the entrance can walk northeast along the lake. After some time, there is a road to the right, which leads to a **jogging path** that follows the lake's edge into the **Zona Family Walk**, passing cute, rentable, apple-shaped pedal boats along the way. This is a paddock with a decent spot for **riding ponies**, complete with a Flintstones' car, a small oasis, caged birds, crocodiles, turtles and civet cats. The area also boasts a **3-D theater**, **performance stage**, **observation tower**, **children's playgrounds** and tiny little tandem bicycles.

The journey home can be challenging if you came by taxi, since traffic along the road back to the toll can be rough. Catching a return taxi is nearly impossible, so it's better to take a local *bemo* up to the overpass and find one there. The taxis won't use a meter, so bargain hard for your ride home. A much better idea is to call for a taxi far in advance and have them wait for you at the entrance to Mekarsari. For the more adventurous, a motorcycle taxi for the first section of the journey will be the quickest way out—if you can find one.

Teluk Betung
Barat

Merbau Mataram

Negeriagung

□ Candipuro

Pasir Sakti

Padang Cermin

Sekampung Pt.

Umbulan Labuhan Ratu

Chapter 5
Beyond Jakarta

Sragi

Palas

P. Mundu

Kalianda ◎

Blambangan

Ketapang

P. Seram

Kalianda Resort ★

Radin Inten Tomb

Hot Spring

P. Sluncal
P. Sijebi

P. Serdang

to Panjang

Wartawan

P. Sebuku

P. Rimau Balak

Pulorido

Puloampel

P. Panjang Bird Sanctuary

P. Tundo

Pulut Pt.

Pontang Pt.

Bakauheni

Tua Pt.

P. Sesi

P. Sangiang

Nature Reserve

Merak

P. Panjang

Bojanegara

Tirtayasa

Kre

Cilegon ◎

to Padang

6°

LAMPUNG
BANTEN

Krakatau Volcano ★

P. Krakatau Kecil

Krakatau National Park

Ciwandan

Banten
Historical Town

Pontang

Binuang

Kres

P. Sertung

Anyer

Anyer

Kramatwatu

Kragilan

to Padang

P. Krakatau

Bedulu

Gede 744m

Serang □

Jakarta-Merak Toll

Ciruas

Bala

Rafting

Raneau Reserve

Cipocokjaya

Curug

Cikande

Jawila

Cilangka

Padarincang

Batukuwung Hot Spring

Baros

Cadasari

Cikeusal

Tanjungteja

Kopo

Ma

Bukit Pesanggrahan Carita Forest Park ★

Aseupan 1175m

Karang 1778m

Pandeglang ◎

S u n d a
S t r a i t

Carita

Mandalawangi Jiput

Banjar

Rangkas Bitung ◎

Labuhan

Pulasari 1346m

Cimanuk

Cikulur

Cipinin

Menes

Saketi

Cimarga

Tanjung Lesung

Pagelaran

Bojong

Cileles

Lebak

Sajira

Parat

Picung

Gunung Kencana

Muncang

Hot Spring

Cipanas

Ujung Kulon National Park

Cemara

Panimbang

Banjarsari

BANTEN

to Panaitan Island

Alang-alang Pt.

Angsana

Munjul

Bojongmanik

Karang Jajar Pt.

Selamatdatang Bay

Sumur

Ciputih

Cijaku

Badui Village

P. Peucang

Cimanggu

Cibaliung Rafting

Cikeusik

Nyungcung 1118m

Mount Halim National Park

Bungalow ★

Bungalow

Bungalow

Cibaliung

Ujung Kulon National Park

Ujung Kulon National Park

Maling ping

Jatake

Cibeber

Guha Kolak Pt.

Cangkuwang Pt.

Sadong Pt.

Binaungeun

Cilangkahan

Panggarangan

Bayah

Hot Spr

P. Deli

Scenic Area ★

Karang Taraje

Panaitan Strait

P. Tinjil

Suwarna Surf Spot

Layar Pt.

Indi
Sur

7°

Ciletuh Be

Sadang Barat Pt.

I N D I A N   O C E A N

Ujung Genteng National Reserve

Sea Turtl

106°

Beyond Jakarta

Jakarta's strategic position, set between mountains and sea, means that both mountain goats and water nymphs can be pleased. There are tropical islands with hammocks, surf breaks and reef and wreck scuba diving spots. There are undulating tea plantations, hot springs, waterfalls, paragliding opportunities and a pair of heavily forested mountains with hiking and mountain biking trails and camping spots. There's a Javan Gibbon reserve and a bird watching island, a pottery village, a gong factory and white-water rafting. And all of these and more are just a drive or a boat ride away from Jakarta.

Set in the Java Sea off north Jakarta are the tiny tropical paradises and dive spots

A tea estate with Mt Salak in the background.

of the **Thousand Islands**. Among these are islands of specific interest to bird watchers, historians and lighthouse enthusiasts, as well as half a dozen for lazy-day seekers.

East of Jakarta is **Jatiluhur Reservoir** buttressed by the jagged peak of **Gunung Parang** (Mount Parang) and the nearby **pottery village of Plered** where visitors can either buy or make their next flower pot.

South of Jakarta is **Sentul**, where both road and mountain bikers have full range to roll, and trail runners can stretch their legs. For horse riders, check out **JPEC Sentul Equestrian Club** and get galloping.

Hop on the train and chug south to Bogor for a great day out. Bogor is Jakarta's baby sister and has **botanical gardens**, a **gong factory**, **puppet makers** and the **presidential palace**. Beyond Bogor is the little-known **Lido Lakes** complex, complete with **microlighting**, **mountain biking**, **trekking** and revving about on **ATVs**. There is also an alternative entry point to the Gede and Prangrango mountains here via the Bodogol National Forest.

Heading southeast into the cool hills is Puncak, an old favorite for weekend getaways. With **mountain trekking**, **tea plantation tours**, **wild animal safaris**, **botanical and flower gardens**, and **paragliding**, there are plenty of reasons to keep going back. Further afield are the waterfalls at the base of the Gede and Pangrango mountains.

On the road to Pelabuhan Ratu is **river rafting** on the often wild Citarik River and **hunting** in Cikadang. Pelabuhan Ratu itself is a great spot for doing nothing but enjoy the beaches, clean sea air and respite from the city. But there are also opportunities for **surfing**, **trekking**, **soaking in hot springs** and taking a **motorbike** tour through the national forest and local plantations.

For those without a car, taking a boat to the Thousand Islands, catching the train to Bogor or taking a bus to Puncak are easy options. If you have a car (and driver), West Java is your watermelon and there's nowhere you can't get to.

Relaxing in a hammock with a good book and a sea view on tropical Macan Island.

Walking Tour 21

PULAU SERIBU

A Speedboat Ride from Jakarta to the Thousand Islands

1. **Rambut Island**
2. **Untung Jawa Island**
3. **Onrust Island**
4. **Kelor Island**
5. **Damar Island**
6. **Alam Kotok Island**
7. **Putri Island**
8. **Macan Island**

Those who think they need to fly to the Gili Islands off Lombok to enjoy a peaceful weekend getaway are sorely mistaken. Roughly 120 islands with the word 'relax' scratched in their sands sit just a flying-fish skip off the north coast of Jakarta. Choices range from kitsch to cool, from family-oriented to silent and serene. Hop on a boat and within an hour or two you can find your own tropical paradise, complete with snorkeling, beach volleyball, cool cocktails and a sun lounger overlooking the baby blue waters of the Java Sea (the farther you get from Jakarta, the bluer the water).

Around 13,000 people live in the area known as the Thousand Islands. Many of the islands are uninhabited and are part of a marine national park. Others are privately owned and serve as the stomping grounds for the rich and famous (think golf courses).

A night on one of the more upscale of the Thousand Islands is fairly expensive as every item must be brought in by boat and the cost of fuel drives up the price. But not all the islands feature big-ticket accommodation. For a more down to earth experience, take a public boat out to a nearby island, stay in ramshackle accommodation and hang out with the local tourists at a very budget-friendly price. The great thing about all the islands is that you can be out of bed at 7am and on an island paradise as early as 9am.

Island hopping day trips are a great way to see a number of the better islands without breaking the bank. Local sailing boats/fishing boats or organized tours make trips out to **Pulau Rambut** (Hair Island), a nature reserve for birds, where a viewing tower allows visitors to scan the skies for the island's winged residents. On the lightly populated **Pulau Untung Jawa** (Javanese Luck Island), you can stroll through a *kampung* blessedly free of cars and other traffic. For beach bums, the large strip of sand is just one big playground.

Pulau Onrust (Island of Unrest), as its name implies, has seen incredible action over its long and varied history. Stroll through the museum, wander among the helter-skelter graves in the Dutch cemetery, picnic under a massive banyan tree and, if weather permits, hire a fishing boat to cruise to nearby **Pulau Kelor** (Moringa Tree Island) to check out a tiny old Dutch fort perched there. Finally, wrap things up on **Pulau Damar** (Oil Lamp Island), which hosts a 60-meter-tall lighthouse that offers bird's-eye views of the island expanse.

> ### FAST FACT
> The very first castle in Batavia was built using coral from the Thousand Islands.

WHO? The Thousand Islands are for everyone, although some are more suitable for couples while others cater to families or groups.

HOW LONG? There are two options: day trips that leave early in the morning and return by late afternoon, or overnight trips that also leave early and return guests by dinner time the following day.

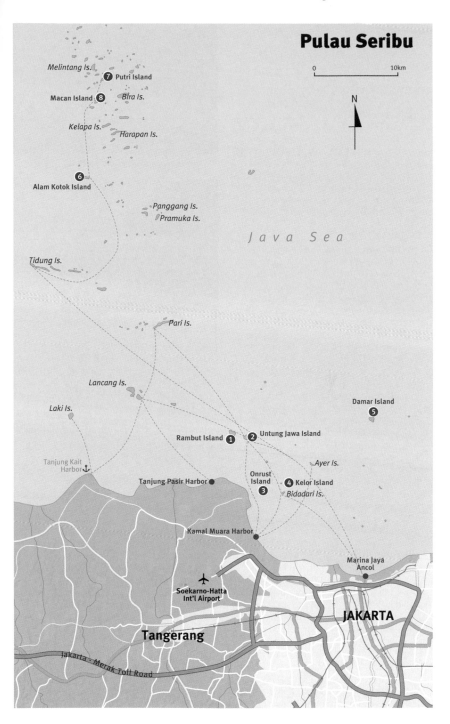

Pulau Seribu

0   10km

N

Melintang Is.

7 **Putri Island**

Macan Island **8**   *Bira Is.*

Kelapa Is.

Harapan Is.

6

Alam Kotok Island

Panggang Is.

Pramuka Is.

J a v a   S e a

Tidung Is.

Pari Is.

Lancang Is.

Laki Is.

Damar Island
5

Rambut Island **1**   **2** **Untung Jawa Island**

Ayer Is.

Tanjung Kait Harbor

Onrust Island
3   **4** **Kelor Island**

Tanjung Pasir Harbor

Bidadari Is.

Kamal Muara Harbor

Marina Jaya Ancol

Soekarno-Hatta Int'l Airport

JAKARTA

Tangerang

Jakarta - Merak Toll Road

HOW FAR? A number of islands are only a 30-minute jaunt from the city, but a 1–2 hour boat ride is required for peace and clean waters.

GETTING STARTED Start at the Marina Office at Ancol at 8am by either coming via the Harbor Toll Road or by taking Busway #5 to the Ancol stop. All speedboats leave from the marina. Fishing boats can be chartered from any number of harbors in north Jakarta.

The following is one example of a solid day trip that is good for a group of singles or families. There are many variations of the following trip, and different companies can put together a range of options and prices.

A day-tripper bird watching on Pulau Rambut.

1 RAMBUT ISLAND

Pulau Rambut (Hair Island) is located just 2km northwest of the Jakarta coast and is one of the last bastions for bird breeding in West Java. Cormorants, flying foxes, egrets, herons, fruit bats, milky storks, swallows and orioles are just some of the 40,000 birds and other winged creatures that live among the mangroves and wetland forest that the government has set aside as a nature reserve. Many of the birds are both rare and protected by law. Nearly 50 species of animals also call this island home.

Tourists combing a beach at Pulau Rambut.

So-named because of the thick head of 'hair' from the dense forest canopy, this 90-hectare island is open year round, but March to September is the best time to see birds feeding their chicks, and the weather at this time is also dry and clear.

When you arrive on the island head around to the left of the administrative buildings. There is a locked gate the island's keeper will open for a small fee. In a perfect world, everyone that came would have a letter of permission from the Jakarta Office of the Natural Resources Conservation Center, but as these are nearly impossible to secure and the local management seems to be ambivalent about this, it seems easiest to skip this step.

Cross the small bridge quietly and immediately be on the lookout for the large monitor lizards that rule the island's undergrowth. Large, boisterous groups will often scare the lizards away, but stealthy, ninja-like trekkers may well be rewarded. While walking up the track, ducking dangling vines and stepping over fallen tree trunks, also keep an eye out for pythons, skinks, large hermit crabs snug inside shells and even the resident lynx that

prowls among the shadows. Butterflies add a fairytale feel to the island, and in the right season the shells of bird hatchlings litter the forest floor.

In the flora department, look for the *jeruk kinkit* (kinkit orange) plant, which does not produce oranges, but does have small red edible berries that freshen the breath, add shine to fingernails and make for good slingshot ammunition. This plant is often used for *bonsai*. The other trees here are much bigger, reaching 10–15m into the air and consist of *kedoya* (iron mahogany), *jambu-jambu* (rose apple), *sago aren* (sago palm) and *kayu hitam* (ebony wood). Countless nests are tucked amid the branches, along with dangling bats, fruit and, of course, perching birds. With so much action above, it's best to wear a hat in case one of the birds decides to drop a little present on you.

The island's main path leads to a 20-meter-tall observation tower, which allows visitors to enjoy the cool breeze and look out over a tree canopy so thick it seems you could walk across the top of it. Take your time to watch the airborne acrobatics of the local population, and try to spot some of the more colorful birds darting from tree to tree. Note the softball-sized green fruit on the *kepuh* tree (silk cotton or kapok) near the tower.

When you've done enough bird watching, return to the dock by following the path back. There are a number of short dead-end side paths to explore, but most have been devoured by nature. For those who have not yet spotted a monitor lizard, try stalking the mangroves along the beach.

Please note that plenty of rag-tag tourists show up and demonstrate how not to act in a wildlife reserve. Playing music, littering, collecting 'souvenirs' and any other behavior that could disturb the wildlife or other visitors must be avoided. Also, while the island is wonderful, it is certainly not pristine. Aside from playing host to a billion birds, the island's beaches and inner waterways are also where Jakarta residents' discarded flipflops and chunks of Styrofoam wash up.

After an hour or two on Hair Island, motor over to Pulau Untung Jawa, just a 10-minute ride away.

② UNTUNG JAWA ISLAND

Pulau Untung Jawa (Javanese Luck Island) is an easy to reach seaside destination complete with beach shelters, playground equipment and bicycle and water flotation rentals. Its close proximity to Jakarta means the water is not pristine and refuse does litter the beach. It is favored by local and Chinese tourists, but fun can be had by all.

Perhaps the best part about the island is the labyrinth of pleasant *kampung* lanes which see more *becaks* than motorbikes and numerous people are on bicycles. Take an hour to just stroll about them, checking out the crab and lobster traps stacked up by the fishing boats or watching the carpenters and craftsmen build new wooden sailing vessels. Buy a seashell wind chime and then chill out at a *warung* and enjoy a cold drink.

At least a dozen budget-priced homestays line the beachfront for those who would like to spend a night practicing their Bahasa Indonesia and getting to know the locals better. There is no need to book in advance.

③ ONRUST ISLAND

A 15-minute boat ride away from Pulau Untung Jawa is **Pulau Onrust** (Island of Unrest). Established in 1615 by the Dutch, the island was originally a docking station and pier for trade ships and fishing vessels. In 1658, the Dutch colonizers built a small fort and, later, warehouses, more docks and a windmill. In 1770, famous world explorer

James Cook docked his ship, the *Endeavour*, here to have it repaired. Then, in the early 1800s, the island was attacked by the British and destroyed. By 1868 it had been reconstructed, and 1,500 free people worked on the island alongside 300 local prisoners who were used for labor. The tsunami sparked by the eruption of Krakatau in 1883 basically wiped the island clean, and the subsequent opening of Tanjung Priok Port in 1886 pushed Pulau Onrust further into obscurity.

FAST FACT

Pulau Onrust is sometimes also referred to as Pulau Kapal (Ship Island).

The island was revived in the early 20th century when it hosted a sanatorium for patients with infectious diseases. Prisoners were also kept there, with the sharks in the surrounding waters acting as infallible guards. The island's dual function continued in 1940, when 1,200 Dutch sympathizers and German civilians were interned on one part of the 7.5-hectare island (down from its original 12 hectares due to erosion). Another area was devoted to Muslims preparing for the Hajj, the annual pilgrimage to Mecca. From 1942 to 1945, Japanese invaders used the island as a prison, and later, political prisoners, beggars and tramps were kept there. In 1972, the island was declared a historical site by then governor of Jakarta, Ali Sadikin.

Most of the island comprises the ruins of days long past, with nature having reclaimed nearly everything but the foundations. A number of signs in English explain what you are seeing, and multiple paths traverse the ruins. A small museum housed in the old doctors' quarters has bilingual signs and artifacts, including iron shoes that held down early scuba divers.

Pulau Onrust is the spot for a picnic lunch, and an open space near the crumbling Dutch graveyard offers views of the sea. The island is most assuredly haunted considering the thousands of lives that have passed here and the cracked tombs. Walking around at dusk is encouraged if you are looking for a spooky atmosphere.

④ KELOR ISLAND

After lunch, try to arrange for a small fishing boat to take you out to the pebble-sized

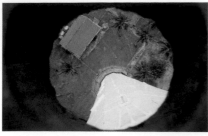

Looking down from the grand 60-meter-high lighthouse on small, wooded Damar Island.

Pulau Kelor (Moringa Tree Island) with its tiny picturesque fort that few have set foot on. Get out to it if the opportunity arises. Note: Only fishing boats can dock here because of the surrounding reef. Because of their small size, however, they can only make the trip if the sea is relatively calm.

5 DAMAR ISLAND
The fifth and final island of the day trip is **Pulau Damar** (Oil Lamp Island). Located 15 minutes from Pulau Onrust, this island has only one attraction—a grand lighthouse rising above the tree line. Built in 1879 by the Dutch, the 60-meter-tall cream-colored lighthouse has 16 floors connected by a spiral staircase made up of 252 stairs. Just below the lamp is a door that opens on to an outer deck encircling the tower. The breeze up here is fantastic after a sweat-inducing climb, and the deck gives 360 degree views of surrounding islands as well as Jakarta, depending on the weather and the haze. For those without a fear of heights, look down to see guard dogs playing and ant-sized fishermen casting their lines off the dock.

Three men guard and man the lighthouse on Pulau Damar, which is otherwise uninhabited. The rest of the small wooded island can be explored via the winding trails. Overnight camping is also an option. Inquire with your trip organizer.

If the breeze atop the lighthouse was not enough, cool off with a swim in the waters off the broken coral beach before taking the speedy 30-minute trip back to the Ancol Marina.

NOTES ON THIS TRIP Ancol Marina is the easiest and most common starting point for trips to the Thousand Islands, but it's also the most expensive. For more of an adventure, try leaving from **Pelabuhan Tanjung Pasir** (Sand Harbor) beyond Tangerang, reached by driving through seas of rice fields and fishing villages. A second option closer to home is **Pelabuhan Kamal Muara** (Kamal Harbor), which houses hundreds of small, colorful fishing boats and the thousands of people who depend on them for survival. The transport at these harbors consists of various sized rough but generally seaworthy fishing boats, most of which don't come with life jackets. Once you have bargained for a vessel and crew, you can enjoy the ride out to the islands while checking out the giant stick insect-like bamboo fishing platforms scattered throughout the waters.

If you do take a local boat and crew, you should plan to tip the help at the end of the day. The boatmen will also expect some small money for lunch and cigarettes. Remember, hungry men can get mutinous, so don't be stingy.

Most boats from Ancol Marina have some sort of flotation protection, so again, Ancol is the safer option.

E-MAIL Cynthia Devi from Jalan Jalan Adventures—cynthia@jalanjalanadventures.com

CHECK OUT www.pulauseribu-resorts.com and jalanjalanadventures.com

ALSO Various travel agents around Ancol Marina can arrange trips.

OTHER Bring water, sun and rain gear (to protect from rain or waves), and wear clothes that will dry quickly if they get wet.

TOP 3 PICKS FOR A WEEKEND GETAWAY
There are numerous overnight options at the Thousand Islands, ranging from just a few hundred thousand rupiah to a couple of million, depending on which island and what room. A good quality one-night stay won't come cheap, but generally the price paid is worth the getaway. The following are a sampling of expat favorites, a number with diving options.

6 ALAM KOTOK ISLAND
Pulau Alam Kotok (Alam Kotok Island) is a wonderful dab of sand the size of a postage stamp that offers great places for reading,

Snorkeling in the waters off Macan Island.

An open-air beach bedroom on Macan Island.

beachside tire swings and, for the water nymphs, snorkeling and diving. Noisy families tend to stay away, so the island is peaceful and quiet. On the far side of the island, the Jakarta Animal Aid Network (JAAN) runs a raptor rehabilitation center. Watch out for the frighteningly large monitor lizards that stalk the restaurant during meal times.

Pulau Kotok House Reefs. The reefs surrounding Kotok have undoubtedly some of the best corals in the Thousand Island chain, particularly along the north and west sides of the island. Turtles, black and white tip reef sharks and schooling sweet lips are common sights, and the gentle sloping reef displays plenty of soft corals and gorgonians. Scuba dives are done off the pier jetty. Note that accommodation can be a bit rough here, with bungalow #14 being the best.

CHECK OUT www.alamkotok.co.id

⑦ PUTRI ISLAND

Pulau Putri (Princess Island), a good place to spend the day or weekend, is one of the more far-flung islands. The 1.5 hour journey is ultimately worth it as the water is clear and fresh and sea life has yet to be hauled out for Jakarta's diners. The activities here focus on undersea adventures with an underwater aquarium, glass-bottom boats, snorkeling and some of the best diving in the Thousand Islands chain. Note that there isn't a real beach here to speak of.

Papa Teo Wreck. The *Papa Teo* sank in 1982 and now lies just east of Papa Teo Island, a short boat ride away from Pulau Putri. The wreck is still in good shape and can be penetrated. The deck is home to both interesting critters and big swimmers, including parrotfish. The occasional reef shark can be found in the deeper water around the stern area. Visibility is usually good on the

deck but decreases rapidly around the stern, where the currents tend to whip around the wreck. Also watch for grouper, barracuda and batfish.

Matahari. This gentle sloping reef is a short boat ride from Pulau Putri and is an interesting dive with a good variety of soft and hard corals. Turtles are frequently seen passing through the site, and the reef is home to moray eels, lionfish and stingrays. Some areas do show evidence of dynamite fishing.

CHECK OUT www.putriisland.com

⑧ MACAN ISLAND

Pulau Macan (Tiger Island) is an eco-resort with quirky decor and a low-key, cozy, tropical ambience. It is definitely an expat favorite and for good reason. The food is excellent, with organic vegetarian options and free-flowing coffee, ginger tea and juice. The beachside sleeping huts are open-air structures made of bamboo, thatch and driftwood. For those who love water, kayaks are available for rent and the snorkeling is good; staff offer snorkel trips to nearby islands. On land, there is beach volleyball, a pool table, a masseuse, myriad hammocks, benches, chairs for sunbathing, a mini-bar and flop chairs for readers and daydreamers. Round up your friends and rent out the entire island—just be ready to pony up for it.

The beachside huts give the feeling of a true island getaway, with the best digs on the island being the Sunset Hut. The ambience of this particular bungalow is excellent and it comes with a sound system that can be hooked up to an iPod. Be warned, however, those who have stayed here have claimed they never want to go home again.

CHECK OUT www.pualaumacan.com

Walking Tour 22

BOGOR
A Visit to the Bogor Botanical Garden and Traditional Craft Workshops

1. **Zebaoth Church**
2. **Bogor Palace**
3. **Ethnobotany Museum**
4. **Bogor Trade Mall**
5. **Gong Factory**
6. **Bogor Botanical Garden**
7. **Zoology Museum**
8. **Orchid Gardens**
9. **Wayang Golek**

Home to more than three million people, Bogor is the largest city in proximity to Jakarta. Although it is no longer the quaint town it once was, as you venture off the main roads and into the neighborhoods you'll still find that it retains much of its former small town charm. Nestled among the mountains of Gede, Pangrango and Salak, Bogor has a cooler, rather fresher climate than Jakarta and is famous as the *hutan kota* (city of rain) as it receives more precipitation than any other municipality in Java. So don't forget your umbrella.

This tour begins with a train ride, leaving from Jakarta's principal train station, Gambir, located near Monas. The train passes the sweeping grounds of the **University of Indonesia**, one of the country's premier institutes of higher learning. It's challenging to fit it into the Bogor day trip, but come back and stroll the campus on another day out.

Bogor's main attraction is the expansive **Kebun Raya Bogor** (Bogor Botanical Garden). The garden is a testament to preservation as well as a showcase of nature's endless ability to awe. The pedestrian-friendly layout allows for hours of strolling and makes it a must-see for newcomers to Jakarta. Do beware that Sundays bring many visitors, along with the concomitant traffic

and crush of schoolchildren eager to ply you with questionnaires and practice their English language skills.

In addition to the gardens, the **Pengrajin Gong** (gong factory) and *wayang golek* (wooden puppet maker) are two highlights of the Bogor trip. The sites offer a window into a handicraft culture that is dying out under the weight of cheap mass production. See sweat-soaked brass-metal workers hammering away over hot coals at the gong factory and then navigate a *kampung* along the river to find an old puppet master, who will show off his wares and teach visitors the history and meaning of *wayang golek*.

Bogor's other great assets are the local residents and their communities. In a perfect world, one walking tour would be devoted strictly to wandering the photogenic back streets of these close-knit neighborhoods. Instead, it will be up to you, the adventurer, to strike your own path.

WHO? Anyone can do this trip, although it involves a solid amount of walking and travel. Wear comfortable shoes, pack snacks and load up on sunscreen.

HOW LONG? This is a full day, including train travel.

HOW FAR? 6km walking; 8.3km including two horse/pedicab rides.

GETTING STARTED Begin at the Gambir Train Station. Drivers can park their cars here for a fee. If coming via the Busway, take corridor #2 and get off at either the Gambir I or Gambir II stops. Once inside the station, look for the window selling Bogor tickets. There is no reason to use a scalper, helper or anyone else selling their services. The station

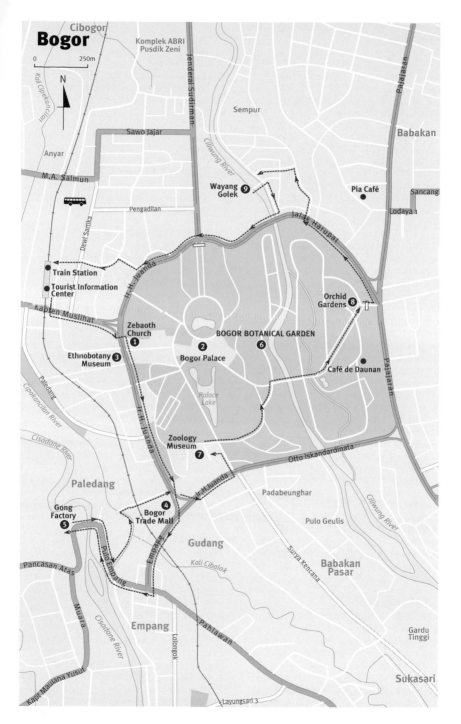

is not often crowded, and its layout is fairly straightforward.

Trains are timely (occasionally leaving a tad early!), but their departure and arrival is not always announced. Be sure to ask if a train pulls up and you think it may be yours. The train to Bogor leaves roughly every half hour, with the recommended times being 7.15am, 7.45am or 8.15am (the full schedule can be seen on Wikipedia by searching Pakuan Express). It should take a little over an hour to cover the 60km from Jakarta, with only a couple of stops along the way. The trains prohibit smoking, eating, drinking and busking, so you should be able to travel unmolested. Look for the Pakuan Express, which is clean, well-lit and air conditioned.

Upon arrival in Bogor, exit the train station and turn right. Either walk along the road with the *bemos*, or along the market area under the makeshift roof on the right. At the end of the road, which ends in a T-junction with Jl. Kapten Muslihat, turn left. Just a few meters up is the sign for the **Tourist Information Center**, which is set back off the road (across from the Matahari department store). Don't worry if the sign isn't immediately visible, it's highly likely one of the Information Center staff will find you. The people who work here are fairly useless, as are their materials. They are mainly interested in getting you into a guided tour, but will also rent themselves out as personal guides. The center says it's open seven days a week, including holidays, from 7am to 6pm, but don't be surprised if the hours are not strictly adhered to.

Walking up the sloped road, visitors will immediately notice that there are sidewalks, a good sign that pedestrians are respected here. At the top of the road, cross the street at the crosswalk and turn right. A directional signpost showing all the points of interest in central Bogor is also located at this intersection. Try to spot the deer behind the fence, across the street.

1 ZEBAOTH CHURCH

The first building of interest, on the side of the street with the botanical garden, is the **Gereja Zebaoth** (Zebaoth Church), nicknamed the 'Rooster Church' because of the chicken statue up in the tower. Built in 1920, the church was exclusively used by Europeans for more than 40 years and the sermons were given in Dutch. The entrance

to Bogor Palace sits next door, but guards prevent visitors from wandering through.

2 BOGOR PALACE

Istana Bogor (Bogor Palace) was built in 1744 and functioned as a country getaway for Dutch colonial governors. Sir Stamford Raffles was one of the most notable. President Sukarno later took up residence there, but it hasn't seen a permanent resident since then. Aside from superb architecture, the palace also boasts an extensive art collection, including 450 paintings and more than 350 sculptures. To get inside, you need to be part of a large group. Enquire at the Tourist Information Office to learn more.

3 ETHNOBOTANY MUSEUM

Just across the street from the palace is the **Museum Etnobotani** (Ethnobotany Museum), which opened in 1982. It contains more than 2,000 artifacts and displays which focus on the relationship between indigenous people and the plants they use.

4 BOGOR TRADE MALL

Continue walking to the main three-way intersection. At the **Bogor Trade Mall** (BTM) (a useful bathroom spot), turn right and head downhill, staying on the right-hand side of the road. After going under the train tracks, the sights become more interesting, with goatskins strung up to dry next to bird sellers, who also offer rabbits and flying foxes. Goatskins can be bought for around Rp150,000 and then made to order into purses or hats, gloves or moccasins.

At the next three-way intersection, turn right and pass a small cemetery. Cross a canal and, later, the river. Continue another 200 meters to the gong factory on the right.

5 GONG FACTORY

The first thing to note is that the **Pengrajin Gong** is anything but a factory. Run by 70-year-old Haji Sukarna, the seventh generation to man the family-run cottage industry, it is a dark, one-room building filled with coal and heat from the fires used to mold the gongs. It is not geared toward tourists, and visitors may feel like they've caught the men working here a bit offguard. The craftsmen, however, are more than happy for the company. They will pose for pictures, let visitors bang on a freshly fired gong and explain the crafting process (though not much English is spoken).

Workers eyeing approaching visitors to the dimly lit, family-run gong factory.

To begin, one man pulls a hot slab of metal alloy (tin and copper) out of the blower-driven flames and lays it on a small platform. A handful of men in various states of undress then hammer away on it, one whack at a time in turn, using large eight-kilo mallets, while another man slowly turns it. After about 30 seconds, the now-cooled metal alloy is slung back into the flames to be reheated. The process is repeated as the slab is slowly beaten into a gong shape.

The workers most certainly expect a tip, and will set a pan out for that purpose. For visitors who have taken a load of photos and played gong maker, don't skimp. Remember, these guys are carrying large tools that could double as weapons (just joking).

Although there is a gong shop next door, the stock is sparse as the factory is working flat out to keep up with back orders, many of which come from outside the country.

6 BOGOR BOTANICAL GARDEN

Leave the gong factory and return toward the botanical garden, crossing first the river and then stopping at the canal. This time, don't cross the canal, but look for a wide concrete path just before it on the left. Turn down this path and follow the canal all the way to the pedestrian bridge that crosses

the water. Cross the bridge, go up the stairs and keep going up until reaching the train tracks. Cross the tracks and follow the path, which runs just to the left of the Bogor Trade Mall. Cross the main street of Jl. Ir. H. Juanda at the pedestrian crosswalk and turn right. Walk with the traffic, circling around the gardens to the notably grand main entrance on the left. Buy an entrance ticket here.

Opened in 1817 by Gustaaf Willem, Java's then Dutch Governor-General, the 87 hectares of natural goodness inside the **Kebun Raya Bogor** (Bogor Botanical Garden) are probably the most visited gardens in Indonesia, and this is for good reason. Nowhere else in the country can you find such accessible flora or so many meandering paths leading to endless leafy surprises.

7 ZOOLOGY MUSEUM

Started as a botanical research center, a mission that continues to this day, the garden has more than 15,000 species of plants, including 400 types of palm trees. Pleasure seekers can wander freely for hours among wonderful collections of exotic, endangered specimens or follow one of the guided walks. A **Museum Zoologi** (Zoological Museum) is also located in the grounds near the Bogor Trade Mall.

A young pineapple plant.

One of the many species in the Orchid Gardens.

GETTING IN 8am to 5pm daily.

Hungry travelers should head to the splendid **Café de Daunan** (Café of Leaves). To get there, go down the stairs just past the ticket booth and continue straight to the main road. Turn right and follow the road, keeping to the right when it branches and heading right again at the crossroads. Look for signposts.

After sitting down in the café, sipping on a fresh juice and looking out across the expansive lawn with the thick crop of massive trees bordering the backdrop, you should be a very happy camper. Try the *nasi timbel* or *nasi langgi* for some excellent sampler platters of fine Indonesian food.

8 ORCHID GARDENS

With lunch complete, head over to the simple but peaceful **Kebun Anggrek** (Orchid Gardens) to see the roughly 3,000 different varieties. To get there, go back down to the main road and turn right. Follow the road up to the park gate and continue along to the garden's entrance on the left.

After the Orchid Gardens, head back the way you came and exit out Gate III. If it's locked, head back to the café and exit through the gate located behind it. Once out on the street, flag down a *dokar/delman* (horse and cart) or grab a *becak* (pedicab) to visit a wooden puppet workshop. Tell the driver you want to go to Jl. Sempur Dalam, which is located to the right of the Ciliwung River. Look for a sports field on your right. Turn right toward it, down a short hill. The field sports a dirt running track around the perimeter, a rock climbing wall and basketball court. Skirt the far side of the field, heading toward the river. Go up the road that runs parallel to the river and stop at the footbridge, across from the SDN Sempur Kidul building.

9 WAYANG GOLEK

Cross the bridge into the tiny lanes of Lebak Kantin neighborhood. Take the first left. At the first T-junction, turn left again. Take the first right after that and the next left. The lanes here are tiny. If you lose your bearings, just ask for **Pak Dase** (say Pak Dah-say). It's highly likely that someone will personally guide you for free to his home. It's not far.

Puppet craftsman Pak Dase has whittled wooden puppets called *wayang golek* for more than 30 years. He learned the trade from his grandfather, and many others in the 12-person family are involved in the business. Pak Dase started selling his handmade puppets at the botanical gardens before moving the business to his home.

The handicrafts are not the flat leather *wayang kulit* used in shadow puppetry, but rather three-dimensional puppets used in Hindu epics and plays about Javanese history. Pak Dase, who speaks good English, can go into detail about how the puppets are made and what the characters represent. Go inside and watch him carve a piece of art from a chunk of whitish softwood called *astonia*. Different styles of puppets hang along the walls. Pak Dase is happy to explain the difference in their craftsmanship and quality.

FAST FACT

The name Dase derives its *Da* from *darajat*, which means 'successful position,' and *se* from *Selasa*, which means Tuesday (the day Pak Dase was born). Pak Dase's last name is Spartacus, the movie his parents were watching when his mother went into labor. He can be reached at 0251-838 3758 or by mobile phone at 0813 8303 9282.

Leave the puppet workshop by returning to the footbridge and then to the rock climbing wall at the sports field you passed earlier. From here, climb the steps to the main road, Jl. Jalak Harupat, and wave down another *dokar* or *becak* to take you back to the train station. For those with a bit of time left, venture over to **Pia** (#10 Jl. Pangrango) for a slice of pie or some dinner before the return trip home.

OTHER OPTIONS One of the station stops on the way to Bogor is the **University of Indonesia** (UI). This university is considered the best in Indonesia, along with the Bandung Institute of Technology and Gajah Mada University in Yogyakarta. UI is also ranked among the top 50 universities in Asia and among the top 200 in the world. It started as a medical school in 1851, only taking its current name in 1950 after the national revolution. The current campus infrastructure is mostly modern, dating from 1987. UI has a student population of 40,000.

The campus is an excellent spot for joggers, power walkers or cyclists because of its myriad paths and nice roads. For others, it offers art shows and music and theater performances.

Exploring the campus the same day as doing the Bogor walking tour is not recommended as it's too much to take on in one day, but the train stop should be noted for future adventures.

To explore UI, leave the train station and enter the campus directly across the road. A long stretch of bicycle parking leading to a broad, tree-covered path greets visitors. To the right is a deer enclosure. Continue along the path and choose one of the numerous splits in the road. One may end up at a giant lake edged by benches, at the stadium or a vibrant bridge that spans a narrow, relatively clean lake. Many of the paths eventually lead to the Central Library, which hosts an eclectic and unexpected range of English language books.

A more adventurous way of getting to UI is to start at the Manggarai station in central Jakarta and take an economy class train for just Rp1,500. Stand in the carriage's open doorway and watch the jumbled, haphazard backyards of Jakarta fly by.

GONE TREKKING A solid outdoor excursion is a climb up the nearby 2211-meter-tall

Wayang golek craftsman Pak Dase and puppet.

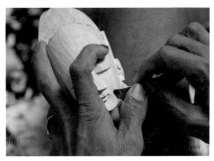

Whittling a puppet head from soft wood.

Gunung Salak (Mount Salak), a short journey from Bogor proper. Although there are seven summits in total, Salak 1, as it is called, is both the most popular and the highest. The hike takes around four hours and, while steep, it is doable by anyone in reasonably good shape.

Another popular climb is to **Kawah Ratu** (Queen's Crater), an active part of the mountain where a trekker can cook an egg in a steam vent and eat it for lunch. A well-marked trail leads there. It's a bit otherworldly, with a moon-like dusty white landscape devoid of vegetation and with clouds of gasses from multiple vents. The hike starts from the Javana Spa (www.javanaspa.co.id).

GETTING THERE To climb to Queen's Crater or the peak, head south on Jl. Raya Sukabumi to Cicurug, 33km outside of Bogor. Head northwest from here following the signs to the Javana Spa, roughly 12km off the toll road.

The trailhead is located a few hundred meters before you reach the Javana Spa. There is a large metal gate on the left with the sign 'Selamat Datang Di Jalur Pendaikan Kawah Ratu Dan Puncak Salak I.' Park employees there will try to get you to take a guide, which can be nice but is not really necessary.

Walking Tour 23

PUNCAK PASS

A Drive to Hills Filled with Mist, Tea Plantations, a Safari Park and the Exhilarating Rush of Paragliding

1. **Safari Park**
2. **Golden Mountain Tea Plantation**
3. **Paragliding**
4. **At-ta'awun Mosque**
5. **Cibodas Botanical Gardens**
6. **National Flower Park**

To escape the heat of the city without having to hop on a plane, train or boat, Puncak, which literally means 'summit,' is a cool getaway just a few hours southeast of Jakarta. There are unlimited paths for ambling, biking, hiking and more through a patchwork of tea plantations, green hills and cool air.

Take the toll road out of the city and stop at **Taman Safari** (Safari Park) for a wild drive-through view of the animal kingdom before continuing up to the bountiful bushes of the **Perkebunan Teh Gunung Mas** (Golden Mountain Tea Plantation). Further on is the launch pad for tandem and solo **paragliding** flights. Vendors around the launch site grill corn cobs on coals for spectators to nibble while watching their daredevil friends.

Hurtle up and over Puncak Pass, the highest point on the road. On the other side of Puncak is the **Kebun Raya Cibodas** (Cibodas Botanical Gardens) for wonderful strolls through nature's buffet of trees, flowers and ferns. Or lace up your hiking boots and tackle the peaks of **Mount Pangrango** and **Mount Gede**. Finally, take the time to continue down the road to **Taman Bunga Nasional** (National Flower Park) to explore the giant hedge maze and wander among the beautiful rose and water gardens.

There is too much to do in Puncak on one weekend, so plan to come back again and again. More than 100 villas are available for rent to overnight visitors.

WHO? The range of activities is diverse. Some, like Taman Safari, were created specifically with families in mind, while others, such as paragliding, are more for those who like an adrenaline kick.

HOW LONG? All day or all weekend.

HOW FAR? From central Jakarta, Taman Safari is 71km, Puncak Pass 78km, the Cibodas Botanical Gardens 88km, and the National Flower Park 90km.

GETTING STARTED The best way to get around Puncak is by car. Drivers should leave before sunrise and take the Jagorawi toll road. Pass Bogor and veer left on to Jl. Puncak Raya just after km 46 (going straight leads to Sukabumi and Pelabuhan Ratu) as the toll road ends. For those without wheels, head to the Kampung Rambutan Bus Terminal near the crossroads of the Jagorawi toll road and Outer Ring Road. Buses leave fairly regularly from here and later they can be flagged down on Puncak Pass for the return trip.

NOTE The road up Puncak is narrow and congested on weekends. As a traffic management strategy, only uphill traffic is permitted on Saturdays and Sundays between 9am and 11.30am, and downhill traffic from 3pm to 5pm Saturday and 3pm to 6pm Sunday. Trips are best done very early in the morning or late at night, and, in a perfect world, on a weekday. Attempting to leave Puncak in the late afternoon on a weekend day or public holiday can mean a very long, slow ride home.

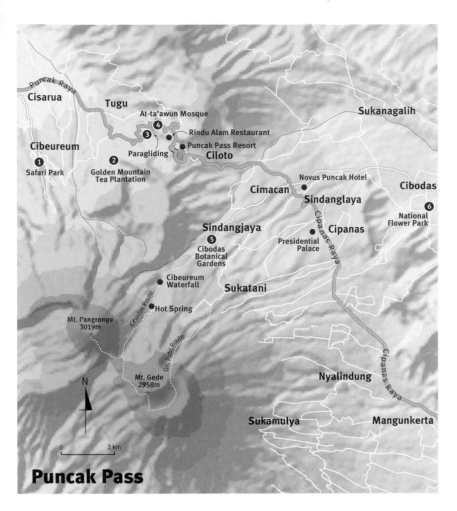

Puncak Pass

1 SAFARI PARK

The first notable stop up Puncak Pass is Taman Safari, just past km 81 on the right.

Taman Safari (Safari Park) is a drive-through animal park. Most of the animals are free to roam among the snaking line of cars crammed with gawking kids and nervous drivers. Along the road in, dozens of roadside vendors sell carrots and bananas for visitors to feed the safari inhabitants—and the animals know this. Once the safari drive has begun, expect just about anything, from a giant ox to a bobbing ostrich to a feisty llama trying to crane its head through the open car window so it can get its teeth on a morning meal.

In between bouts of fending off or luring in these greedy beggars, watch for the hippos, rhinos, giraffes, tapirs, lions, tigers and bears that roam or rest freely along the road. In the more dangerous animal areas, there are signs stressing the importance of keeping car windows closed. When you find a massive lion strolling alongside your car, you'll see the wisdom in these words.

Following the mini-safari drive, head to the safari **Recreation Area** for a carnival ride or animal show. Take a ride on the over-priced gondola for an eagle's-eye view of the park. There is also a Wild West show, a penguin house, primate and reptile gardens, a crocodile farm, elephant and camel rides,

The volcanic Mount Salak, viewed from the 1,000-hectare Golden Mountain Tea Plantation.

hiking trails and the 'Globe of Death,' an enclosed mesh metal ball in which a motor-cyclist defies gravity, and death, while loop-ing at speed in vertical circles. If that's not enough, prepare to get soaked at the newly built water park. After sundown, hop aboard the Safari Bus for the Night Safari. The cover of night makes this safari trip more thrilling and the animals are more active in the dark.

The temperate climate, surrounding forest and well cared for animals make this an attraction worthy of the drive. As with all big attractions anywhere near Jakarta, however, a visit on a weekend or public holiday will be filled with large crowds and gridlock. To avoid children with unruly littering habits and their inattentive parents, try showing up the moment the park opens and be prepared to leave by early afternoon.

CHECK OUT www.tamansafari.com

GETTING IN 9am to 5pm daily.

2 GOLDEN MOUNTAIN TEA PLANTATION

After the turnoff to Taman Safari, the next place of interest is the **Perkebunan Teh Gunung Mas** (Golden Mountain Tea Plantation), the best place to explore Puncak's wealth of tea bushes. Continue up Jl. Puncak Raya and watch for signs on the right-hand side of the road around km 88.

Although **Gunung Mas** translates to Gold Mountain, Green Mountain would be more fitting. The 1,000-hectare plantation, which ranges from 800m to 1,200m above sea level, washes the countryside in a seemingly end-less labyrinth of scrubby green tea bushes. People come here to tour the factory where the leaves are processed, stroll along the paths and photograph the tea pickers with their conical hats and woven baskets strapped securely to their backs.

Though the plantation covers an expansive area, it is rare to get a wide panoramic view due to the contours of the land. The higher you climb, though, the better the view. Groups can take guided tours or just roam about on their own. Horses are available for hire for those who prefer a less strenuous tour. Come early to watch the sunrise light up Gunung Salak, a nearby active volcano.

FAST FACT

Gunung Mas is roughly a hundred years old and produces black tea using the low-cost cut/crush, tear and curl method (CTC), which is most suitable for low-grade leaves meant for teabags. Workers pick each of the fields every three months throughout the year.

After a stroll and a factory tour, dig into a fried banana and wash it down with—what else—a cup of tea.

GETTING IN The plantation is open 7am to 9pm daily. The factory is open 7am to 10am, Tuesday to Sunday.

The road from Gunung Mas becomes very bendy as it wends steeply upwards. Stick your head out of the car window and look up at the sky (unless driving). Depending on the weather and season, there should be numerous paragliders floating through the air like large, colorful ribbons on the breeze.

③ PARAGLIDING

On the right-hand side of the main road is a rough little road leading to the **paragliding launch point** (1,300m), which overlooks the northern side of Puncak. Pay a small fee and drive through to the parking area.

Luckily for extreme sports enthusiasts, this is one of the best spots in the country for paragliding, and a thriving community of birdmen takes to the skies on a regular basis. Some are here for fun, some to compete, while others are waiting for paying tourists to drop by and give it a try. For a one-time thrill, professional paragliders offer tandem flights for a reasonable price.

The dry season is the best time to fly, since the winds are strong and rain won't keep you bound to the ground. Flights can last from 15 minutes to a couple of hours depending on the wind. For those who prefer not to leave the ground, this is also a great place to buy barbequed corn on the cob, drink some *bandrek* (a Sundanese hot ginger drink) and watch the paragliders whirl about on the updrafts.

FAST FACT

Puncak is a popular place for people from the Middle East. The paragliding launch was actually built with Saudi Arabian money and it is common to meet large groups of Saudis during outings here.

First-time paragliders need very little instruction. Simply strap into the harness and clip on to your piloting partner. When he yells 'Run!' do just that. Scurry down the big ramp and moments later your feet will dangle in blue skies while the tea plantations, snaking roads and life's worries are left far below.

Nixon Ray is the founder of Fly Indonesia, and has been the go-to guy for paragliding since the early 1990s. He guarantees a safe flight and has an excellent record to date. He willingly meets guests at Puncak Pass any time to provide lessons, certify solo fliers or do tandem flights. His office is located amongst the strip of *warungs* leading up to the launch point, but it's best to call and arrange a flight ahead.

WHERE TO GO The turnoff is marked by a very small sign, leading to a rough rock and dirt road up to a line of *warungs* and the launch point. It's 3km past the Gunung Mas turnoff and 3.25km before the space age-looking mosque.

CHECK OUT www.paragliding.web.id and www.indonesia-paragliding.com

OTHER Flying times in the rainy season are generally between 9am and 1pm, although if there are too many clouds or rain, no flying at all will happen. The best times to fly in the dry season are from 9am to 5pm. To arrive on time, leave Jakarta at 6am on a weekend and 7am on a weekday.

④ AT-TA'AWUN MOSQUE

After leaving the paragliding launch, continue to grind uphill while watching for the futuristic-looking three-story **Masjid At-ta'awun** (At-Ta'awun Mosque) on the right side of the road. It was built in 1997 and looks like something out of a Jetsons cartoon. Continue on to the top of the pass.

The top of the pass is a popular spot for expat **mountain bikers** to begin their gravity driven downhill blasts, many of whom don't stop until they reach the base of the mountain. Generally, groups descend to the south, heading to the back side of Taman Safari and ending up at Ciawi, while others head north, ending at Ciawi or Sentul. To join these groups, just rock up with your bicycle and ask. To join an Indonesian biking group, a common place to meet is the **Rindu Alam Restaurant** just a short distance from the Puncak peak. Be warned that some groups are looking to ride hard and fast and won't want to wait around much for a newbie, while other groups may stop every 10 minutes for smoking and photo taking. The standard round trip is to drive to the top and have your car and driver meet you at the end point.

One other thing to do at the top of the pass is eat. Pop into the **Puncak Pass Resort**, constructed in 1928, to chow down at one of their numerous restaurants while enjoying the view. The Dutch food is recommended.

Tourists on a day trip to a waterfall on Mount Gede leave from the Cibodas Botanical Gardens.

An overnight stay is possible here in a romantic room with a fireplace. This should be booked in advance.

CHECK OUT www.puncakpassresort.com

5 CIBODAS BOTANICAL GARDENS

Over the pass, the drive downhill begins. Jl. Puncak Raya turns into Jl. Raya Cimacan at this point. On the right, a short way past km 85, look out for Jl. Kebun Raya Cibodas, which leads to the **Kebun Raya Cibodas** (Cibodas Botanical Gardens) and the starting area for mountain treks.

Kebun Raya Cibodas was founded in 1862 and is a wonderfully pleasurable locale with a cool climate. Located 1,300m above sea level, the 125-hectare gardens, nearly as big as Bogor, have a noticeably different floral make-up than those seen at lower elevations, and are a solid spot for forest walks, throwing a Frisbee in open fields, and picnicking (Sundays are not nearly as peaceful due to the crowds). Check out the Moss and Sakura Parks as well as the small waterfall at the Rhododendron Park.

Other notable spots are the medicinal plants and the large fern collection. There are two guesthouses for overnight stays.

CHECK OUT www.krcibodas.lipi.go.id

The Cibodas Botanical Gardens are also a kicking off point for exploring the adjacent Gede and Pangrango Mountains.

Visible from Jakarta on a clear day, **Gunung Pangrango** and **Gunung Gede** are located within the 15,000-hectare Mount Gede Pangrango National Park. Mount Gede, at 2,958m, is the shorter but more famous of the two mountains, as it has a massive caldera that vents columns of gaseous clouds. Mount Pangrango, on the other hand, at 3,019m, is topped by a large, fairly flat prairie of grasses, shrubs and bushes, making it the better camping option of the two.

Both volcanoes are strenuous but wonderful climbs, which a fit climber could knock out in a weekend. To do this, climb Pangrango the first day and camp. Cross the Kandang Badak Saddle and ascend Gede the second day. The descent down the back side of Gede passes through the Suryakancana Meadow before finally ending at the Gunung Putri Park Office. Prepare to be hurting Monday morning. To tackle just one peak, hike up to the Kandang Badak shelter, where the path splits. Head right to go up Pangrango (seven hours to the top from the entrance gate) or left for Gede (five hours to the top).

FAST FACT

Alfred Russel Wallace, a co-founding author of the theory of evolution and natural selection, climbed both these mountains in 1861 while on a collection expedition for his scientific studies.

Shorter hike options include **Air Terjun Cibeureum** (Red Water Waterfalls), roughly an hour from the Cibodas Botanical Gardens, or **Air Panas** (Hot Springs), which are about 2.5 hours from the main gate, an hour past the waterfalls.

Trekkers are supposed to obtain a permit from the park office (usually in advance) and there are times of the year when the park closes the mountains to visitors. These are real mountains and should be taken seriously, so ultimately it's best to register with the park office outside the main gate and to bring a guide if you haven't been up the mountain before (guides are often mandatory anyway). Also, bring plenty of food, water, sunscreen, a headlamp and warm, waterproof clothing. Do not underestimate the descent time needed and never forget how quickly mountain weather can change. Guides and porters can be arranged from your *losmen*, hotel or the park office before setting off. Be sure to call ahead or check the website to get up-to-date information.

CHECK OUT www.gedepangrango.org

OTHER Bring your passport/KTP photocopies for registration.

⑥ NATIONAL FLOWER PARK

After visiting the Cibodas Gardens and marveling at the mountains, head over to Taman Bunga Nusantara. To get there, return to the main road and continue downhill to km 82, watching the Jl. Mariwati turnoff on the left. Take this road to km 7 and look out for the village of Ciwalen.

At only 35 hectares, what **Taman Bunga Nasional** (National Flower Park) lacks in area it makes up for in flowerbeds–around 10,000 square meters of them. Opened in 1995, the attraction boasts ten main gardens, including the Mediterranean, French and crown jewel, Rose Garden. There is an impressive view of the Gede and Pangrango mountains on a clear day which you can sit and gaze at from one of dozens of benches spread throughout the park.

A 29-meter observation tower provides expansive views of the garden kingdom and a hedge maze called **Taman Rahasia** (Secret Garden) is good for a game of hide-and-go-seek. Watch the **Musical Fountain** dance about, stop by the **Flower Carpet** for a photo op, note the massive flower clock and

Navigating the Secret Garden hedge maze in the National Flower Park, here on a rainy day.

wander around the enchanting **Water Park**.

Stroll around the large pond populated by *koi* and swans and overseen by a giant statue of the lovely maiden Kunti from the Hindu epic *Mahabharata*. Check out the various topiary displays, such as the massive peacock and brontosaurus (you should have noticed by now the penchant for dinosaurs around Puncak). When energy levels drop, relax in the **Rafflesia Theater** and watch a short film about the whole complex, then unwrap your precooked lunch and enjoy it in the picnic area.

Before leaving, check out the Dutch-designed greenhouse where visitors can buy flowers from posies to petunias.

CHECK OUT www.tamanbunganusantara.com

GETTING IN 8am to 5pm, Monday to Friday; 8am to 5.30pm, Saturday and Sunday.

SLEEPING OVER With so much to do, it's worth sleeping over. There are over a hundred villas to choose from, many of which are illegally built. Try **Hotel Novus Puncak**. It has slightly faded since its glory days but is comfortable enough for a night. A trip to the high quality spa and a drink at the poolside bar are good rewards after a long day of hikes and adventure.

Cruising the roads at night, you will see guys blinking flashlights. Some are signaling to show a vacant room, others are signaling that they have women to keep lusty guys company.

CHECK OUT www.novuspuncak.com

HOW TO GET THERE It is ¾ km past Jl. Kebun Raya Cibodas on the left.

Walking Tour 24

PELABUHAN RATU

An Action-packed Driving Tour to West Java's Scenic South Coast for Surfing and Relaxing

1. **Bat Cave**
2. **Fish Market**
3. **Pelabuhan Ratu Traditional Market**
4. **Hot Springs**
5. **Manuk Island**

With beautiful, buxom, crashing waves and long slices of sugary beaches stretching for kilometers, the south coast of Java gives sun worshippers, surfers and sand castle makers plenty to celebrate. Hidden coves and rugged cliffs line the coastline, while rice fields and banana plantations enhance the beauty. Curious rock faces and intriguing geological coastal features can be seen, hinting at Java's wildly volcanic past. A number of prime sites sit west of **Pelabuhan Ratu** (Queen's Harbor), a coastal town that makes for a relaxing weekend getaway.

The first stop along the way from Jakarta to the south coast is **Lido Lakes**, good for

Crashing waves on rocky shores along West Java's scenic southern coast.

mountain **biking** and **hiking** in the Bodogol National Forest as well as **microlight** trips and rip-roaring rides on an **ATV**. Farther south from Lido Lakes is **Arung Jeram** (River Rafting). A river rafting company, Arus Liar, offers numerous white-water rafting options. The nearby **Areal Berburu** (Cikidang Hunting Resort), meanwhile, lets people get a gun and shoot their dinner.

After the hunting resort, the road is nearly all downhill to **Pelabuhan Ratu**. Some people come here to unwind in a hotel, occasionally taking a cooling dip in the ocean. For guys called Maverick or Brodie, it's all about the excellent selection of **surfing hot spots**, among the best in the country. If surfing is not your thing, **swimming**, **boogie boarding** and **diving** are also available. On land, you can see bats migrate from their caves at dusk, play in riverine **hot springs** or hike to a nearby **waterfall**. The town of Pelabuhan Ratu has a happening **fish market**, and **fishing boats** can be hired for coastal tours.

Sportier types can **ride their bikes** on very steep hills, take lengthy **coastal walks** or **trek up local volcanoes**.

WHO? Geared to everyone, although the hunting is not for the squeamish or young.

HOW LONG? Try to spend a good two to three days on the trip. River rafting, hunting and all the Lido Lake activities can be done in one day.

HOW FAR? Pelabuhan Ratu is 130km from central Jakarta. Along the way are Lido Lakes (68km), hunting (100km) and river rafting (112km).

GETTING THERE Take the Jagorawi toll road to Ciawi. Go straight through the traffic lights to Jl. Raya Sukabumi. Follow this road through Ciawi and the Cicatih Valley. Mount Salak is visible on the right and Mounts Gede and Pangrango on the left. After 32km, just before the village of Cibadak, turn right (it will be signposted to Cikidang). This hilly, windy road starts as Jl. Cibadak and then turns into Jl. Cikidang. Follow it all the way until it hits the town of Pelabuhan Ratu.

NOTE You can fly along the toll road at off-peak hours, but once the toll road ends the way narrows to one lane and can become quite clogged with trucks and minivans

serving factories along the route. Try early morning or late night trips.

☐ **BAT CAVE**

A rickety fence keeps intrepid explorers out of the guano-reeking **Goa Lalay** (Bat Cave). One whiff may convince most people that they've come far enough. The floor of the cave is an acrid, guano-thick pond of water, and monitor lizards may be spotted lurking about, attempting to snatch up young, infirm or just plain clumsy bats. Watch as hundreds of bats flit about the cave mouth, anxious to depart for their nightly feed.

If there is no rain and the weather in general seems agreeable, anywhere between 5pm and 6pm, the mass exodus will begin. Bats, grouped by the hundreds, spill out of the cave and race overhead, across the road, over the rice fields and toward the sea. There is a small, sheltered observation area near the front of the cave, although crossing the road to the rice field side provides the best views for watching the trailing, serpentine lines of bats heading toward the beachside sunset. For birders, be on the watch for the Savannah Nightjar as well.

GETTING THERE From the fish market in Pelabuhan Ratu, head east over the bridge and take the first right. Follow this road south along the coast for 4km. The bat cave is to the left, 50m off the road.

COASTAL WALKS A hike along the southwest coast reveals protruding headlands, wicked earth formations and sea salt-brushed, breeze-swaying coconut trees. Blue waves scrub the blinding white beaches as fishermen perch on outcroppings, coercing dinner from the froth and foam of the sea. The geology is quite incredible, with large chunks of petrified wood embedded in the ground and cliff faces frozen in time from volcanic eruptions thousands of years ago.

Prepare to leap from one outcropping to the next, ford rivers with your bag over your head and fend off surges of surf. Later, stroll through lime green rice fields and small rubber plantations, chase beach puppies and buy a freshly caught octopus from a local fisherman. Certain sections see you clamber over craggy limestone cliffs, follow paths into the surrounding jungle and stumble upon huts where villagers offer up freshly opened coconuts overflowing with milk.

NOTE The beaches around Pelabuhan Ratu and stretching up toward the Ocean Queen Resort are not that spectacular due to the impact from the local population. To find the beaches described above, start at least 15km west of town, past the Ocean Queen.

HELPFUL HINT

These walks can be done alone, but it's better to hire a local guide from the Ocean Queen Resort. Start anywhere west of the Cibareno River and follow the coast. A few overland forays are necessary when the coast becomes too difficult to traverse. This is where the guides come in handy.

GETTING THERE Head west on Jl. Cisolok-Cilograng until crossing the Cibareno River. Watch for a small lane to the left that leads to the beach.

DEEP SEA FISHING A deep trench off the south coast of Java channels nutrients into the bay off Pelabuhan Ratu, making for excellent trophy fishing. Deep-sea fishermen head out in search of shark, sailfish, marlin and tuna, led by a man named Shane who runs a popular operation out of Pelabuhan Ratu. Twelve-hour trips start at 6am, and the outfit has the best catch record in the area. Trips must be booked in advance and can be done through the Ocean Queen. They don't come cheap but include all the gear and provisions.

2 FISH MARKET
FISHING BOAT COASTAL TRIPS To fully appreciate the coastline near Pelabuhan Ratu, charter a local fishing boat, occasionally bringing it ashore at sights of interest if the surf allows. There are numerous launching points along the coast for a fishing or snorkeling journey, but a common departure spot is the marina next to the **Pasar Ikan** (Fish Market). Strike a deal with a fisherman along the shore or have the staff at the Ocean Queen make a booking. Note: A half or full day of motoring can be expensive due to rising fuel prices.

3 PELABUHAN RATU TRADITIONAL MARKET
FISH MARKET AND TRADITIONAL MARKET Fish markets are some of the most interesting places to explore, especially with a camera, and **Pasar Pelabuhan Ratu** (Pelabuhan Ratu Traditional Market) is no

stranger to tourists. It's easy to move among the covered stalls and check out what's on offer. Expect to see sharks, sailfish, piranha, lobster, crabs, barracuda, eels and groupers. Many are packed in ice or piled high in giant white bowls while others are neatly displayed on long rows of tarp-covered tables.

There are good photo opportunities here, but also take the time to stand back and watch the action. In the back, along the harbor, men hack fish into fist-sized chunks, turning a five kilogram tuna into chop suey in under 60 seconds. Workers here haul around frozen blocks of fish while others sort through the horror show parts that not many want.

Those who love a good fish fry, can buy their fish here and take it back to their villa for an afternoon barbeque. Vendors often raise prices for tourists, however, particularly on the weekends.

After a stroll about the fish market, take a few minutes to check out the fishing boats in the harbor. Across the road is a traditional market selling herbs and spices, dried fish,

Pelabuhan Ratu

0   2 km

N

Bayah

● Rubber
Plantation

⑤
Manuk Island

● Bird/Animal
Watching

● Motor
Bridge

Suwarna
Surf Spot

fruit and vegetables. Just west of here is the Tourist Information Booth. Don't expect too much help there, but they may have information on diving options.

GETTING THERE Head to downtown Pelabuhan Ratu on Jl. Siliwangi.

GETTING IN Some of the earliest fish hauls come in between 3am and 4am, but most of the stalls are up and running between 7am and 8am. If that is still too early, the market hums through the early afternoon.

④ HOT SPRINGS

HOT SPRINGS AND WATERFALL The **Mata Air Panas** (Hot Springs) experience is very much a local one and it's aimed at local tourists. That means most of the bathers are fully clothed. If you come with a group of friends and do just as the locals do, you'll have a fun hour or two splashing about in the hot pools. Note: The infrastructure here is old and poorly maintained, so many of the pools are worn

and the facilities run down. Another option is to just hop into the river, where many visitors soap up under the jets of super-heated water that blast up from the riverbed.

To get to the waterfalls, either cross over the river by bridge and follow the steep, often slippery trail to the falls; take an *ojek* from the hot springs' parking lot or pedal there on a mountain bike if you have one. There is a pool at the bottom of the falls to splash in. If going by bicycle or *ojek*, you will still need to walk a short way by trail.

GETTING THERE From Pelabuhan Ratu, head west on the Jl. Cisolok-Cilograng coastal road until just before the Cisolok River. Watch for the Cipanas sign post, just past the bus terminal, and turn right. Drive up this road another 3km to the hot springs.

MOTORCYCLE EXCURSION Most hotels rent motorcycles that can be driven west along Jl. Cisolok-Cilograng. About 1km past the Ocean Queen is a scenic spot to stop and

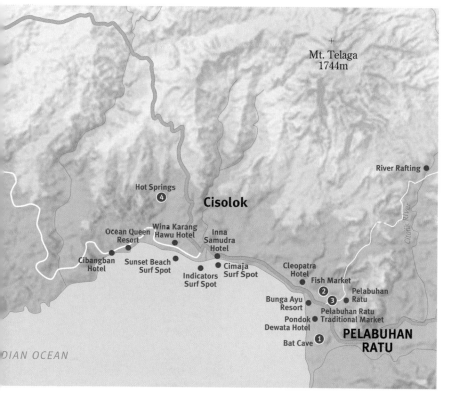

A view of the bay at Pelabuhan Ratu from the Cisolok-Cilograng coastal road.

take a photo of the bay and have a quick *kopi susu* (milky coffee) at one of the *warungs* tacked on to the hillside. Continue on past the Cibareno River, heading north-west along the steep road for 10km until turning left on to a small road (there are two lefts here, and you want the second one). This is a rough road that trends downhill to the small village of Suwarna (One Color).

⑤ MANUK ISLAND

Just past the village, on the left-hand side, is a small wooden suspension bridge that can only be crossed on foot or by motorbike. It leads to the **Lokasi Selancar Suwarna** (Suwarna surf spot). If you continue past the bridge, the road comes parallel with a beach that is worth playing around on. Further down the road is a slice of national forest good for **animal and bird watching**. On the other side of the forest is a reef leading out to **Pulau Manuk** (Bird Island).

Walk out to this wonderful island via the reef (shoes or sandals required) and stroll along the exquisite beaches here. Have a swim, bodysurf a few waves and take a snooze before getting back in the saddle. Note: There have been reports of thievery around Pulau Manuk. Don't trust strangers

around your goods, don't swim without someone guarding your belongings and be prepared to pay someone to watch your motorbike or car.

Continue along the road that parallels the beach and turn right at Jl. Karangtaraje-Darmasari. Pass through rubber plantations and stop to see how the trees are tapped. Also watch for small-scale coal mining done by hand.

It might be prudent to have a local guide follow on a separate motorbike in case your bike malfunctions or you lose your way. While

Hot water in the riverbed at the Hot Springs.

Lush green rice fields separated by bunds near the Ocean Queen Resort.

the road quality is quite good here, remember to always drive with caution.

THE OCEAN QUEEN RESORT The Ocean Queen is the weekend lodging of choice. Run by the nature-loving hiking legend Nick Andrew, the complex of large, four-bedroom, air-conditioned bungalows complete with sea-facing decks, barbeque grills and full kitchens is perfect for families and large groups of friends. A row of newly built rooms is more suited for couples. A swimming pool, foosball table, ping pong and bocce provide other forms of entertainment, while a spa with edible masks and ointments gives visitors a chance to relax. Head out to the beach and lay in a cabana, but beware of the strong undertow and mighty strong waves if you decide to play in the water.

Probably the most important thing about the Ocean Queen is that it can arrange almost all the activities listed in this chapter, and it's a good launching point for swimming, boogie boarding, surfing and coastal walks.

GETTING THERE From Pelabuhan Ratu town, head 17km west on Jl. Cisolok-Cilograng. The turnoff is on the left, a few minutes past the Cisolok River and the turnoff to the Hot Springs. Note that the driveway down to the resort is extremely steep.

CHECK OUT www.oceanqueenresort.com

THE LEGEND OF THE QUEEN OF THE OCEAN There once was a king who had a beautiful wife and daughter. The queen grew envious of the princess, Nyai Loro Kidul, as she couldn't bear to have a daughter more beautiful than herself. The queen gave the king an ultimatum: either the princess goes or she does. To help make the decision an easy one, the king ordered a witch to curse the princess with a terrible skin disease. With that, the king cast his daughter from the palace to appease his wife. Wrought with grief, the princess flung herself into the sea and emerged as a mystical mermaid with a penchant for the color green. As the Queen of the Sea, Nyai Loro Kidul now snatches up fishermen and sailors—and the occasional tourist—particularly those who wear green, a color reserved for her alone.

SURFING Although most people go to Bali to surf, there is no reason to go anywhere near the airport for some solid days on the waves.

The swimming pool and bungalows set amidst coconut palms at the Ocean Queen Resort.

Pelabuhan Ratu offers them up in all shapes and sizes along with rental boards for those without the go-to gear. There are plenty of guys offering lessons at certain areas along the beach. Waves good for all levels strike the coast, with some considered world class.

The best surfing is in the dry season, although waves are good year round in both the morning and afternoon. The swell is generally a southerly one.

Cimaja is one of the most popular and well-known spots in the area, with a good mixture of locals and foreigners surfing there. The beach is made up of round volcanic stones which clatter together on this right-handed point, with waves from one to two meters. Intermediate and advanced surfers should have a real kick with a 100-200m ride possible. Booties are recommended both due to the rocks and the sea urchins lurking below. It's roughly 8km from downtown Pelabuhan Ratu. The access road is a short, chunky drive to a small parking area, just a few minutes' drive from the Ombak Tujuh Restaurant and Desa Resort.

There aren't many facilities here, but there are a number of places to stay in the area, including the **Pondok Kencana Surf Lodge**, connected to the **Ombak Tujuh Pub**.

CHECK OUT www.ombaktujuh.net.

A few hundred meters west of Cimaja is **Lokasi Selancar Indicators** (Indicator's Surf Spot), a tough but exciting spot that is at its best when 2.5-meter waves are breaking. A coral bottom can make a wipeout dangerous, so a helmet is recommended. Indicators is 0.5km west of Cimaja.

Beginning surfers can head to **Karang Hawu** (Sunset Beach), where most of the surf schools are located. The water here has rips and currents, but the sandy bottom makes for softer wipeouts. It's 3km west of Cimaja, and also has an adjacent jutting basalt hill that tourists like to climb all over and photograph.

Just out the back door of the **Ocean Queen** is a fun, right-hand point set in a picturesque fishermens' bay. The waves are not too big and break nicely, making it a popular spot for boogie boarding, body surfing and swimming. The sandy beach works as a good spectator area.

Suwarna is a long, left-hand point break that handles any swell from one meter upwards. It produces nice, smooth waves with a long point break. From Suwarna village, cross a wooden suspension bridge over the

Surfing at the popular Çimaja beach.

Relaxing on the bow of a local fishing boat.

river, and walk 10 minutes through the village. It's a little over an hour's drive west of the Ocean Queen.

The surfing options are extensive, so ask some locals and check in with the surf guide at the Ocean Queen or the Ombak Tujuh Pub for more.

HEADS UP

The seas in this area can be rough and unpredictable. Undertows and currents have killed countless unsuspecting swimmers, surfers and coastal walkers—hence the legend of the Ocean Queen. Make sure you swim only in designated safe areas, never turn your back to the sea and always go with friends.

SCUBA DIVING Pelabuhan Ratu has a number of diving sites near Karang Antuk, a bay roughly a one to two hour boat ride from the town harbor, as well as additional sites south of there. Divers often spot snapper turtles, parrotfish, barracuda, octopus, lionfish, moray eels and eagle rays among the rocky outcrops and canyons, while the volcanic nature of the underwater scenery combined with the coral provides a wonderfully scenic backdrop.

Thea runs the dive trips here, which come with gear and snacks. Two-day overnight dive trips can be arranged through their website. A minimum number of people are required.

CHECK OUT www.octopusdive-pelabuhanratu.com

DIVERSIONS ON THE WAY FROM JAKARTA TO PELABUHAN RATU

Set among palm plantations and forested slopes between the Salak, Gede and Pangrango mountains, the **Lido Lakes** area offers more than enough activities for a day trip.

A dated recreation area marks the entrance to the lakes, which can be explored on a **bamboo platform raft**. Paddleboats are available for some leg exercise and a **flying fox** zip line carries thrill-seekers over the water. **Fishing** areas are available at the upper end of the lake.

Past the recreation area and on the left is the **Lido Lake Hotel** and **LEAD Office** (Lido Empowerment and Adventure Indonesia), where you can arrange guided walks to waterfalls and scenic spots in the **Bodogol National Forest**. These hikes can be done without a guide as well though.

Mountain biking here is recommended. The LEAD Office offers outbound packages, rents out golf carts for cruising and arranges recreational hikes through the hills.

Farther up the road on the right is a rental center for **ATVs**. These four-wheeled mobiles provide a sweet, rip-roaring ride through the hills—blasting through mud puddles, crashing through plantations and in general having a wild toad sort of time. Next door is the Lido airstrip, where microlights take off.

FLYING IN A MICROLIGHT An ultra-light, three-wheeled aircraft with hang glider wings, microlights can carry two people—you and the pilot—and can easily reach as high as 3,000 meters (though they won't go nearly that high when taking a quick jaunt with a customer). How far and high they fly is up to how much a person wants to pay.

Standard flights are 15 or 30 minutes, allowing passengers a spectacular low altitude view of West Java's rural landscape, unveiling heaving hills, meandrous rivers, red-roofed villages and kite flying kids. The sibling mountain peaks of Gede and Pangrango are clearly visible, as is Mount Salak. All the passenger needs to do is don a flight jacket and helmet, squeeze into the backseat behind the pilot and buckle up. Once cleared for takeoff, the little mechanical bird will roll along at 55kph until airborne, after which the hum of the jetski motor seems to disappear and the aircraft dances on wind streams, dipping, gliding and circling like a hawk on the hunt. Unlike a standard airplane, should a microlight have any engine trouble, it can generally just glide to the ground using its hang glider wings.

Both you and the pilot are connected by microphones and headphones built into your helmets so you can ask questions of your pilot about what you are seeing and he can point things out along the way.

With West Java being the most densely populated region in Indonesia, it can be difficult to escape the crowds and get some time away. At 1,000 feet above them all, however, claustrophobia melts away and tranquility takes over.

Continue up the long stretch of asphalt from the microlight center and turn left at the top of the road. Pass the National Park office and, when the road splits, follow the dirt road down to the National Park entrance. This is the starting point for treks and bike rides,

although bike rides can also be started as far back as the National Park office. The wonderful **Javan Gibbon Center**, a rescue and rehabilitation center, is inside the park here and can be visited on a day trip.

GETTING THERE Take the Jagorawi toll road until it ends at Ciawi. Go through the traffic lights and continue for 13km along Jl. Sukabumi Raya. Lido Lakes is on the left. Visitors will need their own car since public transportation here is limited.

MICROLIGHT TRIPS 0251-222-922 or solowings@yahoo.com

CHECK OUT www.lidolakes.com and www.jgcowajawa.blogspot.com (Javan Gibbon Center)

This **Cikidang Hunting Resort** is located at the foothills of Mount Salak, surrounded by palm tree plantations. The basic premise is that a person comes here, rents a gun, shoots an animal and then eats it in the attached restaurant. The animals, which are tame, are raised in pens and released into the hilly, walled-in hunting zone, complete with trees, bushes, a pond and a field of tall grass. A would-be hunter can choose to shoot a rabbit, duck, goose, chicken, turkey, goat, boar or deer and they can hunt on foot, by ATV or from the back of a pick-up truck.

It's best to start the day with some practice rounds on metal silhouettes and paper targets before going off to the killing grounds. There are different package deals available, including one in which a person can shoot five of the smaller quarry, such as two rabbits, a chicken, a turkey and a duck. The deer and boar are more expensive. Once the hunt is through, the kitchen staff cook the game to order. Non-hunters can still do target shooting, horseback riding or go for a swim in the pool. Cabins are available for overnight stays.

Note that shooting to kill is easier said than done. As guns are illegal in Indonesia without a permit, the firepower used here is air-powered and uses pellets rather than bullets. This means, basically, that a person is trying to shoot a pig or deer to death using a BB gun. If the hunter's aim is not spectacular, it can take a dozen shots before the animal is dead—even a little animal. This seems a tad cruel. Crossbows are also available, which may make for a quicker kill.

Microlight aircraft are ideal for viewing West Java's spectacular rural landscape.

WHERE TO GO Cikidang Hunting Resort, approximately 100km from Jakarta.

HOW TO GET THERE Follow the directions toward Pelabuhan Ratu, but after turning off at Cibadak, proceed 13km until reaching the resort on the right.

CHECK OUT www.cikidanghunting.com

Located on the Citarik river, **Arus Liar** (Wild Streams) is the No.1 river rafting company in Java. With professional and enthusiastic guides and sturdy equipment, this is an exceptional way to get the rest of the way to the coast while your car and driver continue on ahead and pick you up at the finishing point, about 3.5km from Pelabuhan Ratu.

Arus Liar floats clients down swift waters and past overhanging cliffs, grassy fields and through sections of thick forest. You may see monitor lizards lazing on river rocks and muddy banks, strong naked farmers scrubbing their tired naked buffalos in the middle of the river, and may be forced to play getaway with gangs of children trying to board your raft like miniature pirates.

Guides bounce rafts through the shock waves of the aptly named 'Dynamite' rapid,

spin them around backwards, butt them up against mid-river boulders and plunge them over whooshing drop-offs. They might also purposely dump a raft full of people into the water for fun and start a water war with the next raft over.

The river does have some slow stretches that grow dark and thick with vegetation, and you may wonder if you aren't actually floating into the 'heart of darkness,' destined to survive on water rats and the occasional barbecued tourist. Just as your mind begins to sink into these dark depths, though, the team will take a pit stop at a roughed-up hut on the river's edge for freshly hacked-open coconuts.

River rafting options are numerous, including half-day, full-day and nighttime rafting.

Beyond just river rafting, Arus Liar offers mountain biking options, kayaking, paintball and camping.

GETTING THERE Follow the directions to Pelabuhan Ratu, and go 25km past the turn off for Cibadak. Watch for signboards for Arus Liar and be sure not to cross the Citarik River Bridge. Arus Liar is on the left.

CHECK OUT www.arusliar.co.id

Walking Tour 25

JATILUHUR RESERVOIR
A Fun Day Trip to a Ceramics Village and Lake-bound Floating Water Village

1. **Ceramics Village**
2. **Mount Parang**
3. **Water Village**

Known as **Waduk Jatiluhur**, this reservoir and accompanying 100-meter-high, 1200-meter-long dam were originally built in the 1950s to produce hydroelectric power. Using six turbines, the dam can crank out nearly 200 megawatts of electricity per hour at maximum capacity. More importantly, though, it now functions as one of Jakarta's main sources of water. The dam also irrigates nearly 250,000 hectares of surrounding farmland, and is home to a successful fisheries industry, which includes more than 10,000 floating hatcheries and aids in flood control. For tourists, the reservoir not only offers cool air and wide open spaces, but the chance to motor out to the **Kampung Air** (Water Village) for a look around. Just up the road from the dam is the small village of **Plered**, best known for its well-priced hand-crafted ceramics.

For those with a sense of adventure, **Gunung Parang** (Machete Mountain) begs for a climb, while others may just want to admire it from the lakeside. As an added bonus, the drive to the reservoir is fairly quick and painless, and even on a weekend this hidden oasis gets few crowds.

WHO? This trip is good for everyone, particularly families.

HOW LONG? This is a day trip and shouldn't be rushed. It is 1.5 hours east of Jakarta, so leave early in the morning and be back by supper.

HOW FAR? 100km out to the reservoir, including a stop in the village of Plered.

GETTING THERE Take the Jakarta-Cikampek toll road toward Bandung via Bekasi. Turn off at Purwakarta and exit the tollway at km 84. At the next intersection, take a right and then drive 11km to Plered. To get to Jatiluhur, turn left at the intersection and then left again before the bridge. It's roughly 9km from there. For those without wheels, take a bus from the Kampung Rambutan bus station to Plered and then hire an *ojek* to get to the reservoir.

GETTING STARTED It is best to begin by visiting Plered so all the shopping and craft-making can be done first. Otherwise, interest may wane after a day out at the dam.

1 CERAMICS VILLAGE
Roughly 20km from Jatiluhur is the wonderful **Kerajinan Keramik** (Ceramics Village) of Plered. To get an inside look at the industry, stop first at the visitor's center on the right side of the road into town. Here, visitors can tour the kiln area and make their own simple ceramic pieces. They can also observe how the whole process works, starting from the moment a raw slug of clay is squeezed through a machine and piled up by hand. Later, craftsmen push the pots into shape using potters' wheels and then fire them in the kilns before adding glaze, paint and fancy detailing. It's worth watching as the final touches are put on to the vases.

Many cottage industries cater to tourists who want a behind the scenes peek at the pottery process, and most will be happy to lead a tour around, particularly if visitors buy something. Drive along the main strip through town to see if one of the pottery shops catches your eye and pop into the traditional market for a stroll around and a taste of village life.

Painting a ceramic pot at Plered pottery village.

Applying decoration prior to glazing and firing.

When stopping off at a shop or small factory, be sure to chat with the pottery sellers. Most are eager to talk about the crafting process and are quite proud of their reputation as one of the go-to spots for pottery in Java. Nearly all the pottery in Plered is made using traditional methods, which means it can take up to a month to complete just one piece, depending on design and complexity. All the clay is locally sourced, but finished pieces are exported both to Jakarta and as far as North America, Europe and Australia.

2 MOUNT PARANG

For hikers looking for a good climb, head to the 915-meter-high **Gunung Parang** (Machete Mountain), which overlooks Jatiluhur Reservoir. To get there, head west out of Plered. The road is mangy and will require a tough SUV or *ojek* to navigate. Pass through the villages of Tegalwaru and Cikakak before finally getting to the trailhead which will be found on the far side of the mountain. There are rock climbing possibilities here, but they are best tackled by those

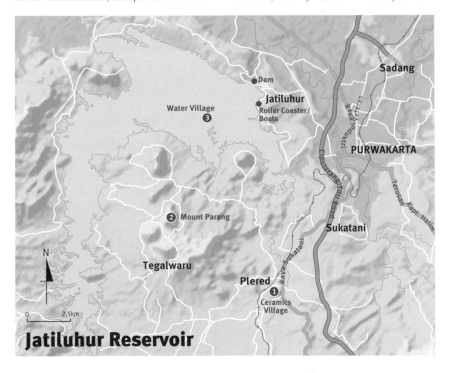

Heading toward the peak of Mount Parang.

with experience. A steep one-hour hike up a fairly well-established trail results in spectacular mountaintop views of the countryside and reservoir. Note that the trailhead is not obvious from the road, so stop frequently and ask the locals for guidance. It shouldn't be too difficult to find a local person to lead you to the top for a reasonable fee.

As when climbing most mountains in Indonesia, it is wise to hire a guide. The track is fairly straightforward, but it's still a good idea to have someone who knows where they are going. Guides can be hired in one of the villages before getting to the trail.

Now it's time to head over to the **Jatiluhur Reservoir**. There is only one road along the water's edge, and it doesn't extend very far. The tourist areas are acutely undeveloped, with only a two-star hotel for overnight stays, but it's the action on the water that is most important. Before getting your feet wet, stop off for a fresh fish lunch at one of the *warungs*. Try the *ikan bakar* (grilled carp or catfish) served with a side of *karedok* (salad made of raw vegetables and peanut dressing).

After lunch, head down to the small beach area next to the **roller coaster** (pedal-powered roller coaster). This is a uniquely adventurous attraction as it requires trusting the rusting 18-year-old wheels as they roll along a track a few stories off the ground. The ride will only go as fast as you can pedal, and while there are no loop-de-loops,

just taking the risk to ride this thing gets you bragging rights.

> ## FAST FACT
> The Indonesian national Dragon Boat teams, winners of numerous gold medals, use the reservoir as one of their training spots.

③ WATER VILLAGE

When you're ready to take to the water, head down to the reservoir's edge, where **banana boats, paddleboats, jet skis, windsurfing boards** and **motorboats** are for rent. The best bet is to bargain for an hour-long trip around the lake in one of the boats, stopping to check out the small islands before reaching the **Kampung Air** (Water Village).

Definitely the highlight of the trip and an experience not to miss, an excursion to the

Tourists on the pedal-powered roller coaster.

The Jatiluhur Reservoir, the largest in Indonesia, is home to the extensive Water Village.

kampung air reveals a very interesting industry and way of life that is rarely mentioned. Comprising hundreds of large floating platforms, each complete with some dogs, chickens, a few ducks and dozens of fish pens, this is where many of Jakarta's freshwater fish come from.

Have the boat's captain pull up to one of the floating fishing homesteads and get permission for you to come aboard and have a chat with the fisherman tending the pens. Once on the platform, stroll along the walkways made of bamboo lengths lashed together and see if the fisherman can be coaxed into explaining the different processes going on, the types of fish, the various stages they're at, the number of fish involved and perhaps give a feeding demonstration.

After motoring back to shore, but before packing up and heading home, stop off at the **Dam**. The security post will ask for an entrance fee as well as a letter of permission to enter, although the letter can generally be overlooked. For a bit of trivia, the dam is the largest in Indonesia and it was purposely constructed in the same fashion and with the same appearance as the Aswan dam in Egypt. In addition, it had to be built with French assistance rather than Dutch, as it was built in the 1950s when Dutch/Indonesian relations were strained.

The long walkway across the top of the dam goes past a monstrous round cement cylinder, where water from the reservoir

Floating fishing platforms at the Water Village.

pours down. The door to this walkway is typically locked, and access will require some sweet talk and perhaps a bit of cash. One final note of interest: Some of the channels that branch off from the Citarum River at the base of the dam and carry water down to canals in Jakarta were built by prisoners, starting in 1959.

Language Guide

Greeting:
Good morning = **Selamat pagi**
Good day (11am–3pm) = **Selamat siang**
Good afternoon (3pm–6pm) = **Selamat sore**
Good evening = **Selamat malam**
Please come in = **Silakan masuk**
See you later! = **Sampai jumpa!**
How are you? = **Apa kabar?**
I'm fine = **Kabar baik**
What's your name? = **Siapa nama anda?**
My name is… = **Nama saya…**
Where are you from? = **Dari mana asalmu?**
I'm from… = **Saya dari…**
Are you married yet? = **Sudah menikah?**
Not yet = **Belum**
Yes, already = **Sudah**

Everyday Speaking:
Good = **Baik**
Bad = **Tidak baik**
Yes = **Iya**
No = **Tidak**
Be careful = **Hati hati**
Excuse me = **Permisi**
Welcome/Please = **Silahkan**
Thank you = **Terima kasih**
You're welcome = **Sama sama**
I'm sorry = **Maaf**
I don't understand = **Saya tidak mengerti**
Oh my! = **Aduh!**

Cashing In:
How much is it? = **Berapa harganya?**
My change? = **Uang kembalian?**
It's expensive = **Mahal, yah?**
The exact price/The final offer = **Harga pas**
Do you have change? = **Ada kembalian?**
Do you have small money? = **Ada uang kecil?**
I don't have = **Tidak ada**

On the Road:
I want to go to… = **Mau ke…**
Where is… = **Di manakah…**
Turn right = **Belok kanan**
Turn left = **Belok kiri**
Keep going straight on = **Terus**
Stop here = **Berhenti di sini**

Go via… = **Jalan lewat…**
How far is it? = **Berapa jauh dari sini?**
What street is this? = **Ini jalan apa?**
Near = **Dekat**
Far = **Jauh**
Next to = **Di samping/Di sebelah**
In front of = **Di depan**
Behind = **Di belakang**
Have you been to Plaza Indonesia before? = **Sudah pernah ke Plaza Indonesia?** (asking the taxi driver to check that he knows where he's going)
Please ask someone (if they know where the location is) = **Silahkan tanya seseorang**

Taking Care of Business:
Where is the bathroom? = **Dimana WCnya?** (prounounced way-say)
Where is a sink to wash my hands? = **Dimana wastafelnya?**
Do you have an ashtray? = **Ada asbak?**
Where is an ATM? = **Di mana ATMnya?** (pronounced ah-tay-em)

Danger Zone:
Help! = **Tolong!**
I'm sick = **Saya sakit**
Go away! = **Pergilah!**
I want to go to the hospital = **Mau ke rumah sakit**
Don't! = **Jangan!**

Getting Stuffed:
Is there a food stall around here? = **Ada warung?**
Is there a restaurant around here? = **Ada rumah makan?**
I'd like to order = **Saya mau pesan**
I'd like to have… = **Saya mau…**
Food = **Makanan**
Drink = **Minuman**
I want to eat… = **Saya mau makan…**
I want to drink… = **Saya mau minum…**
Do you have regular drinking water? = **Ada air putih?**
Without ice = **Tanpa es**
Not too spicy = **Tidak terlalu pedas**

Acknowledgments

This book is dedicated to the four women I love: Melanie, Mom, Naomi and Sommer.

Special thanks also go to:

Adam Bowers
Adolf Heuken and his book,
Historical Sites of Jakarta
Barbara Oravetz
Chad Bouchard
Clarissa Boentaran
Cynthia Devi
Dani Dewanto
Dilla Djalil-Daniel (also credited for the photograph of the horse in the equestrian section of the sports chapter, p. 37)
Doreen Biehle
Eka Alam Sari
Ellen De Man
Gaspar Wosa (also credited for the photograph in the Ultimate Frisbee section of the sports chapter, p. 43)

Harriet Welford
Ina Suhinah
Jakarta Globe
Jakarta Post
Krystyna Krassowska
Kristina Sztucka
Marnix Beugel
Melanie Wood
Mia Tranujaya
Nick Andrew
Nick Elliot
Peter Mitchell
Petty Elliot
Robert Rouphail
Samantha Brotman
Sara Schonhardt
Sarah Wormald
The Indonesian Heritage Society and their book, *The Jakarta Explorer*
Time Out magazine

Trish Anderton
Troy Skaleskog
Tyler Chapman
William Daniel
Zack Peterson
Page 1: Photo © Herminutomo/ Dreamstime
Pages 2–3: Photo © Warrengoldswain/ Dreamstime
Page 88: Photo © Teguhonly/Dreamstime
Page 89: Photo © Photosoup/Dreamstime
Page 94: Photo © Segmed87ru/ Dreamstime
Page 93: Photo © Pandya/Fotolia

Additional Sources of Information

deathrockstar.info (for the latest concert information)
wikitravel.org/en/Jakarta (for comprehensive information on Jakarta)
www.expat.or.id/ (for information on living in Jakarta from expat perspectives)
www.jakarta.go.id (for general Jakarta information)
www.jakarta-tourism.go.id (for general Jakarta activity information)
www.maplandia.com/indonesia (for getting around Jakarta)
www.streetdirectory.co.id (for finding businesses in Jakarta)
www.whatsnewjakarta.com (for up-to-date Jakarta activity information)
Culture Shock! Jakarta: A Survival Guide to Customs and Etiquette, Derek Bacon and Terry Collins (2007).
Jakarta Globe newspaper
Jakarta Inside Out, Daniel Ziv (2002).
Jakarta Java Kini magazine
Jakarta Now! magazine
Jakarta Post newspaper
Jakarta Street Atlas, 2nd edn, Periplus Editions (2008).
Historical Sites of Jakarta, 7th edn, Adolf Heuken (2007).
Museum Encounters: Jakarta, Indonesian Heritage Society (2009).
The Jakarta Explorer: Cultural Tours In and Around the City, 4th edn, Indonesian Heritage Society (2009).

Index